Japanese Horror Culture

Lexington Books Horror Studies

Carl Sederholm, Brigham Young University

Lexington Books Horror Studies is looking for original and interdisciplinary monographs or edited volumes that expand our understanding of horror as an important cultural phenomenon. We are particularly interested in critical approaches to horror that explore why horror is such a common part of culture, why it resonates with audiences so much, and what its popularity reveals about human cultures generally. To that end, the series will cover a wide range of periods, movements, and cultures that are pertinent to horror studies. We will gladly consider work on individual key figures (e.g. directors, authors, show runners, etc.), but the larger aim is to publish work that engages with the place of horror within cultures. Given this broad scope, we are interested in work that addresses a wide range of media, including film, literature, television, comics, pulp magazines, video games, or music. We are also interested in work that engages with the history of horror, including the history of horror-related scholarship.

Titles in the Series

Japanese Horror: New Critical Approaches to History, Narratives, and Aesthetics edited by Fernando Gabriel Pagnoni Berns, Subashish Bhattacharjee, and Ananya Saha

Violence in the Films of Stephen King edited by Michael J. Blouin and Tony Magistrale

Dark Forces at Work: Essays on Social Dynamics and Cinematic Horrors edited by Cynthia J. Miller and A. Bowdoin Van Riper

Japanese Horror

Critical Essays on Film, Literature, Anime, Video Games

Edited by Fernando Gabriel Pagnoni Berns,
Subashish Bhattacharjee, and Ananya Saha

LEXINGTON BOOKS
Lanham • Boulder • New York • London

Published by Lexington Books
An imprint of The Rowman & Littlefield Publishing Group, Inc.
4501 Forbes Boulevard, Suite 200, Lanham, Maryland 20706
www.rowman.com

6 Tinworth Street, London SE11 5AL, United Kingdom

Copyright © 2021 The Rowman & Littlefield Publishing Group, Inc.

All rights reserved. No part of this book may be reproduced in any form or by any electronic or mechanical means, including information storage and retrieval systems, without written permission from the publisher, except by a reviewer who may quote passages in a review.

British Library Cataloguing in Publication Information Available

Library of Congress Cataloging-in-Publication Data

Library of Congress Cataloging-in-Publication Data
Names: Berns, Pagnoni Fernando Gabriel, 1975-editor. | Bhattacharjee, Subashish, editor. | Saha, Ananya, editor.
Title: Japanese Horror Culture: Critical Essays on Film, Literature, Anime, Video Games / edited by Fernando Gabriel Pagnoni Berns, Subashish Bhattacharjee, and Ananya Saha.
Description: Lanham : Lexington Books, [2021] | Series: Lexington Books horror studies | Includes bibliographical references and index. | Summary: "This book investigates the philosophical, socio-cultural, and artistic world of Japanese horror through a varied range of case studies, including video games (Rule of Rose), manga (Uzumaki), and anime (the classic Devilman). Film is represented with well-known works such as Ringu and overlooked filmmakers like Mari Asato"-- Provided by publisher.
Identifiers: LCCN 2021033532 (print) | LCCN 2021033533 (ebook) | ISBN 9781793647054 (cloth) | ISBN 9781793647078 (paper) | ISBN 9781793647061 (ebook)
Subjects: LCSH: Horror films--Japan--History and criticism. | Horror comic books, strips, etc--Japan--History and criticism. | Horror tales, Japanese--History and criticism. | Horror in mass media--Japan.
Classification: LCC PN1995.9.H6 J366 2021 (print) | LCC PN1995.9.H6 (ebook) | DDC 791.43/6164--dc23
LC record available at https://lccn.loc.gov/2021033532
LC ebook record available at https://lccn.loc.gov/2021033533

Contents

Introduction   1
Fernando Gabriel Pagnoni Berns and Subashish Bhattacharjee

PART 1: NATIONAL TRAUMAS AND REPRESSIONS   7

Chapter 1: The Ghost of Imperialism: Japan's Forgotten Horrors in the Shadow of Sadako   9
Calum Waddell

Chapter 2: A Modern Monster: Shin-Godzilla and its Place in the Discourse Concerning 3.11 and National Resilience   21
Barbara Greene

Chapter 3: Cultural Trauma, Cross-Flow of Aesthetics, and the Child: A Comparison Between *Ringu* and *The Ring*   39
Bipasha Mandal

Chapter 4: Space, Smoke, and Mirrors: The Frightening Ambiguity of *Ju-On*: Origins (2020)   51
Daniel Krátký

Chapter 5: The Dead Speak: Horror and the Modern Ghost in Eiji Ōtsuka's *The Kurosagi Corpse Delivery Service*   65
Megan Negrych

PART 2: POSTHUMAN MONSTERS AND GROTESQUE BODIES 83

Chapter 6: "Love in a Chair": Industrialization and Exploitation Edogawa Rampo's "The Human Chair" and Junji Ito's Manga Adaptation 85
Leonie Rowland

Chapter 7: The Monstrous Feminine in Mari Asato J-Horror films 97
Mariana Soledad Zárate and Canela Rodríguez Fontao

Chapter 8: Composite Corpses and Viruses of Viewing: J-Horror as Film and Media Theory 113
William Carroll

Chapter 9: Spiral into Samsara in Junji Ito's J-Horror Masterpiece *Uzumaki* 131
Wayne Stein

Chapter 10: Controlling the Inner Demon: Theological Approaches on *Devilman* 139
Fernando Gabriel Pagnoni Berns

PART 3: CULTURAL FLOWS 155

Chapter 11: The Transpacific Complicity of J-Horror and Hollywood 157
Seán Hudson

Chapter 12: Revisiting the Orphan Girl Narrative in *Rule of Rose* 177
Ingrid Butler

Chapter 13: Idol Culture and Gradations of Reality in Japanese Found Footage Horror Films 191
Dennin Ellis

Chapter 14: Obscure, Reveal, Repeat: Hidden Worlds and Uncertain Truths in Kōji Shiraishi's *The Curse* and *Occult* 211
Lindsay Nelson

Index 227

About the Editors 231

About the Contributors 233

Introduction

Fernando Gabriel Pagnoni Berns and Subashish Bhattacharjee

Ever since the emergence of the J-horror phenomenon in the late 1990s with the opening and critical success of films such as Hideo Nakata's *The Ring* (Ringu, 1998) or Takashi Miike's *Audition* (*Ôdishon*, 1999), Japanese horror has been a staple of both film studies and Western culture. Scholars worldwide have been keen to observe and analyze the popularity and roots of the phenomenon that took the world by storm, producing a corpus of cultural artefacts that still resonate and influence today.

Encompassing a range of genres and media including cinema, manga, video games and television series, the loosely designated genre has often been known to uniquely blend Western cinematic techniques and tropes with traditional narrative styles, visuals and folklores. Tracing back to the early decades of the twentieth century, modern Japanese horror have had tremendous impact on popular culture, introducing many trends which are widely applied in contemporary horror narratives. The hybridity that is often native to Japanese aestheticization is an influential element that has found widespread acceptance in the genres of horror. These include classifications of ghosts as the *yurei* and monsters as the *yōkai*, tentacle erotica or the plight of the suffering individual in modern, industrial society. Furthermore, settings such as damp, dank spaces that reinforce the idea of the morbid are features that have now been unconsciously assimilated into the canon of Hollywood or western horror, and may often be traced back to Japanese horror roots. Besides the often de facto reliance on gore and violence, the psychological motif has been one of the most important aspects of Japanese horror.

J-Horror is term coined by British distribution label *Tartan Video*, which distributed overseas content via their Asian Extreme collection through an extremely astute art of branding. Soon, J-Horror was making waves everywhere, including films such as *Battle Royale* (Batoru Rowaiaru, Kinji Fukasaku, 2000), *Chaos* (Kaosu, Hideo Nakata, 2000), or *Freeze Me* (Furîzu mî, Takashi Ishii, 2000). Yet, the history of Japanese horror culture dates back a long time before the worldwide phenomenon of *Ringu*.

Japanese horror is deeply rooted in the vernacular folklore of its culture, with fairy tale-like ghost stories embedded deeply into the social, cultural and religious fabric. This folklore originated from the Shinto belief system (Japan's largest religion) and Buddhism and was used to reinforce cultural and moral norms. It was not until Irish folklorist Lafcadio Hearn began writing down these stories during the last decade of the 19th century that Japanese and, to some extent, the world, began taking real interest in these tales of ghosts and moral fables beyond folklore. Hearn spent years living in Japan as he compiled a series of *yokai* stories that were published in 1904 as *Kwaidan: Stories and Studies of Strange Things*, now a classic title on horror and Japanese culture.

The book inspired the first vernacular horror films. Aside from Teinosuke Kinugasa's *A Page of Madness* (Kurutta ippêji, 1926), Japan's first venture into full horror exploded with Kaneto Shindo *Onibaba* (1964). The plot follows a widow and her mother-in-law, both poorly living during the warring states period. They survive by killing samurais and selling their belongings for a living. As time goes by, a specter wearing a creepy mask starts haunting the women, now doomed to self-destruction. The tale would fit nicely on Hearn's *Kwaidan*, but it is only with Masaki Kobayashi's *Kaidan* (1964) that the book is adapted to the big screen with a selection of stories from the collection.

Through the late 1960s to mid-80s, Japanese horror became more obscure and hard to notice outside its country of origin. There were exceptions, such as the black and white exercise on creepiness and national trauma that *Godzilla* (Gojira, Ishirô Honda, 1954) was, a hit that spawned a franchise and fell into campy excess through the 1960s and 1970s before returning to serious substance in the 1980s and 1990s with films such as *Godzilla 1985* (Koji Hashimoto and R.J. Kizer, 1985) or *Gojira vs. Biorante* (Kazuki Ohmori, 1989). Nobuhiko Obayashi's 1977 *Hausu*, in the other hand, was a unique mix of experimental surreal cinema, horror and comedy telling the story female vampire who feeds on young women to preserve her eternal youth. The *Guinea Pig* series (comprised of six films, including the infamous *Devil's Experiment*—Satoru Ogura, 1985—and *Flower of Flesh and Blood*— Hideshi Hino, 1985), in turn, gave Japanese horror its fame of being gory and prone to scenes of torture and mayhem.

The 1990s came with bold new directions that mostly left behind the camp of the previous decades but not the art-house style. It is in this decade when the J-Horror phenomenon starts, with straight-to-video and made-for-TV anthologies like *True Scary Stories* (Honto ni Atta Kowai hanashi), created to satisfy consumption within the growing home video market and the translation into English translations of horror manga. The late 1980s and the 1990s were also witnesses of the rise of gory anime, with productions such as *Chôjin densetsu Urotsukidôji* (Hideki Takayama, 1989) or *Ninja Scroll* (Jûbê ninpûchô, Yoshiaki Kawajiri, 1993), animated films that pushed the envelope in terms of gore and sex (including young women being raped by monsters' tentacles). The first entry on the *Resident Evil* franchise (Capcom) debuted in 1996, expanding later into a live-action film series, animated films, television, comic books and other media.

In 1995, a small made-for-TV film opened in Fuji TV called *Ringu* (Chisui Takigawa) and the rest is history. While the TV version is almost forgotten now (especially in the Western part of the world), the most famous theatrical version, directed by Hideo Nakata in 1998, took the horror scenario, not only introducing J-Horror to new audiences worldwide, but also starting a healthy flow between Hollywood and Japan that included remakes and influences. The plot, about a mysterious video tape that evokes an evil ghost called Sadako who kills people within seven days after watching it, was a resounding international hit, introducing audiences to anxieties about technology, virus-like circulations and long-haired pale ghosts coming out from the beyond. Later successes such as *Ju-On* (Takashi Shimizu, 2002), the eerie 2001 film *Pulse* (Kairo, Kiyoshi Kurosawa, 2001), together with the psychological-driven thrillers *Cure* (Kiyoshi Kurosawa, 1997) or *Audition* (Ôdishon, Takashi Miike, 1999), cemented the status of J-Horror as a force to reckon with.

Hollywood took the J-Horror route with gusto, offering Western audiences remakes of *Ringu*—*The Ring*, Gore Verbinski, 2002—, *Ju-On*—*The Grudge*, Takashi Shimizu, 2004—, or Miike's *Chakushin Ari* (2003)—*One Missed Call*, Eric Valette, 2008. Scholarship soon followed, with Jay McRoy's edited collection *Japanese Horror Cinema* (Edinburgh University Press, 2005) introducing readers to some of the most important horror films produced in Japan. The year 2008 saw the publication of two tomes—Colette Balmain's *Introduction to Japanese Horror Film* (Edinburgh University Press) and McRoy's *Nightmare Japan: Contemporary Japanese Horror Cinema* (Rodopi)—further developing the serious study of Japanese horror. Katarzyna Marak's *Japanese and American Horror: A Comparative Study of Film, Fiction, Graphic Novels and Video Games* (McFarland, 2014) and Steven Brown's *Japanese Horror and the Transnational Cinema of Sensations* (Palgrave Macmillan, 2018) were monographs dedicated exclusively to the investigation of the transnational influences taking place between Asia and America, both books the consequences of many Hollywood remakes. As the

J-Horror boom faded, however, critical studies (both monographs and edited collections) slow down, even if new texts, such as Michael Crandol's *Ghost in the Well: The Hidden History of Horror Films in Japan* is announced for publication in 2021 (Bloomsbury).

This edited collection gathers scholars from all over the world investigating J-Horror in many of its manifestations, varying from film to anime and literature, and from theoretical perspectives that include posthumanism, trauma studies, socio-cultural context and theories of abjection, demonstrating that J-horror is alive and still pushing the envelope, both speaking of localized anxieties as much as global fears.

THE BOOK

Our first section, "National Traumas and Repressions" deals with artistic manifestations of trauma within Japan. Via fragmentation, disorientation, ambiguity and flashbacks, the different chapters speak about how the past (both collective and individual) comes back to haunt, being in the form of ghosts or as a giant fire-breathing atomic lizard. The section opens with Calum Waddell's take on the international hit *Ringu*. Following the author, the film reenacts, through a simple ghost story, forgotten memories of war and transnational interventionism. The second chapter, Barbara Greene's "A Modern Monster: *Shin-Godzilla* and its Place in the Discourse Concerning 3.11 and National Resilience," argues that *Shin-Godzilla* metaphorically reworks and reflects the national trauma produced by the Tsunami tragedy of 2011. The monstrous catastrophe and the ineffectual attitude of national authorities are mirrored by this kaiju film, highlighting the importance of how popular culture and history are interlinked via traumatic experiences. In chapter 3, Bipasha Mandal studies the intersections between Nakata's *Ringu* and its American remake, *The Ring*, to unpack underlying cultural patterns and deep-seated social anxieties which play out on and stem from the body of children and women, while also pointing out a cross-cultural flow of aesthetics and modes of storytelling. Chapter 4 and 5 turn to individual trauma and forms of repression. Daniel Krátký's close reading of the overlooked *Ju-On: Origins* (Sho Miyake, 2020) emphasizes ambiguity, flashbacks and mirrors as rhetorical devices fragmenting the story. Complicating the use of flashbacks serves Miyake in his goal to tell about traumatic pasts still haunting the main characters. If, according the author, fragmentation is a common trope of the *Ju-On* franchise, Miyake's film takes this ambiguity to new extremes. The section ends with Megan Negrych's "The Dead Speak: Horror and the Modern Ghost in Eiji Ōtsuka's *The Kurosagi Corpse Delivery Service*." Negrych argues that the power of personal tragedy informs both, the ghosts and the narrative of *The Kurosagi Corpse Delivery Service*, a manga reflecting on Japan's cultural anxieties on death.

The second section, "Posthuman Monsters and Grotesque Bodies," revolves around the emergence of the non-human and the abject in Japanese horror, varying from literature to film and anime. The section opens with Leonie Rowland's analysis of Edogawa Rampo's short story "The Human Chair" (1925). Rowland argues about the impact that modernization and neoliberalism have upon the human body, whereas human–object relations have become stronger than interpersonal ties. In the next chapter, Canela Ailén Rodriguez Fontao and Mariana Zárate study one of Japan's most overlooked female filmmakers: Mari Asato. The authors argue that Asato's use of the figure of the double and corporeal fragmentation serves the director to address the asphyxiating nature of traditional Japanese patriarchal ethos. In "Composite Corpses and Viruses of Viewing: J-Horror as Film and Media Theory," William Carroll addresses the interlinking of bodies on the screen and aesthetics via Bazinian theories of realism and composition using Aoyama Shinji's 1999 J-horror film *EM: Embalming* as case study. Wayne Stein analyzes the disturbing Junji Ito's *Uzumaki* through the lens of Buddhist theology. The sections ends with Fernando Gabriel Pagnoni Berns' analysis of the popular manga *Devilman* (Go Nagai) and its adaptation to anime. Following Pagnoni Berns, the manga and the anime diverge on how both understand their monsters through the linkage of Buddhist philosophy with Japanese demons and posthuman creatures.

The third section, "Cultural Flows," investigates the intertextual imbrications taking place between Japanese horror and foreign narratives. The section opens with Seán Hudson's investigation on the cultural flows between Japanese horror cinema and Hollywood; rather than effacing boundaries, the author argues, the flows are shaped by mechanisms of national consolidation. Ingrid Butler's chapter "Revisiting the Orphan Girl Narrative in Rule of Rose" analyzes a popular video game to unpack the different imbrications between forms of storytelling: Victorian narratives of orphan girls and Japanese horror. Dennin Ellis investigates the interlinking of Otaku culture in Japanese horror, as fiction and reality blurs in some examples of found footage films. The section and the book closes with Lindsay Nelson's chapter "Obscure, Reveal, Repeat: Hidden Worlds and Uncertain Truths in Kōji Shiraishi's *The Curse* and *Occult*." Via philosophy and using found footage horror films as cases for study, the author points to the interlinking of Japanese horror and Lovecraftian cosmology regarding the existence of invisible worlds existing beyond the human eye.

PART 1

National Traumas and Repressions

Chapter 1

The Ghost of Imperialism

Japan's Forgotten Horrors in the Shadow of Sadako

Calum Waddell

If ever one has the opportunity to visit Mainland China and makes a cursory channel surf of the country's television networks at least one thing is almost guaranteed: at some point during the day a small screen period drama depicting local actors as outrageously evil (not to mention bizarrely incompetent) Japanese imperial officers will be broadcast.[1] These predictably patriotic, Communist Party-approved serials frequently end with a Maoist guerrilla fighter sacrificing life and limb to win the day for his Motherland and to usher in The Great Leap Forward and the Cultural Revolution. All cynicism (and dark humor) aside, however, Japan's World War II history—whilst commonly discussed and acknowledged in China and South Korea (it is easy to find copies of Iris Chang's *The Rape of Nanking* in bookstores in either nation)—remains far more secretive, if not even entirely unknown, in The Land of the Rising Sun itself.

Speaking from experience of living in China[2] it is the Nanking massacre, or "rape," that remains pertinent in the popular conscience of today's People's Republic (along with the annexation of Manchuria), even if the authoritarian regime in power may occasionally use such events to sustain sympathy for its historic role as the "Middle Kingdom" (Ringnam 2016, 52). Not for nothing did Mao Zedong, the Chairman of the Communist Party and iron-fisted ruler of the country from 1949 until his death in 1976, initiate a Military Academy in Nanjing, dedicated to spreading his violent ultra-patriotic revolution across the globe. According to research from the historian Julia Lovell, "between 1964 and 1985, the PRC spent between $170 and $220 million in training some 20,000 fighters" (Lovell 2020, 142) from African nations, destabilized as part of Cold War proxy battles, in these establishments. Today's Nanjing, whilst—as with so many a modern Chinese metropolis—dwarfed by hastily erected tourist hotels and bland, nondescript skyscrapers, contains one of the few reminders of the period: an extensive Holocaust museum (dubbed the Memorial Hall of the Victims in Nanjing Massacre by Japanese Invaders) located on the outskirts of the city center. Whilst no such comparable iconography exists as a testament to those who fell to Maoism, it is difficult not to be impacted by the images and descriptions from the time.

However, it is this well-documented conflict between Japan and China that is lacking explicit representation in Japanese cinema *and* popular culture. Even so, one might also argue that this pastness is at least *symbolized* in the nation's most famous horror film: Hideo Nakata's *Ring* (*Ringu*, 1998), itself based on a 1991 novel from Koji Suzuki. Hence, it is the purpose of this chapter to explore this argument further, including with reference to at least two other examples of well-known Japanese genre cinema. Whilst most, if not all, readers of this chapter will have seen Nakata's motion picture, it is worth highlighting some of the clearest references to the Nanking massacre and the wider period of Japanese colonialism that emerge from even the most basic textual analysis.

Ring opens with two teenage girls, Masami (Hitomi Sato) and Tomoko (the late Yuko Takeuchi), who share the legend of a haunted videotape. Once watched, the viewer will receive a phone call and be informed that they have just one week left to live. "Everybody else had heard that story" says Tomoko—introducing the concept of legend and a form of horror that lives on, and sustains itself, solely by word-of-mouth. When Tomoko is mysteriously killed, the attention of the *Ring* story turns to young newspaper journalist Reiko (aunt of Tomoko, played by Nanako Matsushima), who discovers the tape in her niece's bedroom. She enlists her ex-husband Ryūji, a college professor, after their young son, Yōichi (Rikiya Ōtaka) watches the ominous VHS: the youngest generation now haunted by the horrors of an older one. Reiko and Ryūji discover that Sadako, the psychokinetic ghost-girl who lives within the cursed videotape, was the product of an affair between a Doctor called Ikuma (Daisuke Ban) and a local lady (Rie Inō) with psychic powers who was undergoing fresh, but potentially cruel, experimental treatment.

Nevertheless, Ryūji remains skeptical about the Sadako legend: "Nobody starts these kinds of stories. Whatever people feel anxious about becomes rumor and begins to spread" he insists. When he finds out that Ikuma was initially praised for his cutting-edge techniques and then disregarded as a crank and a fiend when someone died during one of his seminars, Ryūji even castigates the newspapers for changing the narrative: "The media still does the same thing." Accusations of fraud emerge—just what is the truth behind Sadako and the "crimes" of her family? Where are the "facts" (and the bodies) buried? What is the older generation keeping quiet? Finally, following Ryūji's climactic death, Nakata offers a stylish end long-shot showing Reiko and Yōichi driving into vast nothingness. In this final moment, *Ring* seems to invite us to ask ourselves if the road to recovery is never-ending—especially when a society fails to acknowledge and come to terms with its past misdeeds. It remains one of horror cinema's most potent and devastating conclusions.

IMAGES OF THE PAST

Before continuing with this analysis of *Ring*, it is perhaps pertinent to touch upon how horror cinema, even in its most exploitative form, has dealt with issues such as war crimes in the past. It is also important to acknowledge how taboo the topic of Nanking, in particular, is within wider Japanese society. Commenting on this collective amnesia, for instance Iris Chang highlights the censorship of a thirty-second scene in Bernardo Bertolucci's classic epic *The Last Emperor* (1987), with the distributor claiming that "his company thought that the Nanking scene was 'too sensational' to be shown in Japan" (Chang 1997, 210). More recently, author Michael Booth has written about the rise of the Japanese far right and their denial of such notorious massacres as those carried out in the former Chinese capital (Booth 2020, 79). Furthermore, Shinzu Abe's visits to the notorious Yasukuni Shrine (in 2013, whilst prime minister, and then again in 2020), the home of Japan's war dead, and also its war criminals, caused inevitable uproar in China and South Korea. Calls from both countries, and beyond (Indonesia, the Philippines, Taiwan and others) for compensation to the wartime comfort women of the Japanese military is ongoing and well-documented, particularly the Wednesday demonstrations in Seoul, but the situation has never been resolved.

Certainly, showing how weaponized this period has become *outside of Japan*, two Hong Kong pro-democracy candidates, Yau Wai-ching and Sixtus "Baggio" Leung, would be removed from the city's legislative council in 2016 after pledging allegiance to "The People's Republic of Shina"—the latter term explained by journalist Tom Phillips in *The Guardian* at the time as "an archaic and derogatory way of referring to China in Japanese" (Phillips 2014). It was also most prevalent during Japanese colonial rule (ironically including Hong Kong itself).[3] Less anyone still believe that this period is now disregarded as "ancient history," director Herman Yau returned to the era of Japanese imperial rule with his Category III extravaganza *The Sleep Curse* in 2017, which was afforded a wide summer theatrical release and accompanying advertising campaign across Hong Kong and Macau (the film also acknowledges the comfort women controversy). It is a rare, recent example of an East Asian horror film that presents "the atrocities of the Japanese" across Chinese territory, including in colonial Hong Kong where "it was the Chinese population who suffered the worst... ten thousand victims of rape: many were [then] bayonetted in the street" (Welsh 1994, 417). Unsurprisingly, and tellingly, a Japanese release is unconfirmed.

Prior to *The Sleep Curse*, the cinematic presentation of Japan's brutal imperial past has been limited to the exploitative, Chinese government-backed *Men Behind the Sun* (T.F. Mou, 1988) and its sequels.[4] The original film was ironically (given its Communist Party links) enthusiastically championed by such "liberal" splatter film critics as Chas Balun: "the *Cannibal Holocaust* of the 80's and about as rough as it comes" (Balun 1992, 51). European filmmakers would also use horror film frameworks and trappings to launch the seventies Nazisploitation cycle. Examples such as the cult, Italian "video nasty" *SS Experiment Camp* (*Lager SSadis Kastrat Kommandantur*, Sergio Garrone, 1976) and the threadbare *Elsa Fräulein SS* (Patrice Rohm, 1977) from France may be both lowbrow and low budget but they do at least raise questions about complicity and silence, whilst presenting fascism as an unsustainable (and outrageous) ideology.

Despite Japan being clustered, unhelpfully, into the bracket of "Asian horror"[5] its twentieth century expansionism, which would eventually encompass the successful, albeit brief, conquest of American, British, French and Dutch territories across the continent, warrants considerable comparison to Western colonialism. Historian Laurence Rees has acknowledged as much, stating that—as Japan began to open up to the foreign powers in the second half of the nineteenth century—"they look at powerful Western nations and learnt that there was one more attribute they needed in order to be considered a powerful, sophisticated nation—colonies" (Rees 2000, 16). Moreover, the dominant Western powers almost certainly fueled a feeling of Japanese antagonism with their own dismissive racism towards the country. The British naval attaché to Tokyo is documented by historian Lawrence James as stating that the Japanese posed little threat to the Empire in Asia as far back as 1934, noting that they had "peculiarly slow brains" (James 1994, 460).

As such, one might expect a similar Japanese cinema of reckoning, even within a more exploitative and/or ghoulish approach comparable to the Nazisploitation film, with events such as Nanking or at least the build-up to imperial aggression. However, none are clearly identifiable. Even the book *Japanese Horror Cinema*, edited by Jay McRoy and released from Edinburgh University Press in 2005, has only one chapter that mentions Nanking—and, in this case, it is only in passing and with the briefest of references to *Battle Royale* (Kinji Fukasaku, 2000) (McRoy 2005). Elizabeth Bridges notes how the recurring (proverbial) "money shot" in the European Nazisploitation thematic is that "the perpetrators meet their gruesome comeuppance, which further draws the audience into an intricate mechanics of pleasure with the thinnest veneer of moral justification" (2012, 75). Yet nowhere do we see representatives of the Imperial Japanese Army, outside of these tawdry Chinese television dramas, meeting their own gory fate at the hands of those they have imprisoned and tortured. Instead, more contemporary, lower-budgeted Japanese exploitation-horror has veered towards pornographic realism such as *Flower of Flesh and Blood* (Hideshi Hino, 1985) or shot-on-video excess like *The Machine Girl* (Noboru Iguchi, 2008) and *Tokyo Gore Police* (Yoshihiro Nishimura, 2008).

The closest parallel to the Italian and French strain of hand-wringing Nazisploitation films, one could perhaps argue, is such iconic Meiko Kaji texts as *Female Prisoner #701: Scorpion* (Shunya Itō, 1972), set in a brutal prison camp and following a familiar exploitation film rape/revenge narrative. The contemporary setting and the concurrency with other women-in-prison narratives, particularly the famous Jack Hill-Roger Corman films of the time such as *The Big Bird Cage* (1971), confuses a more focused reading regarding past crimes, particularly those of comfort women. Even so, as explained by Rees, "There is no exact figure for how many 'comfort women' (though 'victims of forced rape' is a more accurate term) were employed and abused by the Japanese. . . Estimates range from 80,000 to 100,000" (Rees 2000, 36). Consequently, it is surreal, despite a familiar generic pattern to the aforementioned American "sex in cells" texts, that Kaji's frequently abused personas, across a spectrum of Japanese exploitation cinema, is not discussed within the wider spectrum of such brutality. One may even say the same about the Japanese rape-fantasy pornography that is evident on adult tube sites, and sold in X-rated stores across the country, itself as clinical about male dominance/possession over the body of unwilling women as *Flower of Flesh and Blood*.[6] Of course, any such argument doubtlessly also introduces, and likely warrants, a "return of the repressed" approach.

Freud's return of the repressed analogy is, in terms of film studies, most likely associated with the late Robin Wood. Discussing *The Texas Chain Saw Massacre* (Tobe Hooper, 1974), for example, Wood saw the specter of Watergate and Vietnam re-emerging to devour liberal American youth: "as a collective nightmare it brings to a focus a spirit of negativity, an undifferentiated lust for destruction, that seems to lie not far below the surface of the modern collective consciousness" (1986, 93). However, such an approach to *Ring* is dismissed by Eric White who writes, "Sadako's emergence from a well of forgetting cannot finally be explained as the return of the repressed in the sense of an unresolved trauma that has endured in the unconscious, waiting to be exorcised by means of a therapeutic catharsis" (2005, 40). Yet

White never details *why* such a reading is unsuitable to *Ring* (or to any other example of Japanese horror cinema featuring abused females who finally obtain some form of vengeance, such as *Female Prisoner #701: Scorpion*).

Certainly, if one is to accept that Nazisploitation films deliver a minor catharsis with, admittedly after a running time packed full of nudity and sleazy thrills, the death of their vile antagonists, then certain key Japanese horror texts present a similar thematic. Whether it is Kaji as a used and abused mediation of the silent, and silenced, "comfort woman" of imperial pastness, or Sadako as unresolved "truth" that literally destroys the souls of those who engage with her own historical facts, there are clear threads from a small selection of Japanese horror that evoke the crimes of Imperial conflict.

RINGS OF FEAR

Perhaps the most ominous pre-*Ring* expression of this idea is *Evil Dead Trap* (Toshiharu Ikeda, 1988). At least one other author has noted the link between the two films with Richard J. Hand acknowledging it as "a precursor" to the Nakata effort but adding that its most notable influences are foreign: "the influence of Tobe Hooper, Dario Argento and David Cronenberg" (2005, 22). *Evil Dead Trap*, not unlike *Ring*, highlights a young female journalist, Nami[7] (Miyuki Ono), who enters a bunker in the Tokyo countryside to try and locate the "truth" around a snuff video that she has encountered on her news-desk. What she finally encounters, after her colleagues are stalked and slaughtered, is a murderous so-called "mother's boy" (which can certainly be interpreted as loyalty to the nation) who has a conjoined twin. Whilst one "personality" has no connection to the brutal killings, the other does, inviting a reading of a split-identity in contemporary Japan—those aware of the past and *those not*, those complicit and *those not*. At the conclusion of *Evil Dead Trap*, Nami is told by her editor, "maybe you should keep it to yourself... We will remove it from our records." Nami, however, disagrees and argues that she has a responsibility to the victims. In other words, her campaign for justice and factual accuracy will be ongoing. Although *Evil Dead Trap* arrived on the fan scene in the UK as pirated videotape, along with other contraband, hyper-violent, low budget foreign shockers (including, ironically, *Men Behind the Sun*), it remains one of the most intelligent and contemplative modern Japanese horror films.

Nami's own conflict of interests, between responsible journalism and protecting the image of her workplace and country, is a factor that remains prevalent even now. As noted by Booth, and despite an extensive book on the Tokyo War Crimes Trial by Arnold C. Brackman (1990), "today there are Japanese people who deny the Nanjing massacre ever took place. One Japanese historian has written that precisely forty-seven Chinese civilians died. Others quibble about the definition of 'massacre' or the timeframe" (Booth 2020, 251). Taking into account the horrifying images that have survived from the period, including those of imperial soldiers using bound Chinese citizens for bayonet practice, it is telling that the first murder we see in *Evil Dead Trap* is of a young woman who is impaled, multiple times, by the wrath of the film's mysterious stalker. Given the clear and acknowledged influence of *Evil Dead Trap* on *Ring*, to argue that Sadako *does not also* evoke this concept of a repressed evil, forcing contemporary, young Japan—generations of youth raised in the specter of misinformation and denial—to face the facts about a more traumatic period is difficult to accept.

White's conclusion about *Ring*, "a troubled and yet oddly expectant vision of a future in which the great collective psychotronic apparatus of contemporary information technology ceaselessly reconstitutes individual identity" (2005, 46), would infer that the film has considerable transnational commentary (and currency) but minimal localized identity. The same might be said of *Evil Dead Trap*, given its obvious stylistic nods to Argento, Cronenberg and others (and the use of mondo-style, fake-snuff footage actually evokes Italy's *Emanuelle in America* [Aristide Massaccesi, 1977] as much as Cronenberg's *Videodrome* [1983]). Nonetheless, it would be incredible folly *not* to point out such explicit, knowing, smart dialogue *and* imagery across both films. This dialogue and imagery frequently acknowledge the need for journalistic integrity and responsibility when approaching issues of a disputed pastness and results in both *Evil Dead Trap* and *Ring* being framed by plots that progress via investigative research. Whilst this research begins with the respective protagonists of both films expressing cynicism about the "truth," it is eventually established that such doubts are misplaced, even foolish, and rumor becomes reality. This 'reality,' of course, also finally alters the identity politics of both reporters.

Further visual nods are also given to the era of imperial crimes: *Evil Dead Trap* takes place in a bunker marked with the year 1956, the same year when Japan was finally admitted to the United Nations, having quit the precursor League of Nations two decades prior. The new relationship with the UN attested to the country's postwar/post-Hiroshima international co-operation and existence. Moreover, *Ring* opens with its credits unfolding across a vast seascape. It was one particular action on the high seas in December 1937, during the seizure and terrorizing of Nanking, that almost led to friction between Japan and the United States before Pearl Harbor. States Rees: "over-excited pilots sank the US gunboat *Panay* and three American tankers that lay on a nearby river. Two American sailors died in the attack" (2000, 53). Chan also acknowledges the American lack of reaction to the event, maintaining how "the U.S. government was anxious to reach a financial and diplomatic settlement" and noting "the Japanese government also had a large budget for wooing influential newspaper men" (Chang 1997, 149). The sea, therefore, carries an aura of the hidden—literally "what lies beneath"—with Nakata's opening channeling the beginning of Japan's most infamous criminal acts against a foreign nation and concluding with a call for clarity regarding truth (and even reconciliation).

TRANSNATIONAL TERROR

Of course, another transnational analogy could be made regarding *Ring*, per Hyangjin Lee, who raises "The revenge of the female ghost. . . Japanese horror explores transnational film cultures to articulate the national experience of otherness informed by the cultural and religious traditions of the Japanese people such as Buddhism and Shinto" (2013, 24). Even here, however, one can judge this discourse surrounding such "religious traditions" by what is not practiced as much as *what is*. The acts of Japanese soldiers in Nanking have perhaps been difficult for many to accept perhaps *because* the country, when approached and visited as a foreigner, is so genteel and polite. Can we really accept *Ring* as "just" another story of otherness, tradition or even transnationally appealing ghouls and ghosts when Japan itself harbors so many specters of brutal colonial policies and practices that align so perfectly with the film's narrative concept of disjointed video footage and photography, pointing to a past of (secretive) criminal acts among an older generation?

If this reading feels akin to a collective unconscious approach to cinema *ala* Siegfried Kracauer, it might be also worth proposing that *Ring* is viewed alongside *Night of the Living Dead* (George Romero, 1968) as a film that transcends its own genre and grounds a more explicit socio-political approach to the horror thematic. Writing about *Night of the Living Dead*, J. Hoberman describes it as "not bound by Hollywood decorum. . . closer to the raw immediacy of underground movies and cinema verité than to any studio production" (2003, 281). Similarly, *Ring*'s haunted VHS presents us with grainy footage that cannot be dismissed as mere random imagery and which mediates a sense of 'hidden' underground reportage. One moment in particular is especially jarring: grainy footage, shot verité style, of someone with a white sack over their head, as if awaiting execution, pointing at their (offscreen) aggressor. As noted by Chan, the conquest of Nanking and the terrors that ensued were not necessarily a secret even at the time; "Japanese newspapers ran photographs of Chinese men being rounded up for execution, heaps of bodies waiting for disposal by the riverside, the killing contests among the Japanese soldiers and even the shocked commentary of the reporters themselves" (1997, 143).

The other moments in the tape are equally alarming: a beautiful (comfort) woman admiring herself in the mirror but disturbed by a distant figure invading her privacy, disjointed text fighting to align itself into a coherent narrative, floored victims desperately clinging to life and a well—the sight of a makeshift, random, unplanned grave, plus the closeup of an eye, *searching, looking*. It would be an incredible coincidence indeed if these images "just" aligned haphazardly with a story about two young adults attempting to untangle the mystery of a past site of murder and a legend that is whispered about in the halls of high school corridors.

The purpose of this chapter is not to castigate the Japanese government for its broad policy of denialism and failure to answer for calls of compensation to the victims of imperial policy, including those in Nanjin. Ironically, it is because questions of national identity and how to deal with traumatic histories (and present crimes) has never be more relevant. As we have seen with the United Kingdom (and England specifically) such a cultural amnesia around imperialism, and the colonial reasons for immigration and multiculturalism, may be seen to explain the 2016 Brexit vote—indeed, a mandatory search on the internet will introduce all number of journalists and pundits raising this proposition. Certainly, not unlike Japan, Britain's horror cinema has rarely, if ever, acknowledged the brutal crimes of Empire. Instead, colonial wars have been reimagined as heroic stand-offs between opposing men of stature (*Zulu* [Cy Enfield, 1964]) or as something akin to a gung-ho, *Boy's Own* adventure (*Game for Vultures* [James Fargo, 1979] or *The Wild Geese* [Andrew V. McLaglen, 1978]).

In retrospect, one can only wonder what would have come from a genre cinema that more openly discussed and recorded, or at least *symbolized*, the Kenyan concentration camps, the Indian partition or the postwar Malaysian emergency. When seen in this context, even the sleazy bondage and blood of the "nasty Nazi" films from France and Italy have a place in the wider discourse about fascism, and its brief appeal, within the grindhouses of Western Europe. Gaik Cheng Khoo's fascinating essay, "Filling in the Gaps of History: Independent Documentaries Re-Present the Malayan Left" discusses a new movement within Malaysia to rationalize and balance the State of Emergency under British rule and the Communist guerrilla activity, itself influenced by Mao's revolutionary ethos (2010). Might *Ring*, over two decades before, have been an early (and generally missed) sign that Japanese horror cinema could itself be a radical outlet to express symbolism of past crimes, emerging again and again, and never at rest, for as long as the nation itself refuses to acknowledge them? It is a valuable question to ask, and the symbolism of Nanking is clearly evident in *Ring*'s aesthetic frights and its general thematic.

If, as so many of us hope, Japan is the democratic opposite of the Mainland China that today denies its own repressive activities in Xinjiang,[8] and threatens nearby Taiwan with occupation, then the crimes of the imperial age should, nay *need to* have an outlet for expression. Horror cinema, as evidenced by such groundbreaking masterpieces as *The Cabinet of Dr. Caligari* (Robert Wiene, 1920) and *Night of the Living Dead*, is as strong a platform as any to vocalize discrepancies with the national status quo—providing films rich with symbolism but also as upsetting and provocative as any other form of mass entertainment. Seen in this light, and in such esteemed company, *Ring* stands the test of time and invites further deliberation and challenges— a proposition that a nation is not at peace until its past identity is no longer haunting the corners of its existence. One can only wish that further Japanese horror cinema continues to honor its challenging, intelligent and suitably ghoulish landscapes.

REFERENCES

Balun, Chas. 1992. *More Gore Score: Brave New Horrors*. Florida: Chunkblow Press, Florida.

Bernstein, Richard. 2014. *China 1945: Mao's Revolution and America's Fateful Choice*. New York: Vintage.

Booth, Michael. 2020. *Three Tigers, One Mountain*. London: Vintage.

Brackman, Arnold. 1990. *The Other Nuremberg: The Untold Story of the Tokyo War Crimes Trials*. London: Fontana Press.

Bridges, Elizabeth. 2012. "Reproducing the Fourth Reich: Cloning, Nazisploitation and Revival of the Repressed." In *Nazisploitation! The Nazi Image in Low-Brow Cinema and Culture*, edited by Daniel Magilow, Kristin Vander Lugt and Elizabeth Bridges, 72-91. New York: Continuum International Publishing Group.

Chang, Iris. 1997. *The Rape of Nanking*. Basic Books, New York.

Hand, Richard. 2005. "Aesthetics of Cruelty: Traditional Japanese Theatre and the Horror Films." In *Japanese Horror Cinema*, edited by Jay McRoy, 18-28. Edinburgh: Edinburgh University Press.

Hoberman, J. 2003. *The Dream Life, Movies, Media, and the Mythology of the Sixties*. New York: The New Press.

James, Lawrence. 1994. *The Rise & Fall of the British Empire*. London: Little, Brown and Company, London.

Khoo, Gaik Cheng. 2010. "Filling in the Gaps of History: Independent Documentaries Re-Present the Malayan Left." In *Cultures at War: The Cold War and Cultural Expression in Southeast Asia*, edited by Tony Day and Maya Ht Liem 247-264. New York: Cornell University.

Lee, Hyangjin. 2013. "Family, Death and the *Wonhon* in Four Films of the 1960s." In *Korean Horror Cinema*, edited by Alison Peirse and Daniel Martin, 23-34. Edinburgh: Edinburgh University Press.

Lovell, Julia. 2020. *Maoism: A Global History*. London: Vintage.

McRoy, Jay. 2005. *Japanese Horror Cinema*. Edinburgh: Edinburgh University Press.

Parfitt, Troy. 2011. *Why China Will Never Rule the World: Travel in the Two Chinas*. New York: Western Hemisphere Press.
Phillips, Tom. 2014. "Rebel Hong Kong Politicians defy China at Chaotic Swearing-in Ceremony." *The Guardian*, October 12, 2014.
Rees, Laurence. 2000. *Horror in the East*. London: BBC Worldwide Book.
Ringnam, S. 2016. *The Perfect Dictatorship: China in the 21st Century.* Hong Kong University Press, Hong Kong.
Welsh, Frank. 19994. *A History of Hong Kong*. London: HarperCollins.
White, Eric. 2005. "Case Study: Hideo Nakata's *Ringu* and *Ringu 2*." In *Japanese Horror Cinema*, edited by Jay McRoy, 38-47. Edinburgh: Edinburgh University Press.
Wood, Robin. 1986. *From Vietnam to Reagan*. New York: Columbia University Press, New York.

NOTES

1. I should acknowledge here that a similar observation is made by travel writer Troy Parfitt in his excellent book *Why China Will Never Rule the World: Travel in the Two Chinas* (Western Hemisphere Press, 2011). Speaking from experience and testifying to how widely accepted these serials are, it was not uncommon for me to find local passengers watching them on their phones and laptops when traveling by train in China.

2. I lived in Suzhou for three years, a city not far from Nanjing by bullet train, where I gained my first job as a lecturer in Media and Communication. The spelling of Nanking was changed to Nanjing in 1958. I have used both in this chapter depending on the time period discussed.

3. For those seeking a recent book on Japan's retreat from China, and surrounding countries, and then the outbreak of the civil war, I recommend *China 1945: Mao's Revolution and America's Fateful Choice* from Richard Bernstein (New York: Vintage, 2014).

4. *Men Behind the Sun* focuses its horrors on Unit Ei 1644, which was demolished by the Japanese prior to leaving Nanjing. Testament from the Japanese workers is all historians have to go on. Chang offers only a page of discussion about the laboratory in her *The Rape of Nanking*.

5. See for instance Jasper Sharp, long associated with his respected research on Japanese cinema, being credited as an "Asian cinema expert" on the *South Korean* film *JSA* by Arrow Video (JSA—Joint Security Area Blu-ray | Arrow Films)—an Orientalist credit of quite some consideration. It is perhaps worth further acknowledging that Chang's book, which features some impeccable research, was dismissed as "emotive" by Sharp (in his blog review "Japanese Horror Cinema," Midnight Eye, 2005). Given Chang's familial link to the period and her tragic suicide after exposing herself to the evidence of such horrors, accusations of being too "emotive" carry an uncomfortable air of misogyny and possibly even white privilege.

6. It is interesting that *Evil Dead Trap 2* (Izô Hashimoto, 1992) moves away from the slender Japanese antagonist, with the American DVD distributor even once telling me that he suspected that this is why it never sold as well Stateside—with Orientalist assumptions about East Asian appearances being provoked and aptly shattered by the film (which comes recommended).

7. Nami is the name of the recurring protagonist in the notorious Angel Guts series of films of which *Angel Guts: Red Porno* was helmed by *Evil Dead Trap*'s Toshiharu Ikeda. The use of the name might be to subvert expectancies as Ikeda's *Evil Dead Trap* heroine is far from submissive and proves herself to be resourceful and tough.

8. I wish to stress here that I am not necessarily willing to maintain that the actions of the Imperial soldiers in Nanking were (per recent media allegations of the Chinese state in Xinjiang) "genocide"—which carries considerable burden of proof which I am fully unqualified to offer.

Chapter 2

A Modern Monster

Shin-Godzilla and its Place in the Discourse Concerning 3.11 and National Resilience

Barbara Greene

INTRODUCTION

While Japanese cinema has a number of longstanding, cinematic franchises, Godzilla has proven to be one of the most versatile. The Toho producer Tanaka Tomoyuki proposed the first Godzilla, *Gojira*, as a horror film in which the monster would embody the experiences of trauma and feelings of anxiety prevalent in contemporaneous Japan—from the massive loss of life in the Asia-Pacific War and the trauma of both the fire and nuclear bombings to growing Cold War tensions (Tsutsui 2017). During the Cold War, when Japan was closely tied to the United States, Godzilla shifted from a frightening creature embodying nuclear annihilation to a friendly beast that defended humanity in general, and Japanese children in particular. During a period in which the potential of atomic warfare was an omnipresent concern, there was no space in the public imagination for a monster that embodied nuclear annihilation. In the most recent re-boot of the series, 2016's *Shin-Godzilla*, however, Godzilla has returned to the screen as a potent threat.

But why has the franchise shifted back to the horror genre after decades of shifting between family-friendly fare and mild frights? During the mid-afternoon on March 11, 2011, Japan experienced its worst natural disaster within living memory when a powerful earthquake occurred off the coast of north-eastern Japan. The tremor triggered an equally massive tsunami that swept away coastal towns along with thousands of citizens while survivors streamed the catastrophe live over social media. The tsunami also breached the nuclear power plant located in Fukushima, causing one of the most devastating nuclear disasters in human history.[1] At the helm of the Japanese state was Kan Naoto, whose administration's handling of the disaster was lambasted in the press and on social media, resulting in his administration's collapse and his political party's loss to the LDP. The LDP leveraged a pre-existing policy proposal on national resilience—and the hawkish reputation of Kan's successor, Abe Shinzo—to promise a revitalized Japan that would rise out of 3.11 like a phoenix. *Shin-Godzilla* takes the various threads of collective trauma, the perceived failure of the Kan administration, and the hope of a renewed Japan and creates a commentary that succeeds in portraying both the horror of the event as well as the optimism of post-disaster reconstruction. This chapter will place *Shin-Godzilla* into its context within the broader discourse of 3.11 and will explore its commentary on Japan's current political climate and National Resilience Policy.

3.11 AND ITS EVOLUTION IN THE POPULAR IMAGINATION

To understand *Shin-Godzilla*'s commentary, one must first have a thorough understanding of the both the events that occurred after 3.11, particularly within the Kan administration, and how their response is perceived in the public imagination. The disaster occurred during Kan Naoto's tenure as Prime Minister. He was the second prime minister from the Democratic Party of Japan, taking over from Hatoyama Yukio who had led the party to victory against the traditionally ruling party—the Liberal Democratic Party (LDP). Kan was also the first of five previous Japanese prime ministers to serve for more than a year, although the public perception of his response to the disaster meant that he did not last more than seventeen months in office. On the day of the disaster, the Kan administration had mobilized the SDF and set up a centralized crisis response center for the Cabinet by 3 P.M.—approximately twenty minutes after the disaster began. Within days, 100,000 first responders had been deployed to the stricken prefectures. However, this fast response outstripped the organizational capacity of the administration as multiple regional command centers were established and then failed to coordinate personnel and material. Additionally, Kan refused to delegate responsibility effectively and insisted on retaining close control over the response effort— leading multiple meetings himself (Samuels 2013).

Kan's leadership style was known to favor direct action rather than the consensus building that had been the historic practice in Japanese politics.

This departure was initially viewed as strength as it deviated from the leadership tactics of the last few prime ministers whose short tenures destabilized the political system. At first, Kan's tactics appeared to function well, as his Cabinet Crisis Center would be able to collate the information provided by the regional command centers and then relay pertinent data as needed to the disparate command centers. But, when the scale of the disaster became apparent, compounded by the meltdown at Fukushima, the weakness of this leadership style became increasingly obvious as communication between the command centers failed and Kan himself appeared to vacillate as the situation worsened (Kingston 2011). Furthermore, Kan did not have widespread support in traditional media, which began to highlight communication failures and inefficiencies, laying the blame on Kan's management.

The nuclear power plant at Fukushima was located just off the coast. Designed by the U.S. company General Electric (GE), the plant had been contentious even prior to its groundbreaking as it lay close to a shoreline that had been struck by multiple tsunamis in the past. After the disaster, the plant experienced one of the worst nuclear catastrophes to date—with a reactor remaining exposed for an extended period and contaminated seawater continuing to leak from the flooded plant into the ocean for years (Pascale 2017). However, no individual has been held responsible for either the design flaws of the plant or its controversial response to the tsunami. Some commentators have called this a "system of irresponsibility" that is purportedly built into contemporary Japan's political system (Hopson 2013, 3–4). Kan's response to the crisis at the plant was similar to that of the wider disaster, with micro-management and conflicting administrative structures. This would eventually lead the Kan's administration's nuclear energy expert, Kosako Toshiso of Tokyo University, to resign (Samuels 2013). Kan's uncertainty surrounding the situation allowed the government to release only limited bits of information to the general public, stoking fears that a cover-up of an even greater disaster was taking place. Social media in Japan ran rife with rumors that radiation had spread widely from the plant, with some claiming that schools and playgrounds had dangerous levels of contamination.

On August 26, four months after the disaster, Kan would step down as prime minister. While Kan was a target of dissatisfaction in the press and social media, the true death knell for his administration rang from the Diet. There was division between the lower and upper houses, and Kan failed to garner enough votes to override an upper house vote. Even the disaster relief budget was delayed for weeks by the upper house (Kingston 2011). This was viewed not as a failure of multi-party collaboration, but rather as yet another failure of Kan's leadership style. Within the press, Kan and his administration were portrayed as essentially bumbling their way through the disaster, hindering the work of better responders, such as the SDF, and were contrasted with the population as a whole who were characterized as level-headed stoics (Bestor 2013, 765). This narrative—in which Kan and his administration's personal limitations hindered what would have been an effective response to what might otherwise have been a minor issue—arises from the need to pare complicated events down to simplified and more easily digestible tales (Samuels 2013, 27).

Within popular discourse after the disaster, several keywords arose to dominate depictions of the event. While all are telling of the period, only one is heavily used in *Shin-Godzilla*. The most popular was *souteigai* (想定外) or "unprecedented" (Sand 2021). With the disaster broadcast live over social media, the images of devastation shocked the population. The brutality of witnessing individuals swept away by a wall of water while those filming from safe vantage points shouted out in horror was beyond imagination for most prior to this event. Those in charge of planning and disaster preparedness latched onto this term to justify the failure of existing plans, seawalls, and evacuation preparedness. The *souteigai* defense was a cornerstone of the narrative advanced by government regulators and ministries, as well as the power company TEPCO that owned the Fukushima nuclear plant, which claimed that a tsunami and earthquake of such a scale was unimaginable. As such an event was beyond predicting, the logic goes, it could not have been prepared for or mitigated.

This defense is limited, as memorial stones that marked the high-water mark of past tsunamis demonstrated that such waves were indeed possible (Bestor 2013). In July of 2012, over a year after the disaster, the government did ultimately release a statement noting that a disaster of this scale was a clear possibility based off of historical records, that authorities could have been better prepared for such an event, and that policy decisions, both prior to and after the disaster, had exacerbated the destruction (Amano 2014, 332). But, perhaps due to its glaring hindsight, the statement had a limited impact on the public perception of 3.11. For many, the disaster was still beyond imagining, still *souteigai*. It is unsurprising that this term is used to great effect in *Shin-Godzilla*, where the creature is described as such. However, the film, too, demonstrates that the *souteigai* defense is in actuality a failure in imagination, as multiple groups in the films had predicted the existence of Godzilla based off of limited evidence.

The disaster also tied into longstanding fears concerning Japan's perceived precarity. Japan is at risk for a variety of natural disasters, from yearly typhoons and unpredictable earthquakes, but also from regional rivals. Over the last few years the Japanese coast guard has engaged in brinkmanship with South Korean and People's Republic of China naval vessels, as well as missile fly-overs launched from North Korea. This led some to argue that this consistent, low-level anxiety should have resulted in better preparation for internally displaced persons and wide-scale destruction (Samuels 2013). It is unsurprising that Kan's successor was Abe, himself a former prime minister. Not only did Abe belong the historically dominant party, the LDP, that after 3.11 was steadily rebuilding an image of stability and had a policy on national resilience already prepared, but Abe was also known for his emphasis on national security at a time when the public was feeling particularly vulnerable.

Others viewed the disaster as a chance to return to an older value system that prized self-sacrifice and patriotism. While the American media cycle speculated on the worst-case scenario of the Fukushima disaster and rumors that persons living on the western coast of North America were stocking up on iodine tablets, Japanese commentators in turn focused on the negative aspects of globalization and emphasized the importance of Japan becoming more self-reliant in the face of disaster (Ibid). In the film, the U.S. acts both as a supporter of and antagonist against Japan due to its own self-interest. The U.S. provides air support and information, but still leads the charge to once more drop an atomic bomb on a major Japanese city when it believes that the monster could turn and land on American soil. Only through the intercession of one American delegate embedded into the Japanese response effort is the bomb prevented from a precipitous launch, and she is motivated by her own ancestry as the descendant of an atomic bombing survivor.

The belief in a potentially revitalized Japan was predictable, as members of the media have characterized numerous disasters as potential launching points for national revitalization and portrayed such collective thinking as proof that the population of Japan is inherently self-sacrificing (Koikari, 2019; Hopson 2013). Morris-Suzuki (2017) noted that this discourse of hope tied in reoccurring discourse of *Yonaoshi*, or "world-renewal," movements that began in the eighteenth century in response to large-scale disasters such as famine or earthquakes that posit the near-at-hand revelation of a better future. Unsurprisingly, in the immediate aftermath of the disaster arose the Hydrangea Revolution, a new burst of popular protest again nuclear energy. Kan's immediate successor to the position of Prime Minister, Abe, in turn forwarded a Beautiful Country (美□□国) policy that balanced his support of mutual defense between Japan and the United States with Japanese nationalism. Both of these groups, in addition to the media in general, posited *kizuna* (絆), or community ties, as a key aspect of national identity (Morris-Suzuki 2017; Dinitto 2014). *Shin-Godzilla* itself ends on this note of optimism, with radiation levels decreasing rapidly in Tokyo and the understanding that the population will return to their homes within a year. The fictional prime minister states that he will remain in office only until then, when he will resign so that a new generation of politicians and civil servants, whose capabilities were ably demonstrated in the neutralization of the monster threat, can rise to power and once more make Japan a vibrant nation.

MISMANAGEMENT OF AN IMAGINED DISASTER

The film begins with the first of several sequences shot in the manner of "found footage."[2] The first video, taken by members of Japan's Coast Guard, inspects a small pleasure vessel found abandoned in the bay near Haneda Airport. Finding nothing but a sheaf of densely printed papers and a neatly aligned pair of shoes, the sailors decide to call in a tow when the ocean around them begins to steam. The view shifts immediately to a series of videos that mimic dashcams or cellphone cameras of commuters in the Aqua Line[3] that is breached by hot, blood-red water. Commuters flee the tunnel, taking jocular videos for social media. This harkens back to one of the most memorable aspects of 3.11, as Japan already had comprehensive cellphone coverage over the archipelago and a population that adopted the technology quickly (Gottlieb 2010, 397). This meant that both the earthquake and the following tsunami were live-streamed by tens of thousands of individuals during the disaster (Bestor 2013, 764). The film returns to this style of shooting throughout Godzilla's many rampages, often switching back and forth between traditional film-making to found footage, not only to better show the carnage that the creature inflicts on the panicked citizens of Tokyo and its environs, but also to tie the film visually the damage and horror shared online during 3.11.

Just after the stream of videos depicting the first arrival of the monster, the film switches into its first use of traditional filmmaking, which is invariably used whenever a bureaucratic or political member of the government or military are visible on screen. This is the first glimpse that the audience receives of the lead character, Deputy Chief Cabinet Secretary Yaguchi Rando (Hasegawa Hiroki). This is the first of multiple meetings, which number over half a dozen within the first fifteen minutes of the film alone, that make up the bulk of the top-level response to the monster. While this response is quick, beginning within only around ten to twenty minutes of the Aqua-Line being breached, efforts to understand and respond to the disaster are quickly bogged down with the minutiae of both the causes behind the disaster and the potential political fallout of their decisions. This parallels the Kan administration's response, which set up its own Cabinet response center in the same time frame but also quickly became mired in minutia.

Like Kan, this fictional Prime Minister (Osugi Ren) insists on micromanaging the state's response to the disaster. Accordingly, the gathered officials are unable to make any binding decisions before the Prime Minister arrives—almost an hour after the disaster begins. This inertia at the top is constantly juxtaposed with the actions performed by first responders that quickly move the population to safety, but by the midpoint of the film, have clearly become frustrated that they have no information from above that would allow them to operate more effectively. Furthermore, each new meeting is accompanied by a montage of set-up and take-down in which silent underlings effectively ready the room for the Cabinet office and its functionaries who, in turn, do little more than bandy around half-baked ideas and solutions—further juxtaposing high-level stagnation with low-level efficiency.

The inadequacies of the Cabinet are a recurring theme within the first half of the film. Yaguchi demonstrates his forward thinking and active response to the disaster while he and his assistant are glued to his smartphone in order to gather as much online information as possible before the meeting. The rest of the Cabinet is shown to be much more analog in its approach—relying on print-outs and memos generated by their staff and ignoring, as much as possible, any information shared online. Yaguchi's proactive and well-reasoned response to the burgeoning disaster signals his centrality to the narrative despite the numerous other named characters. In fact, Yaguchi's character falls into a popular archetype within Japanese disaster films in which the lead, who is almost always male, responds to catastrophe with self-reflection and ingenuity (Narine, 2010).

But Yaguchi moves beyond his role as a lone stalwart hero when the film demonstrates that his real strength is his ability to find and direct talent. He is not threatened by those around him who may be better informed or more intelligent, nor does he prickle when challenged—unlike his counterparts in the Cabinet. His ability to draw on non-traditional sources of information and reliance on experts who do not have high status or name-recognition is his greatest strength in the film. In addition, he is comfortable with strong women. In the fictional cabinet, the only female member on staff is the Minister of Defense Hanamori (Yo Kimiko), who is competent and direct—but only contributes to the discussion when directly addressed. Under Yaguchi, female staff members are as willing to volunteer information as men, and male staff members are willing to admit their mistakes when challenged by a woman. This continuous commentary on what a truly resilient leader would be remains a key focus throughout the rest of the film, as Yaguchi's actions are consistently contrasted with the old-fashioned and ineffectual response launched by Okochi.

Five minutes into the film, with four separate meetings convening and adjoining, the "Tokyo Bay Multiple Disaster Prime Minister Briefing" commences and, with it, the main action of the film. It is at this point in the film that the characters are identified by name via blocks of text listing the individual's Cabinet position and full name—similar to the manner in which individuals are identified in documentaries or news broadcasts. This, along with the "found footage," is an attempt at verisimilitude that is out of place in a kaiju[4] production. This incongruity serves to highlight the link between the fictional world of the film and its real-world inspiration. The officials in the meeting both demonstrate their lacking critical thinking skills and reveal their inadequate grasp of the situation by proposing a series of potential causes for the disaster that do not match the evidence at hand, but rather fit within their own preconceptions and biases. During the meeting, only Yaguchi demonstrates a complete understanding of the pertinent facts, having properly utilized his support staff.

During these meetings, Yaguchi continues to keep a close watch on social media and becomes the first person in the Cabinet to realize that the cause of the disaster must be an unknown creature. Despite receiving footage showing the monster's massive tail surfacing from the waters of the bay, the remaining ministers are skeptical and instead prefer the already disproven potential causes. In this, the remainder of the Cabinet follows Prime Minister Okochi's lead because he is incredulous that an animal of that size could exist. When Godzilla finally does appear, it immediately becomes apparent that the creature does not resemble the Godzilla seen in previous films—rather like 3.11 itself, the creature metamorphizes constantly in its initial attack.

The Cabinet's obsession with surface-level concerns is further revealed when the creature makes landfall during the press briefing, despite the Prime Minister's simultaneous claim that the creature could not possibly move on land—and in direct contradiction to prior warnings. Notably, the Prime Minister is more embarrassed than concerned by this revelation as he complains that this could damage his image with the electorate. Only after this public embarrassment does the Prime Minister finally begin to delegate authority. Because the Self-Defense Force cannot be deployed until an evacuation is completed, which has not yet been implemented at a level higher than municipal first responders, the Cabinet finally contacts the Tokyo Disaster Control center that is now seen for the first, and last, time in this film to evacuate the areas where the SDF will deploy. It is clear that not only are communications between the central government and the Tokyo disaster center limited, but also that the Tokyo Disaster Control Center can do little but gather information. The Tokyo governor is openly frustrated that the evacuation order had not been issued hours previously despite its obvious necessity, and that he did not have the legal authority to do so himself. Despite Tokyo's dense population and the risk of multiple potentially devastating natural disasters, once again there exists no prior evacuation plan. The lack of planning and communication bottlenecks too is an issue that is addressed by the National Resilience Policy, which is designed to facilitate the create of elaborate plans to prevent the loss of life and infrastructure as well as creating multiple channels of communication that could not be broken despite loss of personnel or the collapse communication networks (Cabinet Secretariat 2018).

The film then shows the consequences of this oversight. Streets are jammed with cars that inhibit the movement of fleeing pedestrians. Police officers and firefighters work to direct the crowds, but clearly do not know where they should be guiding the people, nor have they developed any efficient means of communicating clearly with the public, screaming directions over the panicked voices of those rushing past instead. These responders also have to stay behind despite the clear danger that approaches them. After 3.11, video surfaced online of Endo Miki, a twenty-five-year-old civil servant, giving evacuation directions over her town's loudspeaker system—and forfeiting her own chance of escape as she continued to give guidance as best she could until the tsunami ripped through her office, killing her (Yamashita 2017). The parallels between her heroic acts and those of the cinematic first responders are clear, further elevating the acts of local responders to those at the national level both fictitiously and in reality.

The elderly and the immobile must rely on the assistance of their neighbors to evacuate from their homes. One family is killed when Godzilla pushes over their apartment block—they were not warned that they were in the direct path of the creature despite its moving in a straight line through the city. This too draws from 3.11, where evacuation plans were vague or poorly implemented—such as the Okawa Elementary School, where the principal followed a manual directing the evacuation to a field away from the school despite a nearby hill offering closer and higher sanctuary. Only four students and one teacher survived (Parry 2017). *Shin-Godzilla* highlights within its narrative the need for the enhanced networking and strategic planning of the National Resilience Policy by demonstrating the consequences of the lack of such policy would be for the general population.

Notably, unlike their civilian counterparts, the SDF is shown to be decisive in their decision making, with each member of the command structure knowledgeable about the situation at hand and all avoiding the bickering that hinders the Cabinet's action. Additionally, unlike the Prime Minister whose panic seeps into each Cabinet meeting, the top military officer from the SDF never interrupts his staff with panicked questions, making well-reasoned decisions quickly. In the next scene, an officer is briefing the pilots on the mission and asks for volunteers, noting that the situation is volatile and dangerous. The pilots respond that none will volunteer, but will adhere to that day's roster of on-duty pilots, as this was a risk they accepted when they joined the Self-Defense Force. Despite the apparent conclusion that the SDF will not succeed in destroying Godzilla, the personnel continue the attack at the risk of their lives. This is in contrast to the Cabinet, who, with the exception of Yaguchi, will flee Tokyo when the creature reaches the city-center during its second attack. *Shin-Godzilla*'s depiction of the SDF mirrors the shifting public perception of the organization following 3.11, where civilian policy makers at the highest levels were viewed as bumbling their way through the disaster as clear-headed and forward-thinking members of the SDF sacrificed their well-being for the good of the nation (Bestor 2013, 765).

The day after the disaster, the Cabinet gathers, again wearing the garb of the rescue crew to survey the damage caused by Godzilla. Like Kan's Cabinet, this fictional one appears not to feel any emotional connection to the scale of the harm inflicted upon the lives of those in the devastated communities (Kingston 2011). Members of the Cabinet also appear to be oblivious that much of this damage was due to their delayed decision-making, one even using *souteigai* to justify their late response. However, Yaguchi counters these claims with the argument that, "No, we had two hours to mount an initial response—disappointing," which offends the other Cabinet members. It is apparent that this visit is merely a photo-op, so that the Cabinet can be seen behaving as if they were active members of the response disaster.

While the Cabinet spends their morning at a photo-op, the SDF tracks Godzilla to a trench just off the coast. With the possibility that Godzilla would once more make landfall, Yaguchi back-channels to form the "Unidentified Creature Response Task Force." This is a horizontally organized task force, and the members are selected according to their talent rather than seniority—a complete reversal of the Cabinet's composition. There is only a single individual selected to join the group due to political concerns, Kayoco[5] Anne Patterson (Ishihara Satomi), who is sent by the U.S. to embed herself in the response to the monster. It is telling that she is with Yaguchi rather than with the Cabinet; the Cabinet placed her with this taskforce because they viewed her as an onerous intrusion demanded by an ally, and figured that this was the simplest means of keeping her out of their way. Despite being the most successful response to the monster, the Cabinet treats this group as an irrelevant after-thought, a safe place to dump potential trouble-makers. Notably, this taskforce is also an example of what the National Resilience Policy intends to foster within Japan (DeWit 2016).

However, Kayoco is pleased with her assignment as this taskforce is the only group likely to be effective, and accordingly introduces data from the American intelligence community concerning Godzilla and Dr. Mori—who left a puzzle on the composition of the monster behind on the vessel that was boarded at the beginning of the film. Damning for the Japanese intelligence community, she has a copy of Dr. Mori's notes—meaning that no one in Japan recognized their importance despite his vessel's proximity to the first Godzilla incident. Rather, the Americans were able to obtain it. In another signal that demonstrates the fossilized and unimaginative thinking of the Okochi government, Yaguchi himself was not selected due to talent but rather due to inter-party politics as the descendent of a powerful political dynasty in a country where nearly a quarter of politicians comes from such families (Smith 2018). By assisting Yaguchi's taskforce, Kayoco can ensure that the U.S. will have a positive relationship with a probable future Prime Minister—another example of forward thinking that the Okochi Cabinet fails to fully utilize.

It is only now, almost fifty minutes into the film that has largely consisted of bureaucratic stagnation, that the historic Godzilla finally make its appearance to the original score of the 1954 film. From this point onward, music and scenes from *Evangelion* are no longer used or replicated within this film, replaced instead by the original soundtrack. The film has returned to its roots of Godzilla as a nuclear horror, no longer a creature that shakes the Earth or causes tsunami but rather an embodied Fukushima. The tone of the film does not yet shift, however, as the Cabinet's response to the monster is to bring together the United States and SDF in a quicker response to defend Tokyo. By the time this alliance is fully mobilized; the creature is nearing Tokyo despite making landfall on the other side of the Miura peninsula near Kamakura—over fifty kilometers away. Here, the film demonstrates the Cabinet's final act of ineptitude, as the order to attack the monster must move through layers of command: first the pilot must ask for permission to fire from their commander, who then asks for permission from the Minister of Defense, who then has to receive final approval from the Prime Minister, and then the final order must be relayed back through the same people to the pilot. And this must be done for each escalation of the attack, even though it was clear from the first encounter with Godzilla that many of the available weapons would likely fail. Later, Yaguchi would develop a plan consisting of pre-approved, multi-tiered responses so that the response to Godzilla would be swifter and more efficient.

As the SDF is unable to stop the creature, the Cabinet decides to call in an American airstrike. The U.S. has been pressuring Japan to allow for the use of much more powerful missiles, due to the fear that Godzilla would reach the nearest nuclear facility outside of Tokyo. Given the creature's trajectory, the nearest plant would have been that at Fukushima. This means that the population of the city center would require evacuation into the subways and basements because once again, the Cabinet had again not ordered it until the last possible moment. This would ultimately result in countless needless deaths, as even Yaguchi's team found themselves at half-power after the strike, many of the team having been unable to find shelter in time. The U.S. airstrike entails a firebombing of the creature—an image that harkens back to the first film's reenactment of the U.S. firebombing in Tokyo that killed hundreds of thousands in one night. As the film returns to traditional Godzilla imagery, this use of the original film's motifs adds an additional layer to the ambivalence toward the United States, perhaps alluding to public opinion about the American reaction to 3.11—where lower ranking American soldiers who participated in search and rescue were lauded while the high level embedding of American personnel, as well as the American media's response, were viewed as overbearing. This strike also means that it is ultimately the Americans who are responsible for the death of the Okochi Cabinet, with the exception of Asakusa and Yaguchi, who elect to remain behind and join with the civilians sheltering in the city. Godzilla's response to the U.S. strike is to produce innumerable laser-like blasts from its body followed by intense flames that reduce the center of Tokyo to a wall of flames. While the airstrike stuns Godzilla, who becomes inert over Tokyo Station, the city is rendered uninhabitable due to radioactive fallout.

Under the haphazardly composed Cabinet of junior ministers and the elderly Agricultural Minister, now Prime Minister, Satomi (Hiraizumi Sei), the evacuation of Tokyo is started. Satomi, like Yaguchi, obtained his position due to political considerations—in this case, his long-service to the party—and was not included in the initial response, having been viewed as unnecessary. Ironically, under Satomi the evacuation of Tokyo is undertaken in an orderly fashion and, when international opinion shifts against Japan, he is able to effectively leverage UN Security Council members against each other. It is here where *Shin-Godzilla* shifts completely from a focus on the 3.11 Disaster towards positing a future for post-disaster Japan. While the monster may be in its original form, it is inert and this allows for a short window where Japan can blaze a new path to a different future as *Shin-Godzilla*'s heroes band together to neutralize the creature and revitalize their country.

MUTUAL ASSISTANCE AND RESILIENCE

Yaguchi and his team hypothesize that Godzilla could be rendered permanently inert via a chemical compound; however, they lack the computational power to run the simulations. Unlike their American counterparts, who are hesitant to share information, no matter how pertinent, with others, Yaguchi has his team distribute their information to as many groups as possible both domestically and internationally. This allows a German university to research and discover the precise chemical formulation required, and offers Yaguchi and his team a chance to reach out to private corporations throughout Japan to manufacture it. Since the Japanese bureaucracy is known for its close ties to heavy industry, chemical manufacturing, and construction, it is no surprise that Yaguchi leverages these ties to initiate a massive project that combines chemical production, the privately-held transportation sector, and the nation's construction industry to develop a multi-stage attack on Godzilla. Furthermore, strengthening ties between the private sector and the public sector are a key part of the National Resilience Policy—which have expanded to include work with international organizations and companies (DeWit, Shaw and Djalante 2020).

On the day of the attack, Yaguchi remains as close to the action as possible but, unlike Okochi, does not require that the teams report to him—rather they are to do their duties according to the plan and according to local conditions in order to keep the effort as focused and swift as possible. He, too, dons the clothing of the first responders, but, unlike the Okochi Cabinet, Yaguchi does so to take-part in the attack on Godzilla and wears them for protection just like everyone else. The final battle takes up a small, almost anti-climactic portion of the film, as the majority of screen time was dominated by meetings and human collaboration.

After this partnership, both Yaguchi and Kayoco comment that this may not be the last time that they will work together. Both have their eyes on the highest political posts in their country—aspirations that are now within reach due to their successful negotiation of the Godzilla crisis, valuing teamwork and ingenuity rather than short-sighted political considerations. They both also represent a new hope for Japan-U.S. relations, where both stand upon an equal footing. The Satomi Cabinet in turns plans to resign within the year, stating that they are nothing more than a caretaker government that wishes to hand over a stabilized Japan to a new generation of leaders who can direct the nation towards a brighter future. Over these more optimistic plans, however, hangs the frozen body of Godzilla and the knowledge that if it begins moving, the United States is prepared to undertake a nuclear strike within three minutes. The last shot of the film pans over the seemingly fixed monster, only to reveal that there is one final mutation on the original form of the monster—on its tail, we see humanoid forms pulling away from Godzilla's flesh. Godzilla's last action responded to the threat of teamwork with a team of its own. Therefore, it follows, Japan will never be safe unless it, too, continues to evolve.

The last segment of the film is a treatise on the policy of National Resilience and the Beautiful Japan policies. It is notable that, unlike past Godzilla films, the monster is not defeated with firepower but rather through the collaboration of the state with private industry. Only by working in collaboration with private industry and academia do Yaguchi and his team devise and implement the plan that saves Japan from destruction—not at the hands of the creature but rather from the incompetence of the old political order and the self-interest of global rivals. This intersection of the state, industry, and a new generation of experts who are not bound by traditional power structures but instead focus on innovation are all key discursive points of the policies.

The national resilience policy and investment in self-reliance existed prior to 3.11. During the disaster, the limitations in technology and planning became quickly apparent. Despite existing policies that encouraged collaboration between ward-level public servants and national-level ministries so that they could both continue to operate and support each other smoothly in the event of a natural disaster, key personnel in local level governance experienced heavy casualties—like Yaguchi's team in the film. Without a clear chain of command, the response slowed and failed to readily address local needs (Aoki 2015). Even on an individual level, such as the "all-electric homes," which were partially powered by solar panels and touted by TEPCO as black-out and disaster-proof, virtually all failed after the initial quake (Sand 2012, 317). Originally proposed in 2009, the National Resilience Policy focused on the re-development of aging infrastructure, the strengthening of local resources, and increased planning to prevent large-scale loss of life in a massive natural disaster. This decision to emphasize the concept of disaster-proofing as an opposition party proved fortuitous, as the LDP could readily highlight this as a contrast to the perceived inadequacy of Kan's response to 3.11 (Koikari 2019).

The LDP's National Resilience Policy (国土強靭化) is complex, as it tries to reinforce the networks between localities and national ministries so that they can equally withstand the devastating loss of life and damaged infrastructure that had been so easily ruptured during 3.11 (Kazuhiko 2017). According to policy documents, the goal is to ultimately shift from reacting to disaster to proactively working to mitigate damage to property and the loss of life with four key goals. The primary goal is the preservation of as many individuals as possible in the case of a repeated Triple Disaster. The second is to maintain a functioning state and society with the support of the third goal, which is to maintain the integrity of infrastructure. Lastly, the policy encourages the creation of effective plans so that recovery efforts are swift and effective (Cabinet Secretariat 2018). This is a major aspect of the film's commentary as well. Due to the slow response of Okochi's fictive Cabinet, lives are lost when Godzilla first makes landfall after its slow ascent up the Tama River. The lack of communication between those coordinating the national response and the first responders is shown repeatedly, as well as the innumerable and ineffective Cabinet meetings that take up the first third of the film. Damningly, both the United States and a poorly funded academic had realized the existence and potential scale of Godzilla and had planned accordingly. Godzilla is a destructive force insofar as incompetency and limited imagination of the state-level response allows it to run rampage through Japan. Thorough planning and resourceful redirection of both Japan's ministries and use of their ties with private industry is the backbone of Yaguchi's effective response—notably, a key aspect of the National Resilience Policy itself. Even Godzilla, rendered inert at the end of the film, recognizes this as a strength. The last shot of the film pans up to the creature's tail where a group of humanoid beings are rising out of the monster's flesh—it is forming its own network of experts. Lastly, the film's final Prime Minister does not take advantage of the situation to launch himself into a long tenure as Prime Minister. He states that he shall resign once everyone is able to return to Tokyo so that the new generation can lead Japan into a revitalized future—a comment no doubt levied at Abe by the filmmakers.

National Resilience also plays a role in the both former Prime Minister Abe and current Prime Minister Suga's administration's fiscal policy, "Abenomics," which is predicated on principles of quantitative easing, deregulation, and increasing privatization. With its emphasis on protecting infrastructure and rebuilding trust between local governments and industry, National Resilience is intended to assist in the implementation of the last two aspects of Abenomics (DeWit 2015). GE, the American company that built the Fukushima plant, was tapped to create an "industrial internet that could link together both public and private infrastructure to streamline both the sharing of data and communications during a disaster" (DeWit 2013, 1). As early as 2013, the spending on the National Resilience Policy had resulted in the investment of almost ¥12 million by private industry alone—largely focused on the expansion of solar power and renewed energy infrastructure (DeWit 2016). In addition, local governments and individuals are also expected to invest in strengthening local capabilities and infrastructure (Cabinet Secretariat 2018). On the individual level, there has been an increase in consumer products (危機管理) that purport to enhance crisis response and management for an average household. In 2013, a convention in an upscale district in Tokyo drew visitors with the promise that mothers could more readily protect their family through a variety of gadgets (Korikari 2019). But this is an extension of past political policies that had failed to mitigate the damage of 3.11. The film's call for new ideas and renewal thereby both supports and undermines the National Resilience Policy, as it posits that such initiatives should be led by the new generation of civilly minded youth who have been fired up by disaster.

CONCLUSION

Shin-Godzilla is a unique distillation of the discourse surrounding 3.11 and the National Resilience Policy. Even its title, best rendered in English as "A New Godzilla," signals that the film is a commentary on a new era in Japanese history—borne out of disaster like the original, 1954 film. The creature reenacts 3.11, beginning with tremors that breach the Aqua Line with seawater and then sweeps inland via the coast and ocean-connected rivers. Even its initial shape, clumsy and amorphous, seems to bring Godzilla to a primitive, elemental level as an unintelligent and unguided force of nature. However, its final form demonstrates a level of creative thinking and planning that places it on a more human level above that of a simple natural force. However, it is not Godzilla that brings disaster but rather the incompetence of Japan's politicians and indifference of its allies. Like 3.11, Godzilla destroys this ineffectual Cabinet and brings an opportunity for national renewal. Despite the creature's destructive power, it offers Japan a chance to sweep away stagnation and offers a map written in blood and debris for how Japan could make itself resilient against all potential threats. It is through open-collaboration, innovation, both public and private, and the cooperation of industry that Japan can save itself. However, with Yaguchi, the creators posit that a new political order must, too, be established.

REFERENCES

Amano, Ikuho. 2014. "From Mourning to Allegory: Post-3.11. *Space Battleship Yamato* in Motion." *Japan Forum*, 26:3 (May): 325–339.

Aoki, Naomi. 2015. "Wide-area Collaboration in the Aftermath of the March 11 Disasters in Japan: Implications for Responsible Disaster Management." *International Review of Administrative Science*, 81:1 (October): 196–213.

Bestor, Theodore C. 2013. "Disasters, Natural and Unnatural: Reflections on March 11, 2011, and Its Aftermath." *The Journal of Asian Studies*, 72:4 (November): 763–782. JSTOR.

Brougher, Kerry. "Art and Nuclear Culture." *Bulletin of Atomic Scientists*, 69:6 (November): 11–18.

Cabinet Secretariat. 2018. "Fundamental Plan for National Resilience." *Fundamental Plan for National Resilience*. Accessed may 1, 2021. www.cas.go.jp/jp/seisaku/kokudo_kyoujinka/en/fundamental_plan.pdf.

DeWit, Andrew. 2013. "Can Abenomics Cope With Environmental Disaster?" *The Asia-Pacific Journal: Japan Focus*, 11:43 (October): 1–9. Accessed May 21, 2021. https://apjjf.org/2013/11/43/Andrew-DeWit/4016/article.html.

———.2015. "Disaster Risk Reduction and Resilience as Structural Reform in Abenomics." *The Asia-Pacific Journal: Japan Focus*, 13:1, (January): 1–10. Accessed March 17, 2021. https://apjjf.org/2015/13/1/Andrew-DeWit/4248.html.

———. 2016. "Japan's National Resilience and the Legacy of 3-11." *The Asia-Pacific Journal: Japan Focus*, 14:6 (March): 1–6. Accessed March 11, 2021. https://apjjf.org/2016/06/DeWit.html.

DeWit, Andrew, Rajib Shaw, and Riyanti Djalante. 2020. "An Integrated Approach to Sustainable Development, National Resilience, and COVID-19 Responses: The Case Study of Japan." *International Journal of Disaster Risk Reduction*, 51 (December): 1–6.

Dinitto, Rachel. 2014."Narrating the Cultural Trauma of 3/11: The Debris of Post-Fukushima Literature and Film." *Japan Forum*, 26:3 (May): 340–360.

Fruhstuck, Sabine. 2007. *Uneasy Warriors: Gender, Memory, and Popular Culture in the Japanese Army*. Berkeley: University of California Press.

Gottlieb, Nanette. 2020. "Playing with Language in E-Japan: Old Wine in New Bottles." *Japanese Studies*, 30:3 (November): 393–407.

Hopson, Nathan. 2013. "Systems of Irresponsibility and Japan's Internal Colony." *The Asia-Pacific Journal: Japan Focus*, 11:52 (December): 1–9. Accessed May 12, 2021. https://apjjf.org/2013/11/52/Nathan-Hopson/4053/article.html.

Kazuhiko, Terao. 2017. "Basic Concept of National Resilience and Policy of the Government of Japan: Resilient Japan." 農村計画学会誌, 36:3 (2017): 398–401.

Kingston, Jeff. 2011. "Ousting Kan Naoto: The Politics of Nuclear Crisis and Renewable Energy in Japan." *The Asia-Pacific Journal: Japan Focus*, 9:39 (September): 1–14. Accessed May 12, 2021. https://apjjf.org/2011/9/39/Jeff-Kingston/3610/article.html.

Koikari, Mire. 2019. "Re-masculinizing the Nation: Gender, Disaster, and the Politics of National Resilience in Post-3.11 Japan." *Japan Forum*, 31:2 (October): 143–164.

Morris-Suzuki, Tessa. 2017. "Disaster and Utopia: Looking Back on 3/11." *Japanese Studies*, 37:2 (August): 171–190.

Narine, Neil. 2010. "Global Trauma and Narrative Cinema." *Theory, Culture & Society*, 27:4 (August): 119–145.

Pascale, Celine-Marie. 2017. "Vernacular epistemologies of risk: The crisis in Fukushima." *Current Sociology*, 65:1 (March): 3–20.

Parry, Richard Lloyd. 2017. *Ghosts of the Tsunami: Death and Life in Japan's Disaster Zone*. MCD/Farrar, Straus and Giroux.

Samuels, Richard. 2013. *3.11 Disaster and Change in Japan*. Ithaca: Cornell University Press.

Sand, Jordan. "Living with Uncertainty after March 11, 2011." *The Journal of Asian Studies*, 71:2 (May): 313–318.

Smith, Daniel M. 2018. *Dynasties and Democracy*. Stanford: Stanford University Press, 2018.

Tsutsui, William. 2017. *Godzilla on My Mind: Fifty Years of the King of the Monsters*. New York: St. Martin's Press.

Yamashita, Michael. 2017. "The Calm Before the Wave." *National Geographic*, 14 Sept. 2017. Accessed March 15, 2021. www.nationalgeographic.com/magazine/2012/02/tsunami-science/.

NOTES

1. For the remainder this chapter the combination disaster will be referred to as 3.11.
2. Diegetic videos taken by individuals within the narrative.
3. The undersea tunnel that runs under that section of the bay.

4. The term for a large monster film in Japan. Other examples would be the American monster King Kong.

5. This name should have been Romanized as "Kayoko," this error is a signal that while she is of Japanese descent she is disconnected from Japanese culture and norms.

Chapter 3

Cultural Trauma, Cross-Flow of Aesthetics, and the Child

A Comparison Between Ringu *and* The Ring

Bipasha Mandal

After the A-bombing of Hiroshima and Nagasaki in 1945, the survivors of the man-made catastrophe had to suffer the insufferable. Subsequently, in a parallel thread, what ensued is a complete reevaluation of the Japanese culture and society which, in turn, also facilitated the already deeply traumatized citizens a sort of disintegration not only of the idyllic concept of nationhood, but also simultaneous scrutiny of the individuated identity in the midst of shared collective grief and loss. Any artistic artifact to emerge out of such a culturally traumatized context, be it visual or otherwise, would be deeply rooted in, originate from, and subsume the collective trauma to signify the absences, the silenced, as a form of testimony to speak of the unspeakable. In an age characterized by neo-colonialist invasion made a spectacle by the rise of news media, the genre horror's appeal as a form of popular culture also points to the audiences' collective urge to take into considerations the traumatic past while at the same time also looking into the representation of such trauma.

The release of Hideo Nakata's *Ringu* (1998) at the turn of the millennium perhaps gave momentum to trans-cultural and trans-national dissemination of the symbol of the uncanny child with its characteristic pale-white face with ink-black lanky hair. The subsequent reception of the movie, and the fact that Hollywood picked this movie up for a remake not only points to the appeal of the genre of horror, but more than that, it brings to the surface the collective effort to understand past trauma and bring into question the concept of nationhood and what it demands of the individuals: for the individuals to be a reflection of a nation promulgated by varied ideologies. In the Japanese movies of the 1960s onwards, a telling pattern of a female ghost/corpse returning from the dead to wreak vengeance upon those who have wronged her could easily be deciphered. It is imperative to mention here that this trope of a female ghost haunting often with a disfigured body is not an exclusive one for either Japan or the United States. The same trope could be seen in the movies of other countries and cultures as well. Both the narratives of *Ringu* and *The Ring* (Gore Verbinski, 2002) are built on the Japanese *onryō* tradition of storytelling that focuses on exposing the hidden yet unhealed wounds inflicted upon the nation, and thereby, on the psyche of the populace. The introduction and enforcement of the Showa Constitution following Japan's defeat and the subsequent invasion of Japan by America, which set out to rewrite Japan's ideals on the basis of American propaganda and as a pseudo-means to end the right-wing militaristic zeal prevalent in Japan, called into question the nation's renegotiation of its own historic past.

The phenomenon of Hollywood adopting and remaking Japanese films in the American vein is not something new, and could be traced back to Hollywood's remakes of Kurosawa Akira's movies. Although the two films in question, *Ringu* and *The Ring* are culturally different, in both of these films symbols are used to denote and signify the coherent narrative that seems to be missing from the main drive of the plot: why is the ghost killing whomever she is killing? These symbols offer audiences richly potent pathways into uncovering the underlying cultural patterns that inform the attitudes towards the supernatural while at the same time offering a distinct perspective of both the nations through difference in a very Bhabha-like third space.

As mentioned earlier, within the Japanese tradition the spectral female ghost with pale face and jet-black hair has also become the stock-image of any strain of storytelling based supernatural entity or simply a horror story. Arguably, cinema is the youngest form of storytelling and therefore, it is not surprising that it will be influenced, and inspired by a long-established tradition of storytelling that uses the female ghost trope. "*Yurei*, or female ghosts, are central figures in numerous myths and folktales dating back to the Edo period (1603–1867). *Tokaido Totsuya Kaidan* (*Ghost Story of Totsuya*), *Bancho Sarayashiki* (*The Story of Okiku*), and *Kuroneko* (*Black Cat*) are just three of the more popular kaidan (literally "supernatural tale" or Japanese ghost story), many of which feature innocent women who are victimized and brutally murdered by men" points out Valerie Wee (2011, 49). The spirit of the murdered woman comes back to wreak vengeance upon those who have wronged her, and upon society in general. It would be interesting to note here that this narrative does not enjoy an enduring influence only within the Japanese culture; in India, too, horror films to come out of Bollywood also employ this narrative where a wronged woman haunts those who have wronged her. The most recent among the plethora of such movies would be the Bollywood movie *Stree* (2018), directed by Amar Kaushik.

It must be acknowledged here that the aesthetic that underlines Japanese movies did not develop and does not exist in a cultural vacuum, that is to say, we have to acknowledge the cross-cultural influence and the globalization that clearly marks the turn of the century. Japan as a nation had to navigate or negotiate between the two sides of capitalist modern Japan: between the "otherness" that the Japanese civilization went through postwar and that of the clinging on to an "authentic" Japaneseness; this unyielding tension resulted in what Paul David Grainge in a commentary on Arjun Appadurai has called a "deterritorialized community" (2000, 137). By the late 1970s, the kaidan tales themselves came under the direct influence of American and European horror narratives, and the Hideo Nakata movie *Ringu* (1998) cannot be said to embody a long tradition of authentic Japanese storytelling. The effect of Sadako (played by Rie Inō) from *Ringu* also became a synecdoche and a point of reference for horror movies outside of Japan, and this movie also helped to establish a new genre known outside of Japan as J-horror.

Ringu's Japan is a hugely Americanized Japan with its baseball games, western-style living conditions, and of course, technology-laden everyday life. Reiko, (played by Nanako Matsushima) the mother, is a career-oriented modern woman molded in the American style, pursuing a career in media. When she encounters the murdering video, the images shown do not immediately form a coherent pattern giving rise to a whole narrative that is easily decipherable. There appears to be no connection between a woman combing her hair, and a bunch of people walking uphill: this could perhaps be read, alongside the literary modernist narratives that come with their own sets of incoherent narrative. But more than that perhaps it is precisely the intention of Nakata to produce an incoherent sequence and situating it inside a film that is also characterized by ambiguity. What Reiko discovers from these fragmented images, the fact that Sadako's mother Shizuko (played by Masako) was a psychic who predicted a volcanic eruption which, in turn, explains the people struggling uphill, and what she interprets from these images are never contextualized, their meaning never established. In other words, the stringing of the images to form a narrative coherent which in some way uncovers the meaning underneath it all, is applicable only to Reiko; since we are not given the truth about these images, this same set of images would mean something else entirely for someone outside of this socio-political context. Interestingly, this perspective perhaps also stems from the influence of Hollywood which strictly adheres to the sequential development in a plot with a beginning, a middle, and an end, a plot which, more often than not, demands an organic and singular meaning to come out of the visual experience. Richie notes, "the kind of narrative tightness so prized in the West is not found in Japanese films. The idea that each unit or scene should push the story through to its conclusion is not one to which Japanese literature, drama, or film subscribes" (1990, 8). Not privileging the narrative coherence not only situates the influence of the long-standing Japanese aesthetics but also inadvertently plays the part of creating an atmosphere of unease, full of anxiety, unpredictability and the fear of the unknown. Moreover, the deadly images and symbols of the video also serve as the means to refer to contexts outside the film narrative, and within the broader Japanese aesthetic realm. In this case, the several images used in the video refers directly to the traditional *Kaidan* or ghost stories. Sadako, therefore, belongs to the already established long-line of traditional Japanese ghosts which, in turn, clearly shows the influence of traditional Japanese art and by means of association, broader Japanese cultural influence on the film.

As mentioned before the narrative of *Ringu* is marked by ambiguity and incoherent development. For example, how the videotape was created in the first place or why the seven days interval between the watching of the video and the subsequent killing, are never explained. However, the ambiguity can never be associated with or categorized as unintentional gaps in the plot. As argued above, these gaps act as a referent to the well-established Japanese cultural contexts. Wee similarly argues, "These narrative gaps can be related to the Japanese Buddhism derived aesthetic concept *mujo,* which can be translated loosely as the practice of 'leaving things incomplete' (2011, 49). This *mujo* deliberately leaves things incomplete so that the individual goes on to weave a complete narrative of their own, stringing referents together to form a meaningful unit. According to Richie, in Japanese films "the collection of scenes which makes up the sequence is sometimes . . . empty in that narrative information (in the Western sense) is missing—'nothing' occurs, though this nothing may be filled with another kind of information or something other than information" (1988, 20). Establishing the film within the broader Japanese cultural context and its unique and exquisite mode of horror storytelling would be to do injustice to Nakata who although was indeed inspired by the Japanese-ness of the ghost stories, masterfully situated the film in contemporary times, and thereby, also provided a commentary on the anxieties stemming from the economic stagnation of the 1970s and the weight of the Lost Decade, a period of economic stagnation which lasted from the year 1991 to 2001 following the asset price bubble's collapse in the late 90s when the strong economic growth of Japan ended abruptly. Sadako ultimately is a child and she serves as an embodiment of the internal "other" of Japan as a nation. Napier has pointed out that this internal other is related with the changing ideas about selfhood paralleled with Japan's slow transition into a country that embraces modernity and the Western ideals: "the fantastic Other may be seen as an important means by which post-Restoration Japanese began to construct a Westernized sense of self [. . .] working out their explorations of the self against such textual elements as dreams, ghosts, monsters and *doppelgängers*" (1995, 97). This internal other perhaps has an overwhelming influence irrespective of different culture; moreover, the child as a site where deep-seated national anxieties are given a voice resonated deeply with the American audiences which, in part, would explain the very successful American remake of the movie.

In most contexts, a child represents the future of a nation: a child symbolizes "the continuation of the nation-state itself" (Lury 2010, 26). However, Tanaka suggests that in premodern and early Japan children were not thought of as embodying the futuristic ventures and goals of a nation-state. Rather they existed and were thought of mainly as a part of the locale, just existing alongside other citizens, bearing no special responsibility. Kathleen Uno argues that during the Meiji Restoration the children became the site upon which the national progress was inscribed (1999, 8). Interestingly, Brian Platt makes a similar argument:

> Japanese leaders during the early decades of the Meiji period (1868–1912) believed that the source of Western power and the key to Japan's national survival in the face of Western imperialism lay in the nation-state's capacity for mobilizing human resources. When they set about creating institutions to accomplish this goal, they recognized the particular importance of the school, which extended the project of mobilization to Japanese children. In turn, they opened up the child to public inquiry, generating within an emerging mass society a new awareness of childhood. [. . .] the modern concept of childhood was "created" in the context of Japan's encounter with modernity. (2005, 965–66)

The proliferation of children as facilitators of horror narrative forced to surface the suppressed ideologies that ran parallel to Japan's quest for modernity while at the same time burying the traumatic past following WWII and the Lost Decade. Jessica Balanzategui makes a point about the Imperial Rescript which the children would recite to pledge their allegiance to the Emperor (2018, 166). Later, the Imperial Rescript was proved to be null and void, and it was thought of as a site for militaristic aggression which prefers nationalistic zeal over the individuality of its citizen; in the long run, any form of excessive nationalism proves to be cancerous. Furthermore, Balanzategui also points out that in 2013 the mayor of Osaka, Hashimoto made a controversial claim stating that Japan's wartime sex slaves were necessary to comfort the soldiers torn by the experience of war (Ibid). These are only two examples, among many, which show that Japan is still a long way from coming to terms with the atrocities committed in WWII. Broadly speaking, the horror movies, and the child as the main perpetrator of those movies highlight these tensions and anxieties, albeit in a very subtle manner.

While the discussion above points that *Ringu* originates from a distinct traditional Japanese root, further extending the branch of its own mode of storytelling which is something exclusive to the cultural context of Japan, and that the film acts as a site to bring to the surface the age-old anxieties intensified by the war and Japan's quest for modernity, there are elements in the film that are directly influenced by an avant-garde perspective. To make a claim that *Ringu* retains the cultural authenticity of Japan in an age of globalism or rather in an age of neo-imperialism, would be simplistic. Several sequences of the film refer directly to Hollywood and its influence on the film. Richard Hand in "Aesthetics of Cruelty" notes that in the opening scene of the film where two teenagers, Tomoko and Masami, talk about a mysterious video footage some moments before Tomoko dies under mysterious circumstances is a direct product of Hollywood's popular teen slasher films (2005, 22). The fact that Reiko acts as the film's sole "protagonist," in the sense that she is the only person who discovers the mystery behind the killer video or decides to investigate further to understand Sadako resonates strongly with Hollywood's focus on a single "larger-than-life" hero who could do it all. Hollywood rings loudly in the sequence where Sadako finally makes her appearance on screen. Notably, at that point her corpse had been found and rescued from the well which gave both Reiko and Ryuji the impression that the curse had been redeemed, Sadako had been freed from the bonds, and that they are safe. However, the deeply haunting images of Sadako's contorted figure crawling out of the screen to occupy a space in the "real" world yet again is a sequence that stems directly from its Hollywood roots. Julie Rauer notes that Japan was "tragically splintered by defeat, subjugation, humiliation, and inconceivable horrors—unable to command a return to a unified monolithic persona, the ordered cerebral imperative and societal dignity of pre-nuclear innocence [. . .] World War II left indelible stains on the Japanese psyche" (2005). After the war, images of the disfigured bodies haunted the psyche of the whole of Japan, and especially the bodies of women as a site of violence became a symbol of suffering, and thereby, of a victim. In fact, the image of the child as a suffering victim found its permanent place among the statues of the Peace Park which commemorates precisely the hardships faced by the Japanese citizens. Balanzategui points out that the statue of Sadako Sasaki, a young girl who died of radiation-induced leukemia, has "become the most recognizable symbol of the postwar valiant victim" (173). It is, therefore, not a coincidence that the ghost-protagonist of *Ringu* shares the same first name as that of Sasaki. But unlike the unfortunate fate that most Japanese children had to face, the film reaches a cathartic climax where Reiko clutches the corpse of Sadako and cries, thereby, symbolizing collective mourning for a past and the lives unfairly lost. Wee contends,

> Although *Ringu* borrows from, and pays homage to, classical *Kaidan* in its narrative, characterization, and visual imagery, it also deviates from the traditional Japanese industry's practice of simply retelling a familiar ghost story. Instead, *Ringu* reinterprets these traditional narratives, immersing the ghost story within a contemporary structure and plot that reflect influences from other national cinemas. These complex inter-textual echoes and references highlight the intricate matrix of influences across textual and cultural boundaries that characterize not only the history of horror cinema, but also the process of filmmaking in general. (Wee 2011, 54)

But Sadako's suffering does not end with Reiko's show of acknowledgement of her pain; she emerges out of Ryuji's television screen to kill him indicating that Sadako will continue on her journey until the whole of Japan falls victim to her curse. The final redemption that Hollywood drills into most of its movies is not to be sought here. *Ringu* demands a reevaluation of the supernatural, of the thin boundary between what we know as reality and the other world, that emerges from an intricate mixture of textual and cultural traditions expanding a whole of culture, materialized in the form of a J-horror movie.

In contrast, mainstream Hollywood movies do not offer the same blurred lines between reality and the fantastical/supernatural. Hollywood films, but a few experimental ones such as Adrian Lyne's 1990 movie *Jacob's Ladder*, and Martin Scorsese's neo-noir thriller *Shutter Island* (2010), are geared towards portraying the reality as it is with minimum deviation, even when a subject matter such as the one being discussed is taken up as a kind of source material. Realism has been a major part of Hollywood, with its protagonists possessing the demi-god-like ability to overcome every single hurdle thrown at them, while being devoid of hamartia, at least partially, putting the classical characters to shame. More often than not, it advocates for a linear progression, and although the order might be thrown into chaos mid-movie, the ending would resonate with the order expressed during the first half of the movie. However, the early 1970s underwent a development that comes very close to the anxieties expressed in the J-horror movies. If dug deeper, there is sure to be deep-seated cultural anxiety as a source of this shift from realism; however,

> it can also be interpreted as part of a broader tendency within American cinema's adoption of art cinema storytelling that culminated in Hollywood's turn toward the New American Cinema movement in the 1970s. The contemporary horror film's break from its classical roots is expressed in the propensity for

open-ended narratives, minimal plot developments, and the creation of unappealing characters who challenge audience identification, features associated with modernism, art cinema, and, to some extent, the New American Cinema. (Wee 2011, 55)

The Ring perfectly embodies Hollywood's shift from the conventional and traditional portrayal of the linear, realistic narratives to embracing a more open-ended, ambiguous ending. The Hollywood remake of *Ringu* attempts to close the narrative gaps prevalent in the Japanese film, and offer a more coherent narrative that will reinstate the binary opposition between the "real" world and the "supernatural" world, keeping the two worlds separate. *The Ring*'s killer video sequence is much longer than that of *Ringu;* however, that does not guarantee that the shots of seemingly unrelated objects portrayed in the video signify a message that is coherently meaningful. On the contrary, the close-up shots of a horse's eye, of maggots, of a centipede, of water, at its face value, appear as fragmented as the reflections off of a broken mirror. But these images perform as a referent, pointing to a specific meaning which, in a collective format, offer coherence. As Bordwell and Thompson note, "looking is purposeful; what we look at is guided by our assumptions and expectations about what to look *for*" (1990, 141). Therefore, the shot of the woman combing her hair establishes a relation with the young girl's distorted image. The mirror above a wood paneling suggests that both of these women are in the same room; further, the image of a house with its shadowy figure that remains at the window suggests that this is where the women live, thereby, establishing a possible familial relationship between them. Seen in the overall context of the movie, the images of the video appear to be coherent, something that is glaringly absent in the Japanese version. The video sequence of the American version point to the vital events that drive the whole narrative, and it also provides Rachel with the vital information that furthers her investigation into the murdering video. Rachel discovers about the life of Samara whose arrival at Anna and Richard Morgan's farm, her adopted parents, triggered a series of mysterious events. What ensues is Samara's visit to the psychiatric ward only to be confined to a barn when she comes back to live with the Morgans, and ultimately, Samara's murder and Anna's suicide. All of these details can be deciphered from the seemingly unrelated shots of the videotape; all of the shots in the video not only narrate the events that had occurred, but some of them also provide vital information to Rachel and Noah. This is not to imply that all of the elements suspended in the videotape acts as a referent to a certain meaning; some of the images in the videotape elude falling into a coherent narrative whole.

One other important point of divergence from the Japanese version, which also provides a vital piece of information, thereby, an explanation, is that the video sequence in the American version attempts at explaining the seven-day gap between watching the videotape and the imminent death. Hollywood's version of the film goes to such an extent to explain the seven-day lag by giving Rachel an eye for details, who also was able to establish the fact that it must have taken Samara seven days to die after being trapped inside the well, and while being forcefully confined to the barn, a TV must have been her only connection with the outside world; after her death, the TV also becomes a vessel for her for the same reason.

More recent horror movies to come out of Hollywood tend to serve as a political commentary on the socio-economic conditions of the States, such as Jordan Peele's brilliant movie *Get Out*, which does not include the element of the supernatural but the unease of uncertainty and unpredictability keeps the audience at the edge of their seats, or even those films that do feature the supernatural as its driving force, such as Ari Aster's 2018 film *Hereditary*, do not always follow the pattern of progressing from the order through a stage of chaos to reach an orderly stable state again. However, coming back to *The Ring*, the fact that the film tries to provide an explanation and a logical coherence only serve to intensify the underlying anxiety, and thereby, creates a menacing presence of the supernatural other, of the uncanny, an embodiment of the cultural "oddity" the suppression of which becomes necessary for a dominant hegemonic power to strive, to further maintain its power relations to other hegemonic powers. Wee similarly argues:

> in *The Ring*, the explanations, clarifications, and scientific rationalizations uncovered by Rachel and Noah are ultimately irrelevant and immaterial in combating the ambiguous, unknown, irrational power of Samara's evil. By emphasizing reason, information, and knowledge, and subsequently undermining their power and consequence, the film reflects a declining confidence and sense of security in humanity's ability to harness our intellect to control and determine our reality and destiny. What The Ring dramatizes is the failure and inconsequence of humanity's ongoing reliance on logic, science, and reason against a destructive supernatural force. (2011, 59)

Samara never conformed to the boundaries set in place, not when she was alive, certainly not after death. A few scholars have pointed out Samara's transgressive abjection by highlighting the fact that Samara enters into "reality" by stepping out of the television to kill her subjects: thereby, the boundary of any kind does not exist for her. Mary Douglas (1966) has argued that *The Ring* conforms to the Hollywood, western ideas and definition of horror precisely by disregarding the boundaries that exist for anything that could not be put into binary oppositions and something which consistently transgresses the culturally defined boundaries, especially that between "us" and "them" is seen to embody destructive supernatural power. At the end of the film although both Rachel and Noah unearth the mystery, acknowledging the harm done to Samara, they fail to neutralize the evil, which directly reflects Hollywood's growing acceptance of ambiguities and open-endedness.

CONCLUSIONS

Both the films, the original *Ringu* and the Hollywood remake *The Ring* have been shaped by the existing socio-cultural context of the nation the films are set in. Although there are dissimilarities between the movies which also could be explained in terms of different artistic visions of the directors, the films act as a site where the cultural paranoia and anxieties surface in the form of a distorted body and evil other to, in a way, subvert the hegemonic dominance or the insistence on the nation-state's part to bury the bloody past only to impose a notion of modernity on all of its citizens to maintain the status quo. However, *Ringu* does portray the cultural acceptance of the existence of the otherworldly, the opening sequence clearly showing an influence of the American films. On the other hand, *The Ring*, although accepting the ambiguities, showcases Hollywood's attempt at providing a more coherent, logical narrative underpinned by reasoning. The child and women-centred proliferation of horror movies are perhaps reactionary of the national cultural trauma. Unease prevalent in the horror movies give voice to the anxiety that otherwise becomes increasingly difficult to acknowledge under the weight of hegemony, but both the films are nonetheless "deterritorialized to refract the cultural 'between-ness' of transnational cinema" (Balanzategui 2018, 237); however, it also creates a two-way cultural flow of the art of storytelling and aesthetics to come up with new ways to jointly disrupt the status quo.

REFERENCES

Bordwell, David and Kristin Thompson. 1990. *Film Art: An Introduction*. New York: McGraw-Hill.

Balanzategui, Jessica. 2018. *The Uncanny Child in Transnational Cinema: Ghosts of Futurity at the Turn of the Twenty-first Century*. Amsterdam: Amsterdam University Press.

Douglas, Mary. 1966. *Purity and Danger*. London: Routledge.

Hand, Richard. 2005. "Aesthetics of Cruelty: Traditional Japanese Theatre and the Horror Film." In *Japanese Horror Cinema*, edited by Jay McRoy, 18–28. Edinburgh: Edinburgh University Press.

Grainge, Paul David. 2000. "Advertising the Archive: Nostalgia and the (Post) national Imaginary." *American Studies* 41, no. 2/3 (Summer/Fall): 137–157.
Lury, Karen. 2010. *The Child in Film*. London: I.B. Tauris & Co. Ltd.
Napier, Susan. 1995. *The Fantastic in Modern Japanese Literature*. Tokyo: The Nissan Institute/Routledge Japanese Studies.
Platt, Brian. 2005. "Japanese Childhood, Modern Childhood: The Nation-State, the School, and 19th-Century Globalization." *Journal of Social History* 38, no. 4 (Summer): 965–85.
Rauer, Julie. 2005. "Persistence of a Genetic Scar: Japanese Anime, Manga, and Otaku Culture Fill an Open National Wound." *AsianArt.com: The on-line journal for the study and exhibition of the arts in Asia.* June 13, 2005. Accessed March 27, 2021. http://asianart.com/exhibitions/littleboy/intro.html.
Richie, Donald. 1990. *Japanese Cinema*. London: Oxford University Press.
———. 1988. "Viewing Japanese Films: Some Considerations." In *Cinema and Cultural Identity: Reflections on Films from Japan, India, and China*, edited by Wimal Dissanayake, 19–31. New York: University Press of America.
Tanaka, Stefan. 1997. "Childhood: Naturalization of Development in a Japanese Space." In *Cultures of Scholarship*, edited by Sarah C. Humphreys, 21–56. Ann Arbor: The University of Michigan Press.
Uno, Kathleen. 1999. *Passages to Modernity: Motherhood, Childhood, and Social Reform in Early Twentieth Century Japan.* Honolulu: University of Hawai'i Press.
Wee, Valerie. 2011. "Visual Aesthetics and Ways of Seeing: Comparing *Ringu* and *The Ring*." *Cinema Journal 50*, no. 2 (Winter): 41–60.

Chapter 4

Space, Smoke, and Mirrors
The Frightening Ambiguity of Ju-On: Origins (2020)

Daniel Krátký

The narrative of the Japanese series *Ju-On: Origins* (Netflix, Sho Miyake, 2020) can seem confusing at times. However, it makes such an impression on purpose. Being a part of a long-lasting franchise brings certain expectations and conventions. *Ju-On* has always crafted its narratives with many intertwined episodes and quite a few characters. The first direct-to-video feature *Ju-On* (Takashi Shimizu, 2000) consists of six narrative segments named after central characters: Toshio, Yuki, Mizuho, Kanna, Kayako, and Kyoko. Most of them are told out of chronological order. Such storytelling principle applied to further instalments such as *Ju-On: White Ghost* (Ryuta Miyake, 2009) and *Ju-On: The Beginning of the End* (Masayuki Ochiai, 2014).

There has always been a sense of narrative disruption in the franchise. As a formalist might say, the series utilizes "syuzhet," meaning, explicitly deformed fabula. Classical fabula represent events in chronological order within a certain time and space while syuzhet: "is the actual arrangement and presentation of the fabula in the film" (Bordwell 1985, 49–50). *Ju-On: Origins* builds upon this legacy, thus complicating the recollection of events for the viewers, not only from a narrative standpoint. The disruption can be found in other aspects as well—storytelling comes hand in hand with film style. Camera, editing, sound and mise-en-scène take this ambiguity further. More accurately, *Ju-On: Origins* creates ambiguous spatial and temporal relations between shots which systematically blurs the line between past and present along with objective or subjective storytelling. To put it bluntly, *Origins* goes out of its way to confuse us. In this chapter, I will analyze two categorically connected features of *Ju-On: Origins*.

At first, mirrors will serve as my entryway. What is glass, if not a culturally and metaphorically burdened deception? Refraction of light can be seen as a gateway into another world in folklore studies or as a symbolic code for Lacanian psychoanalytic theory. For me, however, mirrors will not be as interpreted, but rather analyzed as a visual reoccurring motif. A motif that fractures the spatial relations and foreshadows narrative breaks. What I will unpack is not the role of mirrors as a reflection of society and a mythos deeply rooted in Japanese folklore and culture, but the role of mirrors as a filmic device, therefore, moving from a hermeneutical perspective to an epistemic one. Looking glasses have been an integral part of the *Ju-On* franchise since its first instalment. Furthermore, they are an essential component of modern horror, notably as a scare trope.[1] *Origins* transforms said trope into a stylistic instrument which is bending spatial relations and foreshadows important narrative instances.

Secondly, I want to move further. Mirrors are only one part of a complex system which subverts our expectations regarding narrative development. If one particular motif reshapes the way we understand space, *Ju-On: Origins* as a whole alters the way we grasp the narrative dichotomies of *past/present* and *subjective/objective*. If—not only Japanese—horror film usually leaves flashbacks and subjective narrative perspective in clear boundaries, distinct from the objective and present, *Origins* blurs those boundaries. In other words, tension and expectation in the series are rooted in its temporal and perspective. We never know what to expect. At what point are we seeing a subjective vision and when this vision *leaks* into objective reality? *Origins* works hard to rupture our understanding of the apparent through a heavy emphasis on ambiguity. I will therefore analyze the narrative and stylistic strategies the film utilizes to create this sense of ambiguity and how does the latest *Ju-On* instalment distributes its cues—sort of narrative breadcrumbs—to lead its viewers into the uncomfortable position of uncertainty. Same applies to subjectivity and objectivity and characters themselves. They all seem to be mentally impenetrable, distant and ambiguous. *Origins* goes further than any other instalment of the *Ju-On* series. It not only continues to work with ambiguity on the level of narrative, but it also mirrors it with ambiguous style. But let me start with connecting *Origins* to the narrative context of the franchise.

HOW TO MIRROR A FRANCHISE

The franchise of *Ju-On* is different from other popular J-Horrors such as *Ring* (Chisui Takigawa, 1995), the better-known adaptation *Ring* (Hideo Nakata, 1998), *Spiral* (George Iida, 1998), *Pulse* (Kiyoshi Kurosawa, 2001) or parts of the *J-Horror Theater*: *Infection* (Masayuki Ochiai, 2004). *Ju-On* started with an intertextual narrative network consisting of two shorts *Katasumi* (Takashi Shimizu, 1998) and *4444444444* (Takashi Shimizu, 1998) as well as two feature direct-to-video films *Ju-On* (Takashi Shimizu, 2000) and *Ju-On 2* (Takashi Shimizu, 2000). Why an intertextual network?[2] For the reason that some kind of narrative disruption has always been part of it. A disturbance in chronologic order, a gap filled with other kinds of texts. All four films compose an intertwined narrative space that transcends each one of them alone.

Ju-On (2000) has two critical narrative ellipses which never really explain what happened with three other characters. Schoolgirls Kanna (Kanna Kashima) and Hisayo (Ayako Omura) leave their—cursed—house and are later mentioned briefly when their remains are found. Similar ellipsis removes Kanna's brother, Tsuyoshi (Kazushi Ando), yet another important character who leaves for school to meet his girlfriend. However, he never reappears later in the film. We might ask the obvious question: where are they and what happened to them? It seems the narrative leans toward an explanation; however, it never reveals it fully. We should not assume that viewers of *Ju-On* in 2000 were fully aware of two short-films made by Shimizu in 1998 as a part of television horror anthology *Gakkô no kaidan G* (Kiyoshi Kurosawa, Tetsu Maeda, Takashi Shimizu, 1998). Nonetheless, both gaps can be filled by watching *Katasumi* and *4444444444*. In each the fate of—at that time—anonymous characters are revealed. While both shorts were sort of a filmmaking exercise at that time, both were recontextualized by the feature film in 2000.

Furthermore, almost twenty minutes of *Ju-On 2* recapitulates the events of *Ju-On* by not recalling but literally showing the entire ending of the later. Thus, the second film creates two different types of viewers: (a) ones familiar with *Ju-On* and (b) others unaware of it. For first group, it might feel narratively redundant. However, both films were distributed on home video (Kalata 2007, 280). A media without the initial fast impact of a short-term cinema run, in the early 2000s home video were not as much simultaneously bought as successively rented. In that context, redundancy refreshes context and memory. Second group, newcomers, might find nothing redundant about it—first twenty minutes establishes what the curse is and how it transfers from person to person. The ending of *Ju-On* might therefore work as an introduction for the second film. Thus, these examples create an intertextual—or better, transcompositional[3]—overreaching narrative. Four films, four non-chronological, transmedia elliptical narratives.

If we take a look at the first few minutes of *Ju-On: Origins* this intertextual network is still very much there. A voice-over tells us: "*Ju-On* was inspired by true events. All of these events originated from one house. However, the real events were far more frightening than the movies." It implicitly explains its relationship to the original franchise. Those were only movies; this is the real deal. This rhetorical figure constitutes a meta-fiction relationship where *Origins* does not share the same narrative space as the original *Ju-On*. In fact, in the fictional world of *Origins*, *Ju-On* is implicitly acknowledged to be a movie franchise. Or non-existing. Thus, the series complicates simple terms such as remake, reboot, sequel or prequel. There is the narrative intertextual network again. One of the most fascinating aspects of this franchise is the relationship of each new installment to the entire fictional mythos. At certain points *Ju-On* might seem to be a linked chain of events regarding one house, same recurring ghosts and curses, although their relationship is far more complex. Each new film and/or series recontextualizes what came before. There is always a sense of ambiguity. My point is, *Ju-On: Origins* is not narratively complicated for the sake of being complicated. It follows an established pattern of narrative complexity which was laid by the franchise so far.

Said complexity is conveyed even with the *Ju-On* approach to a protagonist—there is none. Each instalment consists of intertwined segments featuring at least six important characters. All of them switch perspectives through the narrative and the only unifying factor is the curse itself. A curse born out of anger and violence, which is rooted in a haunted house in Tokyo. The curse can spread like an epidemic—or pandemic, if you will—from person to person, from one household to another. And it always kills.

Such context is important, because *Ju-On: Origins*, while not as medially fragmented, relies on similar narrative strategies, telling a story, yet again, focused on a cursed house in six episodes through the years 1988–1997. Paranormal investigator Odajima (Yoshiyoshi Arakawa) tries to uncover dark secrets revolving around a house in Nerima, Tokyo. His story unifies all six episodes. He is not only an investigator but had a direct contact with the haunting when he was a child. Therefore, is searching for a closure. Another important character is a schoolgirl Kiyomi (Ririka) who is abused by her mother Mina (Izumi Matsuoka) and later raped by a school bully Yudai (Koki Osamura) with the help of two girls, Yoshie (Nana Owada) and Mai (Hitomi Hazuki). Kiyomi later marries Yudai and are raising a boy named Toshiki (Atsuki Yamada) in a very toxic and abusive environment. Even more characters enter the picture; a teacher of Kiyomi named Noguchi (Tomomitsu Adachi), actress Haruka (Yuina Kuroshima), her boyfriend Tetsuya (Kai Inowaki) and list could go on. Again, the main goal of the narrative is not to focus on characters, but it is the curse that takes the stage. A curse jumping from one character to another through shared suffering. There are almost ten parallel—and sometimes intertwined—narratives. Odajima confronting his past, Kiyomi surviving rape and dealing with Yudai and a child, Haruka and her boyfriend Tetsuya who becomes the first one to be haunted and so on. There is much suffering condensed in the series. Sexual abuse, bullying, drugs, mutilation and even murders. Everything negative seems to be always intertwined and related to the central curse. And always preceded by a shot of a mirror.

MIRROR, MIRROR ON THE WALL

There is a popular Surimono—Japanese woodblock print—named *White Cat Hissing at Its Reflection in a Black Lacquer Mirror Stand* by the artist named Gakutei which was created in the nineteenth century. A white cat on the left looks as if it was scared by its reflection. Rightfully so, because on the other side, the cat in the mirror is darker and somehow frightening. This artwork seems to—at least for many critics[4]—encapsulate the complicated position of mirrors in Japanese folklore and mythology. As tempting as it may seem, I only want to use this image/idea as the starting point of my analysis. I do not think mirrors in *Ju-On: Origins* open a gateway into another world, or even to the other side. I do think, however, that mirrors do a great deal of foreshadowing and spatial disturbances in the series.

Even the first off-stage conversation between investigator Odajima and actress Haruka (Kuroshima) happens in front of a giant mirror in the fifth minute of episode one. The mirror here deepens the space and allows viewers to see not only her but the incoming investigator throughout most of their discussion regarding the house. A few seconds later a cut to an over-the-shoulder shot reveals Haruka's confused yet excited expression, the mirror staying in the frame. What the glass does is sort of a visual defamiliarization of the space itself. Staging a scene through a mirror is quite a popular technique in for example, Hong Kong cinema. It offers an interesting visual experience while keeping the cost low.[5] Same principle probably applies here. Later, when Haruka's boyfriend Tetsuya is looking for a new place where both could live, he enters the cursed house for the first time. The first thing audiences see is a mirror on the wall. As unimportant as it may seem, this mirror particularly appears more than twenty times during the series to accompany violence and abuse. It comes back later in the first episode, to accompany the sexual abuse of Kiyomi. Especially crucial is only seconds before the end of episode one, where the rape is happening off-screen and the only thing we see is a mirror on the wall.

This is just a selection from the first episode which demonstrates how important the visual motif of a mirror is. Further into *Origins* mirrors do not only appear when a bad thing is about to happen but even to create complex spatial relations, quite more intriguing than the one with Haruka and Odajima. Mirrors do help deepen the space and keep us aware of the people inside the room. Furthermore, mirrors can mislead us. In a key scene, a phone rings. Haruka's friend picks it up while her fiancé sits in the background. At first, this shot seems fairly normal. Our attention is divided between two levels of action. A girl in the foreground is central because she is answering the call, yet we still know where Haruka is through the composition. Staging is showing her in the unfocused background. It is a piece of important spatial information for us because the phone is for her. Therefore, the girl in the foreground turns away to Haruka. Then, something visually striking happens. Haruka gets up and leaves the frame. When she re-enters, it is not from the side she exited (right) but from the exact opposite (left). How is that possible? The next shot reveals that the scene was not framed by the background-foreground relationship we might expect; it has been a mirror's reflection all time long. The mirror not only allowed the style to establish a complex spatial relation; furthermore, it accompanied more bad news—Tetsuya has passed away.

Ju-On: Origins offers such a complex play of camera and staging with mirrors quite often, creating sophisticated and elusive spatial relations. Right after the intense sexual abuse of Kiyomi in the opening scene of episode two, a mirror takes the central stage. She stands in the middle of the frame in close shot, while listening to disturbing meowing upstairs. She leaves the frame, yet the camera never moves. We only see Kiyomi briefly walking on the stairs in the reflection of a small mirror on the wall. Whereas in classical filmmaking we would see a cut following the character, *Origins'* camera does not move. It stays there, fixated on the mirror. In stasis. Kiyomi has crossed to the other side on two levels. Firstly, literally on the other side of the room. However, more importantly, psychologically. She hears a disturbing sound luring her deeper into the cursed house. Deeper into her own trauma, she listens and follows. There is only a reflection of hers because the abusive experience changed her. Later, Kiyomi fights with her mother and eventually leaves her home. The entire scene is shot through a pair of mirrors constantly reflecting both characters. Again, we might ask why would a filmmaker choose to do that? There are dozens of stylistic approaches to stage a scene, so why mirrors? Both characters are yet again ephemeral—traumatized Kiyomi never uncovers her plans and acts somehow irrational (as someone who just survived a traumatic event) and her volatile mother Mina is psychologically unapproachable as well. We can never grasp them; we only see literal and psychological reflections. Furthermore, mirrors can work as a way to destabilize the house's architecture. Space is repeatedly fragmented and inaccessible as the characters.

Thus, ambiguity of space runs parallel with the ambiguity of central characters. The viewers are denied clear construction of space and psychology as we might be used to see in classical cinema. If the classical character is "psychologically defined individual who struggles to solve a clear-cut problem" (Bordwell 1985, 157) in *Origins*, we have individuals who are psychologically distant and elusive. This unattainability is reflected in the construction of ambiguous spaces through the mirrors. The entire narrative of *Ju-On Origins* feels distant. Furthermore, in the next section I will argue how this ambiguity lives and thrives in the process of narration, blurring the lines between subjective and objective reality. Characters, spaces, and perspectives—nothing is as simple as it seems in *Ju-On: Origins*.

THE FLASHBACK

Episode five starts with paranormal investigator Odajima meeting detective Kosaka. Their conversation is centered about a cursed house where it seems like the same accidents keep happening over and over again. Odajima, however, reveals a personal secret—he used to live there, and his sister seemed to be one of the victims. One thing is worth pointing out; both men are sitting in a coffee shop and the space is constructed in a fairly classical fashion. Most of the time we see two figures in a medium shot with occasional close-ups. Medium shots dominate most of the scene, yet close-ups have the simple function of guiding our attention to facial expressions and newspaper headlines. Colors are worth mentioning as well. So far, they seem quite normal and multi-chromatic. That changes, however, when Odajima starts remembering his past. There is a trauma deeply rooted in his memory regarding the house, his father, sister and a curse. An abrupt cut takes us to a tonally different place—a place of the subjective past, a memory in black and white. We watch an older man in the left side of the frame and a small child in the background. Audiences are seeing a flashback.

It is interesting how this flashback is constructed. Firstly, there is the successive relation between the scene in the coffee shop and a monochromatic flashback at the cursed house. To scene A (coffee shop) succeeds scene B (the house in the flashback). Secondly, Odajima creates a causal relation by mentioning his father. One cut and an older man appears. This sets up a stronger connection and temporal clarity between the two shots with a device called a dialogue hook. Film historian Kristin Thompson describes it as such: "at the end of a scene a character will mention what he or she is going to do and then will immediately be seen doing it early in the next scene" (1999, 20). And thirdly, we should pay attention to color. Maureen Turim in her inspiring book *Flashbacks in Film* names just a few ways of how a filmic text can articulate temporal reference—a flashback can differentiate itself by the use of a voice-over, a dissolve cut or "changes in image qualities such as color to black and white" (2014, 15–16). *Ju-On: Origins* follows this pattern, and its flashback utilizes black and white photography with slightly overexposed image to differentiate itself from the present, thus creating a tighter connection between scene A (coffee shop) and scene B (the house). After the flashback the narrative moves back to the coffee shop with a shot centering the investigator, therefore framing it as *his* evoking of past events. Shot of Odajima (present) is succeeded by a shot of Odajima and his father (past), his father from the perspective of young Odajima (past) and back to Odajima (present). So far, this has been a fairly classical flashback.

The flashback consists of two shots: a father in the foreground and a small Odajima in the background; and a central composition of the man alone. Shot number two is especially important because it opens up another important part of flashbacks I briefly mentioned: subjectivity and a point-of-view. Both are terms with a complicated history. As Edward Branigan puts it, if we understand narration as a process, a textual activity of telling, "subjectivity, then, may be conceived as a specific instance or level of narration where the telling is attributed to a character in the narrative and received by us as if we were in the situation of the character" (1984, 73).

The history of POV is quite complicated. We are used to certain simplifications, usually meaning an instance when the camera is placed approximately where the character's eyes would be. That could bring up to mind the opening sequence of John Carpenter's *Halloween* (1978) where we witness a brutal attack from the perspective of six-year-old Michael Myers. Point-of-view in film studies, however, refers to a certain technique of perceptual subjectivity where the film style "confides itself to the character's optical or auditory experience" (Bordwell 1985, 58). Or what Edward Branigan calls an optical POV (1984, 80–81). Point-of-view might also refer to a broader concept in the realm of subjectivity within the process of narration. Branigan in his book *Point of View in the Cinema* explains in detail how subjectivity can *leak* from an optical POV into the *objective* reality and *objective* style (1984, 80–82). Subjectivity transcends a simple POV shot in many contemporary and classical films. Take flashbacks in Hollywood cinema, for example: not many of them are shot through perceptual subjectivity of POV shot. Yet, they are subjective. Flashback's origin lies in a character and therefore creates a subjective conception of fictional time and space.

The first shot of *Ju-On*'s flashback (the one with Odajima in the background watching his father) is not an optical POV shot; in fact, the second one is (the one where viewers are watching Odajimas' father through the boy's eyes). Yet both are subjective. The narration frames the flashback as a memory of Odajima. Based on the relation to other shots and a dialogue hook, we can say the memory is something Branigan might call a *character projection* (1984, 95). Odajima's character is the *origin* of those two shots from the past. While the scene in a coffee shop might be called an objective-narration the flashback would be a subjective-narration. Let me update the sequence of shots I proposed before: shot of Odajima (present-objective) is succeeded by a shot of Odajima and his father (past-subjective), his father from the perspective of Odajima (past-subjective) and back to Odajima (present-objective). All of this might seem like an unnecessarily complicated way of stating the obvious. However, nothing about the flashback is as simple as it looks. Even when the narrative tells its story from a perspective of Odajima in few instances, his character is quite ambiguous. As with the mirrors, we only see fragments and visual reflections like those short subjective flashbacks. *Ju-On: Origins* establishes these simple and clear patterns of past/present and subjective/objective stylistic differentiations just to blur them later.

A FRIGHTFUL VISION

I will follow my analysis moving past these four shots. Odajima persuades the detective to take him to a cursed house. His main goal here is to remember the past and his former home might serve as a trigger. In the next scene, both men approach the infamous house which is now a crime scene following a murder inside. After entering, Odajima slowly moves across the hall into the kitchen. Here he speaks to the detective while looking all over the crime scene. Few seconds in, Odajima looks towards the camera, astonished and almost frightened. Space is, yet again, constructed clearly. We see him on the left side of the frame in a full shot, while the detective stands on the right. A cut moves the camera in the over-the-shoulder shot of Odajima, revealing what he was looking at—a glass door to the garden. This now makes a visual connection to the flashback scene in the coffee shop, where we saw a little boy watching his father in a garden through a glass door. This is the place where his memory came from. A glass breaks; Odajima—visibly shaken—turns back at the glass door while the detective seems uncomfortably apathetic. The detective's reaction tells viewers there was no sound in the objective reality; however, audiences—through perceptual subjectivity—share Odajima's auditory experience. Next cut reveals the source of that sound, another flashback, now leaking into present. Camera reveals the glass doors yet again, however, now in the flashbacks' monochromatic color. A small boy—supposedly young Odajima—is running across the room with a baby in his hands. We can clearly see a table in the left bottom corner of the frame, which gives us an idea of the line of sight. The camera is not behind Odajima but inside his head, auditory experience is now accompanied by the visual one. This is the POV shot we know and saw in the first flashback. Back to objective-reality, with a normal color spectrum and no boy whatsoever.

So far, the narrative and stylistic strategies are quite clear about their intentions. The present is multichromatic and objective, past monochromatic and subjective with Odajima as its origin. In the present, he is an adult and in the past a boy. That changes in the next few shots. The investigator runs in panic upstairs and enters a small bedroom. Now audiences see a dramatic shift in *Ju-On*'s representation of time and space—upon opening the bedroom door, Odajima enters it as an adult, however in the black and white photography which was so far linked only to flashbacks. Odajima literally enters within his memory. He looks around the room in a short POV shot and continues exploring the bedroom, always in black and white. The detective follows him upstairs and another temporal switch happens—at the first glance this shot seems to be rooted in objective reality. But in the background, we see two moving persons in school uniforms which seem to be the already dead girls. They seem to be ghosts of the past roaming the house in the present, blurring the lines between two different times. Not only that Odajima from the present has just entered his own memory, but ghosts of the past are also haunting the detective as well. *Ju-On: Origins* makes sure to confuse its viewers by complicating spatial and temporal relations between shots, not only in this sequence. But as interesting as it might sound, there is an obvious question—why? The question might be answered on the level of (i) one scene and secondly, (ii) the entire series.

THE TENSION OF INSECURITY

There are quite a few scenes or sequences in *Ju-On: Origins* which work in the same fashion as this one. Furthermore, the complication of past and presents seems to be one of the most important ways the series builds tension. The horror is rooted in uncertainty. As some critics rightfully noticed, *Ju-On: Origins* is practically without the so-called *jump scare*, a technique based on "fast editing, disturbing visuals, and loud sounds" which "prey[s] on an evolutionary reaction that exists in many different species; the startle response" (Seyler 2021). *Origins* on the other hand tend to create tension through a combination of narrative and stylistic techniques resting on the opposite spectrum: narrative ambiguity and longer takes. I will analyze the Odajimas experience in the haunted house as an example.

The entire visit lasts for three minutes and eighteen seconds and consists of thirty-one shots. That means an average shot length of about 6.4 seconds, which is quite long,[6] even if not for the *Ju-On* franchise. Mohsen Nasrin (2021) measured the average shot length for the *Ju-On* (2002) as high as 8.8 seconds. We can see an oscillation between shots as short as two seconds and longer up to sixteen seconds. That creates a rhythm. A long take can help with building tension and expectation—it is usually accompanied by increasingly louder sounds while a character is looking for something. Odajima hears his own memories happening all over again when he visits the house. When they start looking for the source of it, we usually watch them through longer takes. Rapid cuts follow. A sound is heard, a character appears and a ghost stumbles across the room in the background. Those are the shorter and much more condensed shots filled with information. Thanks to them the viewers can feel anxious during the longer ones, expecting yet another scary gruesome discovery, a revelation of personal trauma and much more. Longer and shorter takes help with creating a rhythmic pattern of uncertainty underlining the narrative and its temporal, spatial and causal ambiguity. We do not need jump-scares. *Ju-On: Origins* is scary because of its unpredictability not only story-wise but even on the level of spatial construction and editing. We never know what is coming.

HOW DOES IT ALL COME TOGETHER?

Horror often plays with ambiguity—it can create visions of something unreal just to scare us. A character in *Sinister* (Scott Derrickson, 2012) sees a disturbing figure outside of his house and only seconds later the figure is gone. *Ju-On Origins*, however, takes this ambiguity further. Not only that certain narrative instances are enigmatic to build tension, but the Netflix series also takes ambiguity as its central principle of construction. It never shows us the full picture. Only fragments and reflections. Everything revolves around unclarity. Formalists might call it a dominant theme, film's critics a concept.

First, the intertextual relationship of *Origins* and the rest of *Ju-On* franchise remains quite ambiguous. The only (meta)narrative commentary in the first episode frames the TV series as the *real* story behind the films. Second, its narrative space, the literal construction of spatial relation inside the fictional world of *Origins* remains unclear or subversive at many instances. When something important or frightening happens, we might only get to see a fragment. As little as a reflection in a small mirror on the wall. Such mirror can even deceive us, creating an illusion of a deep space. Third, narrative time gets twisted as well. What might seem as past and present reveals itself to be intertwined and complicated. Same applies to subjectivity and objectivity and characters themselves. They all seem to be mentally impenetrable, distant and ambiguous. *Ju-On: Origins* is a slow-burn sort of series with complicated narrative without explicit jump-scares. Yet that should not be understood as flaws but pragmatic intention. A play with narrative ambiguity. *Ju-On: Origins* continues an old story that has already been told in at least nine Japanese feature installments and four American ones. Yet writers Hiroshi Takahashi and Takashige Ichise with the director Sho Miyake managed to evolve it even further. What was a story based on fragmentation and displacement of narrative segments, became even more intriguing by making the style ambiguous as well? *Origins* subverts our expectations by creating conflicting spaces while blurring the borders between subjective, objective, past and present events.

REFERENCES

Bordwell, David. 1985. *Narration in the Fiction Film*. Madison: The University of Wisconsin Press.

———. 2000. *Planet Hong Kong: Popular Cinema and the Art of Entertainment*. Harvard University Press.

Bordwell, David, Kristin Thompson, and Jeff Smith. 2020. *Film Art: An Introduction*. Madison: McGraw-Hill Education.

Branigan, Edward. 1984. *Point of View in the Cinema: A Theory of Narration and Subjectivity in Classical Film*. Amsterdam: Mouton Publishers.

Goodwin, John. 2014. "The Horror of Stigma: Psychosis and Mental Health Care Environments in Twenty-First-Century Horror Film (Part II)." *Perspect Psychiatric Care* no. 50 (October): 224–234.

Kalat, David. 2007. *J-Horror: The Definitive Guide to The Ring, The Grudge and Beyond*. New York: Vertical Inc.

Kok, D. P. 2017. "Visualizing the Classics: Reading Surimono and Kyōka Books as Social and Cultural History." *PhD diss.*, Leiden: Leiden University.

Kokeš, Radomír D. 2015. *Rozbor filmu*. Brno: MUNI Press.

Kokeš, Radomír D. 2021. "Film-Shot-Counter." Accessed April 21, 2021. http://www.douglaskokes.cz/pdz/

Nasrin, Mohsen. 2013. *Cinemetrics, JU-ON (2002, Japan)*. Accessed May 29, 2021. http://www.cinemetrics.lv/movie.php?movie_ID=14047.

Seyler, Sarah. 2019. "What Are You So Scared About?: Understanding the False Fear Response to Horror Films." *NC DOCS*. Accessed May 29, 2021. https://libres.uncg.edu/ir/uncg/f/S_Seyler_What_2019.pdf.

Thompson, Kristin. 1999. *Storytelling in the New Hollywood: Understanding Classical Narrative Technique*. Cambridge, London: Harvard University Press.

Tsivian, Yuri, and Gunars Civjans. *Cinemetrics Database*. Accessed March 29, 2021. http://www.cinemetrics.lv/database.php.

Turim, Maureen. 2014. *Flashbacks in Film Memory & History*. London and New York: Routledge Taylor & Francis Group.

Uricchio, William, and Roberta E. Pearson. 1993. *Reframing Culture: The Case of the Vitagraph Quality Films*. Princeton: Princeton University Press.

Vedger. *Vegder's Blog*. 2015. Accessed April 14, 2021. https://printsofjapan.wordpress.com/2015/11/05/mirrors-and-the-soul-in-japanese-art-and-elsewhere-part-one/.

NOTES

1. See John Goodwin, "The Horror of Stigma: Psychosis and Mental Health Care Environments in Twenty-First-Century Horror Film (Part II)," Perspect Psychiatr Care no. 50 (2014): 224–234.

2. I chose this term as an allusion to the *intertextual grid* used by Roberta Pearson and William Uricchio. Both argued that silent films such as *Uncle Tom's Cabin* (William Robert Daly, 1914) are built upon high degree of audience knowledge which could fill the narrative ellipses. They mention not only books but postcards and showmen accompanying the screenings. Therefore, if something is missing in the filmic text itself, audience knowledge can fill the gaps. *Intertextual grid* is, however, very deeply rotted in the study of silent cinema and a sort of different type of viewer-text-paratext relationship than *Ju-On* offers. More in: William Uricchio and Roberta E Pearson, *Reframing Culture: The Case of the Vitagraph Quality Films*, Princeton: Princeton University Press, 1993.

3. A term transcompositional was proposed by a Czech film historian Radomír D. Kokeš. A theoretical hybrid between transtextual and compositional motivations derived from the works of David Bordwell and Kristin Thompson. While transtextual links together two and more works of art, compositional motivates a particular thing inside one narrative. Transcompositional links together two or more films (trans) which share the same fictional universe (compositional). David Bordwell, Kristin Thompshon and Jeff Smith, *Film Art: An Introduction* (Madison: McGraw-Hill Education, 2020); Radomír D. Kokeš, *Rozbor filmu* (Brno: MUNI Press, 2015).

4. A good start might be a wonderful blog series by Jerry Vegder or inspiring dissertation on Surimono. *Mirrors and the Soul in Japanese Art and Elsewhere—Part One*, Vegder's Blog, https://printsofjapan.wordpress.com/2015/11/05/mirrors-and-the-soul-in-japanese-art-and-elsewhere-part-one/. D. P. Kok, "Visualizing the Classics: Reading Surimono and Kyōka Books as Social and Cultural History" (PhD Thesis, Leiden University, 2017).

5. More on this topic in David Bordwell, *Planet Hong Kong: Popular Cinema and the Art of Entertainment* (Harvard University Press, 2000).

6. Further data on the average shot length in (not only) contemporary films and TV can be found on Cinemetrics or personal database of Czech academic Radomír D. Kokeš. Yuri Tsivian and Gunars Civjans, "Cinemetrics Database," http://www.cinemetrics.lv/database.php; Radomír D. Kokeš, "Film-Shot-Counter," http://www.douglaskokes.cz/pdz/.

Chapter 5

The Dead Speak

Horror and the Modern Ghost in Eiji Ōtsuka's The Kurosagi Corpse Delivery Service

Megan Negrych

There is something about a ghost story that calls to the very heart of what it means to be human. Likewise, there is something about horror that makes us feel alive. Perhaps this is the reason why Japanese horror manga has such a devoted following. From the monstrously supernatural horror of Shigeru Mizuki's classic *GeGeGe No Kitaro* (*Kitaro of the Graveyeard, 1960–1969*) to the bone-chilling grotesqueries of Junji Itō's *Tomie* (1987–2000), *Gyo* (2001–2002), and *Uzumaki* (1998–1999), horror manga is an interesting niche in modern popular culture. The stories can be alarming and graphic but are deeply rooted in literary and artistic traditions. Haunted by *yūrei* (ghosts or spirits), these stories modernize the *kaidan* (strange recited narrative) to reflect contemporary social and cultural anxieties.[1] When not focused on apocalyptic alternate realities or zombies, many of the stories are informed by history, traditional social and cultural concerns about the ability of the restless dead to return to cause harm, and the responsibilities the living have to make sure they are treated with the proper respect.

Between Mizuki's *Kitarō* and Junji Itō's entire body of work, there is the dark, multilayered, and wonderfully interesting series *Kurosagi Shitai Takuhaibin* (*The Kurosagi Corpse Delivery Service*, 2000–present).[2] Author Eiji Ōtsuka (1958–) is a well-known social critic and media theorist with a background in anthropology and women's folklore. These influences can be seen in his work with *Kurosagi*. Paired with Housui Yamazaki's art, *Kurosagi* becomes a beautiful, chilling, and thought-provoking horror manga series. Before *Kurosagi*, Ōtsuka had made a name for himself in the world of manga and the horror genre in the past with *Multiple Personality Detective Psycho (Tajū-Jinkaku Tantei Saiko,* 1997–2016), which has been adapted by renown graphic horror mastermind Takashi Miike. Ōtsuka's attention to detail and his ability to deftly incorporate believable horror in *Kurosagi* creates a compelling series of tales that, while supernatural, are very human at their core. Ōtsuka has stated that his goal while writing *Kurosagi* is to return to an orthodox horror and "get back to the fear any real person would feel, should death's work appear to be unfinished" (Ōtsuka, 2005 vol. 3, 215). As such, Kurosagi's horror elements are informed by literary, artistic, and religious traditions, and grounded in history and contemporary socio-cultural anxieties about the dead, the return of the buried past, and the harm both can cause the living when not handled properly. *Kurosagi* serves as a modern horror anthology, composed of shorter, self-contained stories within an overarching plot, and serves as an exploration of the continuing role of ghost stories in modern society, in which the living and life itself are often much more horrific than the spirits that haunt them.

Historically, Japanese *kaidan* addressing horror and the supernatural were shaped by cultural and social ideas regarding death and the concern that the restless dead could visit misfortune on the living. These ghost stories date to the Edo period (1603–1867). They take concepts from religious doctrine, including Shintō and Buddhism (Balmain 2008, 52), and are typically enriched with folkloric and didactic elements. Largely these ghost stories focus on spirits who cannot move on due to improper or absent funerary rites, those caught in repetitive cycles of suffering at the location of their death, those who die with unfulfilled obligations or wishes, or in gruesome and violent ways away from home. Elements of horror and the grotesque in visual art can be traced to at least the ninth Century in the form of hanging and hand scrolls brought to Japan by Buddhists to be used as teaching tools. In addition to *kaidan*, contemporary horror manga also draws from modern Japanese literature and pulp fiction, specifically a genre known as *Ero-guro-nansensu* (erotic grotesque nonsense), which emerged during the 1920s as "a bourgeois cultural phenomenon that devoted itself to explorations of the deviant, the bizarre, and the ridiculous" (Reichert 2001, 114). After 1945 became part of the horror genre and was considered "dark, perverse, and increasingly centered on eroticizing boundary violation [and] dismemberment" (Tinsley 2017, 30).

As important to horror as its history are its ghosts. There are many ways in which the dead manifest as *yūrei,* and important to note that they "are part of the everyday, wielding influence over the living" (Davisson 2015). Three types of spirit stand out in the *Kurosagi* stories selected for analysis. At the forefront are the *muenbotoke* (unassociated spirit); generally thought of as the anxious and jealous spirits who have not been honoured properly after death, they could linger at the places of their death for years (Iwakasa and Toelken 1994, 79), bringing misfortune to anyone who comes across them. In contrast to the somewhat ambiguous manifestation of the *muenbotoke*, the *onryō* (vengeful or wrathful spirit) tends to focus its energy on tormenting the ones responsible for their suffering. They are typically women who were victims of extreme violence and if unappeased they can also torment those who enter their space. While not the only other spirit in Japanese *kaidan*, the *ubume* (birthing woman ghost), is the ghost of a mother who died either during childbirth or with children left uncared for. Their energy is usually consumed by attempting to provide for their children, and their hauntings are far less violent than the *onryō*. It is important to note that these spirits, no matter how they manifest, died "under great emotional stress [creating] an energy which is not easily dissipated; these *yūrei*, thus, have an impact on the local environment and are vivid proof of the seriousness of breaking codes [of proper behaviour]" (Iwakasa and Toelken 1994, 82).

In the following pages, three stories will be analyzed independently from the series as a whole and examined in detail. First, *If You Should Die* will be given a considerably detailed treatment due to the multilayered nature of its depictions of horror and the poignant nature of its content. Next *Waltz* and *The Look I Had 'til Yesterday* will be examined briefly to show how Ōtsuka creates horror from socio-cultural anxieties throughout the series. Finally, the character of Kuro Karatsu will be examined to show how it falls to individuals like Karatsu to help the restless dead fulfill their final wish and lay them to rest because it is "the job of the living to provide the proper ritualized order in which the dead may rest, the living may prosper, and the community (for the time being) will be safe" (Iwakasa and Toelken 1994, 66). Horror in Japanese manga runs much deeper than a shambling zombie horde, a psychotic killer, or a malevolent spirit possessing technological devices to expand the reach of their anger. Instead, the horror comes from how the ghosts are created in the first place, and the lack of proper acknowledgment and treatment of the dead that empowers these *yūrei* to negatively affect the living around them, drawing everyone to repeated tragedy until they are properly laid to rest.

MEET THE *KUROSAGI CORPSE DELIVERY SERVICE*

To begin, an overview of Ōtsuka's main characters will be provided. The main protagonist of *Kurosagi* is Kuro Karatsu, a student Buddhist monk from a non-religious family attending an average Buddhist university. He can hear the voices of the dead when he touches them, and return their lingering spirits to their bodies to help them fulfill their remaining worldly obligations or wishes. Whether he is entirely aware or not, he is followed by the spirit dressed in white, a mysterious figure still not completely explained. As a monk, even only a novice, Karatsu takes on the role of custodian and caretaker of the dead (Tamura 2000, 214), a responsibility that he does not take lightly. He is referred to as Mr. Itako by other members of the Kurosagi Corpse Delivery Service, referring to a tradition of blind women who underwent intense training to become mediums who could communicate with the vast array of Japanese spirits (Yoshida 2015, 207–208). It is through contact with Karatsu that the spirits of the dead regain their agency and are able to be pacified. No matter the circumstance, Karatsu never rejects a request for help made by the dead, even if it means exposing himself to danger.

The rest of the Kurosagi Corpse Delivery Service is made up of students at the same university, all looking to put their somewhat unorthodox skills to use. Numata is a dowser who can find corpses instead of water, tough on the outside, but no abler to turn away a call for help than Karatsu, though far more driven by monetary gain. Sasaki is a hacker with a nose for business who acts as the organizer and job finder for the group, who uses her skills to get information not readily available to the public. Makino has studied as an embalmer, but since Japan deals with their dead mostly through cremation, she tends to act as an impromptu medical examiner, letting the others know the gruesome ways in which their clients died. Yata is a channeler, but his useful skill is his knowledge of Japanese myths, urban legends, and pop culture; his observations tend to help the others piece things together. Finally, there is Sasayama of the Shinjuku Municipal Social Welfare Office, who relies on Karatsu and the others to help him identify individuals who are found dead with no identification. A former cop, Sasayama's many skills and experiences often help Karatsu and the others navigate the more mundane problems they encounter. Though the members of the Kurosagi Corpse Delivery Service come together with their eyes on making money, they never turn their backs on a client, even when they know that all they will be left with after the job is done is a sense of satisfaction.

PRESERVING ATROCITIES

Perhaps the most insidious story Ōtsuka has written for *Kurosagi* is *If You Should Die,* which recreates the atrocities committed by the Japanese Army during the Second Sino-Japanese War (1937–1945) at the infamous Unit 731, the Buddhist artistic tradition of *kusōzu,* as well as urban legend and real-world controversy. As a result, it can be read as a condemnation of the dangers of ignoring and forgetting the past and how, when left unaddressed, previous actions can return in new and horrific ways to cause further suffering. *If You Should Die* pulls no punches in its judgment of Japanese military history, and the editor of the manga as a whole takes the time to reflect that this is the first time they can remember Unit 731 being mentioned in a manga, though the first true expose on Unit 731 was *The Devil's Gluttony* by Seiichi Morimura in 1983.[3]

While visiting "The Mysteries of the Corpse," an exhibit of preserved, dismembered, and dissected human bodies created by Nunokusa Biological Preservation and Research, Karatsu and Numata contemplate the idea that their next client might be found among the displays. While Karatsu hears voices when he touches the displays, none of them speak Japanese, leaving Numata and Karatsu to rely on Yata's observation that they speak Mandarin. But the display entitled "Woman Holding Her Head"[4] stands out to Karatsu, though before he can investigate the sense of deep yearning he feels from her, the director of the exhibit, Takahashi Nunokusa, stops him. He had previously employed Makino to help fix some damage done to that particular display, given her background with embalming and body preparation. With Makino's grudging help, Karatsu manages to take the woman's decapitated head back to the university for further examination.

Once Karatsu fully touches the woman's head, he discovers that she was a Japanese student abducted while travelling in China. She was then tortured, dissected, and preserved alive before being put on display. Numata comments on the eerie similarity between the woman's experience and The Daruma Woman,[5] an urban legend they had been discussing earlier. Makino is unconvinced as Nunokusa Preservation states that they acquire bodies through legal donations and that they are backed by reputable medical companies and science schools. Sasaki provides further evidence to Karatsu's concerns when she uncovers that Nunokusa Preservation has sole control over the acquisition creation of the displays and that the reputable backers only donate money and space. Together, Karatsu and Sasayama agree that it seems like someone is using the urban legend of the Daruma Woman to hide their crimes, knowing that "if people who hear any rumors stop to think . . . they'll end up assuming it's fake" (Ōtsuka 2015 Vol.4, 71).

Driven to help the woman, they head back to the exhibit only to discover that it has packed up and moved overnight, leaving no trace of where they went. For Karatsu this is proof that Takahashi is up to something nefarious, and since the woman is their client, he will do what it takes to free her spirit. Makino finds an address on the box in which the woman's head had been stored, leading them to Harbin, China. Already involved and wanting to see justice done, Sasayami travels with them as their Mandarin interpreter, and

Sasaki stays in Japan to uncover more information. The address takes them to the site of the "Remnants of the Invading Japanese Army Unit 731," a dark place of horrific historical importance. However, with no sign of either Takahashi or Nunokusa Preservation, the groups must wait for Sasaki to find more information. While they wait Makino is abducted from a change room, once again recreating the story of the Daruma Woman as well as the experience of the woman they are trying to help. Karatsu and the others chase Makino's abductor and fall right into Takahashi's trap. Once they arrive at the Nunokusa Facilities, Takahashi reveals that he belongs to "The Grandchildren," meaning he is a descendant of a doctor who worked at Unit 731 during the Second Sino-Japanese War. In typical villain fashion, Takahashi monologues at length about his sadistic experiments, and how the postwar chaos allowed his grandfather to escape and find a place to continue his human experimentation. As Karatsu and the others are locked away, Takahashi prepares to do to Makino what he did to the woman before, and to countless others, all while she is awake and able to feel every moment of it.

While Takahashi torments Makino with the gruesome details of his work, Karatsu sets to work calling out to the souls of the restless dead that Nunokusa Biological Preservation has created, using his powers to grant them agency once more. With Karatsu's help the various dismembered, dissected, and mutilated corpses converge on Takahashi in an unstoppable wave, their preserved bodies a haunting account of Takahashi's reprehensible experiments. Takahashi is dragged down by the corpses he has made and his facility burns, the ghosts of the dead finally able to find rest, no longer trapped as the fire consumes their corpses and releases them from their torturous prisons. Their final wish is for Karatsu and the others to return the woman's body to her home so that she can have the proper funerary rites to be at rest. Karatsu accepts the job without a second thought knowing that it is the right thing to do.

Ōtsuka's narrative treatment, paired with Yamazaki's delicate yet horrific rendering of the corpses, is deeply informed not only by Buddhist practices, including but not limited to the responsibility the living have to the dead, but also of the underlying fear that the action of the past can return to haunt and bring further destruction to the living when care is not taken to acknowledge, rectify, and change harmful and immoral patterns of behavior. In the words of writer Lafcadio Hearn (Yakumo Koizumi, 1850–1904), "the hand of the dead was heavy: it is heavy even on the living today."[6] If the past is swept away and justice is not administered for the victims of atrocities, then they can never find an escape from their suffering as it persists as if it were still occurring. In *If You Should Die* the failure to properly examine and learn from past wrongs served is personified by Takahashi, who perpetuates the sins of the past without remorse, filling the world with *muenbotoke* and perpetuating the cycle of violence and destruction from the war.

Ōtsuka's decision to characterize Takahashi as one of "The Grandchildren" underscores the connection between the vivisection and preservation methods he uses to create his displays and the human experimentation and atrocities that occurred at Unit 731. This connection is key to understanding the horror Ōtsuka evokes with this story; he is creating a return of the traumatic past and utilizes persistent social anxieties emerging from wartime guilt. Similar to *Gojira* (Ishirō Honda, 1954) or Junji Itō's *Gyo*, this return of a disregard for human life that occurred during the war returns in new and interesting ways to bring further chaos and destruction is an underlying trope in Japanese horror. Moreover, the *yūrei* presented in the story are robbed of their agency; not only can they not find rest, but they are unable to actively seek their revenge without help from the living, as they are trapped within their own preserved bodies, controlled in both life and death by Takahashi's cruel agenda. It is as if they are the true voices of the forgotten dead of Unit 731, trapped and lost without justice even decades later, almost as if forgotten.

The experiments which took place at Unit 731 are deep wounds, still open, that affect Japanese international relations to this day. While not as well documented, or taught, as the crimes committed at Nazi concentration camps, they are never the less one of the darkest points in Japan's colonial past. In fact, "determining the full extent and nature of Unit 731's work is further complicated by postwar American Policies" (Cook and Cook 2000, 159), and the fact that it was never even presented at the Tokyo War Crimes Tribunal. This is important to note as Numata and the others, despite being university students, do not know what Unit 731 was, [7] to which Sasayama exclaims "Don't you kids learn anything these days...?! [...]Of course, now that they're teaching 'patriotism' in the schools again, maybe it wasn't in your history books" (Ōtsuka 2015 Vol.4, 78). The atrocities committed at Unit 731 are perhaps less remembered by the general public since many of those responsible escaped justice following the war, despite the atrocities committed against civilians in the form of biological research[8] and medical experimentation.[9] Many of those in positions of power were able to return to normal life post-war and "continued to work actively in related fields [and even managed to climb] the ladder in medical-academic circles to become professors at major university and research institutes" (Cook and Cook 2000, 159). At one point, after Takahashi has revealed the pleasure and pride he takes in his horrific actions as well as those of his ancestors, Karatsu admonishes him:

Karatsu: It's because of people like you that suffering continues

even after war ends.

Takahashi: No, Mr. Karatsu. Suffering comes from the desire for

power . . . and the willingness to look, yet not see. (Ōtsuka 2015 Vol.4, 90)

This can be read as Ōtsuka's direct reproach to the fact that in the aftermath of the war many of the key figures responsible for the atrocities were granted immunity from persecution by the Americans, in exchange for "their knowledge of bacteriological warfare techniques and defenses against it, together with the records of their human experiments," for the further development of American research (Cook and Cook 2000, 159). Interviews conducted by Haruko and Theodore Cook in *Japan at War: An Oral History* reveal that some enjoyed the process like Takahashi,[10] who gleefully confesses to Makino that " you're not the first person I've done this to . . . no, not the tenth or even the twentieth . . . the truth is, I so enjoy seeing that expression of fear and shame upon your face" (Ōtsuka 2015 vol. 4, 94). There were those like Yoshio Tamura who at sixteen was deployed to Unit 731, who admits that he felt no pity for the victims at the time, but later admitted her saw himself as "a war criminal because of the things [he] actually did" (Cook and Cook 2000, 159) and that "[those involved, including himself] had to struggle with [their] humanity afterwards" (Cook and Cook 2000, 164). Takahashi not only feels pride in his sadistic activities, but he also flaunts them; they are a testament to his power, an ever-enduring record of his cruelty that he can parade to the unsuspecting public.

Despite this, Ōtsuka's characterization of Takahashi strikes at the heart of human horror because it contains just enough truth to blur the line between fact and fiction. He serves as a contemporary reflection of the fears that those who were not held responsible, or those who idolize the actions of those individuals can perpetuate further horror on the living. Takahashi hides his crimes in plain sight, even receiving accolades and active praise for them; they are a form of morbid immortality for not only himself but his predecessors. In his words "[The Grandchildren of the staff of Unit 731] remain proud commanders of sickness, of pain, and of death" (Ōtsuka 2015 vol. 4, 88–89). Part of his perverse joy comes from the fact that "in the old days our material would have disappeared into a gas oven. Now [the corpses of our victims] can be flaunted objects—still earning money in a world hungry for spectacle" (Ōtsuka 2015 vol. 4, 90). He revels in his ability not only to murder without recourse but to showcase his depravity disguised as a marvelous innovation for scientific and medical study. The reason Takahashi can continue to torture and murder without repercussion is based on the fact that his predecessors escaped without facing justice for their actions. Takahashi's reign of terror is only brought to an end by Karatsu's acknowledgment of the voices of the dead, and his ability to grant them the agency they need to take justice into their own hands since no one else would do it for them or those who had experienced similar violence. Unlike the majority of those who worked at Unit 731, Takashi has no immunity from the wrath of the *muenbotoke* he has created, and no one to blame for his downfall but himself.

Aside from the historic atrocities used to give Takahashi his truly menacing manifestation as a horror villain, Ōtsuka's "Mysteries of the Corpse" is a mirror image of anatomist Gunther von Hagens' popular *Body Worlds* exhibits. This serves to further mix history with urban legend as Hagens' work has a rather controversial existence. Hagans was born in 1945, the son of a Nazi SS officer, and has made a name for himself through his development of the plastination process used to preserve corpses for dissection, exhibition, and scientific study. In horror manga, as with film, there is always the fear of what people are willing to do in the pursuit of further scientific discovery, or what those technologies can be used for in the wrong hands. Takahashi is modelled after Hagens, only relieved of moral obligations and freed from the constraint of ethics. Hagens' work has seen its fair share of ethical and social backlash, from being openly accused of using the bodies of criminals and psychiatric patients to the shadow cast by his father's past. Where Hagens and Takahashi differ is in the fact that Hagens' organization has made public extensive records regarding the donation of bodies to his organization.

In addition to the unsettling and stark connection to real events, *If You Should Die* also relies on a connection to the Buddhist practice of *kusozu*, wherein an observer meditates on a depiction of a decaying female corpse in order to understand their own impermanence and "recognize oneself in the disintegrating body" (Tinsley 2017, 21). Together, Ōtsuka and Yamazaki circumvent the implied lesson of these depictions of dismemberment and decay by creating a corpse that is permanently preserved, with "no decay [and] no odor" (Ōtsuka 2015 vol. 4, 63). Instead of contemplating his mortality and impermanence, Takahashi creates an enduring symbol of his control over his victims, casting himself as a powerful and merciless god with "power over [them]. [Their] lives, [their] death, belong to [him]" (Ōtsuka 2015 vol. 4, 101). By preserving them, he is trapping them in their flesh, even their spirits cannot escape until Karatsu offers them a path. In his quest for a permanent record of his crimes, Takahashi engineers his death; had he not created and kept their bodies as trophies, they could not have been there to hold him down while his legacy burnt to the ground. Their only wish was to no longer be looked at but to return to the earth, and in helping them achieve their desires and freeing them from their cycle of suffering, Karatsu and the others are saved, able to escape their most dangerous experience to date. This story acts as a cautionary tale of horror that attempts to convey to the audience the dangers that can arise from failing to acknowledge historical atrocities and respect the victims of them. By actively opposing ongoing horrors and cruelty, there can be growth and salvation instead of the perpetuation of past mistakes. Just because something occurred in the past does not mean that similar violence is not continuing. By ignoring rather than acknowledging the past, it is allowed to reemerge, more insidiously and possibly in the guise of something for "the greater good."

The use of the perversion of the *Kusōzu* practice in this particular chapter of Ōtsuka's work becomes even more interesting when looking at the history of Japanese horror literature, in particular that of Edogawa Ranpo, the father of *ero-guro-nansensu* in modern Japanese literature. Again in a call back to Ōtsuka's desire to write orthodox horror in *Kurosagi*, *If You Should Die* bears great similarities to both *Hakuchūmu (The Daydream*, 1925) and *Mōjū (Moju the Blind Beast, 1931)*; both tales involve the display of corpses by their murders, either as a mannequin made up of the dismembered body parts of all their victims, or in the guise of a wax anatomical model in the window of a pharmacy. Both of the murderers get sadistic pleasure not only from the acts of violence they commit but their ability to flaunt them under the unsuspecting noses of the public, just like Takashi. The corpse of "Woman Holding Her Head" brings together the female corpse central to the *kusōzu* depictions and the Erotic Grotesque tradition to highlight Takahashi's deliberate cruelty. Her corpse is skinned save for her breasts and pubic area which have been left untouched by the knife, her lower ribs and spine exposed. She holds her head at arms-length, her eyes permanently closed. He has posed her as if in contemplation but made her unable to see. It can be argued that because she can neither contemplate her corpse or decay, she is purposefully kept from being able to move on by Takahashi's deliberate articulation of her corpse. While both Ranpo stories were written before the atrocities at Unit 731 could occur, Ōtsuka's adoption and modernization of these elements to reflect contemporary social anxieties and fears is a masterful turn and deepens the horror of the story in a meaningful way.

HAUNTED SPACES AND THE WORDLESS VORTEX

While *If You Should Die* calls out specific historical events as a source of horror, *Waltz* highlights the dangers posed by *yūrei* created by the merciless drudgery of modern life. In her monograph, *The Price of Death*, social anthropologist Hikaru Suzuki states that *muenbotoke* fall into certain categories: often they are those who have died while travelling, either by "natural catastrophe or through violence" (Suzuki 2000, 32) and adds that "non-kin who have died by violence away from home are always considered harmful and dangerous" (Suzuki 2000, 32). In a city where the vast majority of individuals have to commute every day, this creates a surplus of travelers who could potentially meet violence undertaking the tasks of daily life. It is this type of spirit that Ōtsuka uses to populate modern-day Tokyo in *Waltz*; they are ambiguous and created as a result of daily life rather than deliberate actions taken by one party against another. The tale begins with an apparent suicide at the Shinjuku train station and the discovery of an ear in a magazine.[11] Karatsu is unable to speak with the ear as he did the woman in *If You Should Die*; instead, he hears a haunting, disjointed melody, presumably the last thing the individual heard before he was killed. Over the course of the story Karatsu and the others uncover a series of similar suicides at a nearby train crossing. Ōtsuka presents the reader with a series of events which leads the group to discover an entire host of *muenbotoke* are tied to this particular location, drawing more victims to them, not through active manifestation but through the disjointed conglomeration of sounds which have become routine background noise to the daily commute; the alarm bells on the crossing arms, the melancholic jingle of the recycling truck and, the school bells signaling the end of the day all come together to create an atmosphere of overwhelming hopelessness in what Karatsu calls the "lure of meaningless life to meaningless death" (Ōtsuka 2015 vol. 3, 187). It is not until Karatsu asks the truck driver to change his vehicle's song to something less sad that the cycle is finally broken, but not before Karatsu and his spirit have to intervene to save Sasaki from being pulled into the void. It is fitting then, that these spirits are as equally deserving of pity as they are fear because even though they are not vengefully seeking out victims they continue to "cause the living trouble if not appeased or pacified" (Barrett 1989, 81).

In *In Ghostly Japan* (1899), Lafcadio Hearn presents a similar tale, *At Yaidzu,* where the mingling sounds of the ocean and the dead converge to create a vortex of death. Hearn emphasizes that "the sounds together, of a certain place are said to be the voices of the Drowned" (Hearn 1971, 238). Ōtsuka creates a modern-day equivalent with the everyday sounds carrying the spirit of the dead who have become trapped, drawing others to share their fate, since they can never escape and return home to be properly laid to rest. As Sasayama informs Karatsu "there was [carnage] scattered over tens of meters of track. [He had] even heard of an incident when a dried-out arm from a corpse fell off a platform ceiling . . . months after its owner's suicide" (Ōtsuka 2015 vol. 3, 159). This alludes to the idea that a portion of the soul of the living can remain unappeased, unable to pass on as the vortex will not let them escape. Ōtsuka further follows the literary tradition of Hearn's ghost story by establishing a specific window during which these ghosts are actively able to draw others to them. In his work, Hearn states that a certain hour is said to be the most powerful time for spirits to affect the living. Historically speaking this was believed to be the hours between 2 A.M. and 4 A.M. commonly referred to as the Hour of the Ox (Hearn 1971, 211). In *Waltz*, Ōtsuka shifts this to 3 P.M. (2015 vol. 3, 171), which is the time when many people would be on their way home for the evening. The *kaidan* element in this tale manifests in how the spirits are linked by misfortune to a certain location and continue to call the living to them, seemingly jealous of what they can no longer have. Those lured by *muenbotoke* must join them in their cycle of suffering, luring others to experience their pain so long as the conditions that led to their deaths remain unchanged. Ōtsuka evokes the inner hopelessness present in modern life with these spirits; they can affect anyone, regardless of whether or not the victim seems to have their life together, they can still be dragged into the void and crushed, like a body on the train tracks.

This type of phenomenon is not isolated or new and has been a trope in Japanese horror cinema since the 1990s. It recalls the horror in *Kyua* (The Cure, Kiyoshi Kurosawa, 1997) in which hypnotism originating first through recorded sound and later through the pull of an enigmatic amnesiac causes others to commit murder, with no memory of their actions or what drove them to it. Likely, it is similar to *Jisatsu Sākuru* (Suicide Circle, Sion Sono, 2001), in which seemingly innocuous pop songs heard every day in every home drive individuals and groups to commit suicide, where they are asked "are you connected to yourself?" Ōtsuka takes these tales of horror and shifts yet again; instead of making his *muenbotoke* actively seek their victims, he makes them a consequence of everyday life, of the endless monotony of modern life, where anyone can fall victim through no fault of their own.

VENGEFUL GHOSTS AND OBLIGATION

Up until now, we have examined *muenbotoke* presented as a host of nameless spirits, where the violence experienced by and committed against them is impersonal. They are all victims of opportunity, rather than targets of personally directed rage or jealousy. In *The Look I Had 'til Yesterday*, Ōtsuka has heightened the traditional presentation of the *onryō* and combined it with the concept of the *ubume* to give rise to a singular spirit enacting her vengeance against the individual who wronged them while also caring for the child she left behind. She remains connected to the world of the living not only by the violence committed against her but by the obligation she has to the child left behind. Aside from a tale of revenge, it is also a reflection on the persistent lack of compassion in the world and a didactic lesson on the dangers of jealousy.

During an afternoon at Saigoyama Park in Tokyo, Sasaki tells a story about how the bodies of many children were found buried in the park at the beginning of the Shōwa Era (1926–1989); they were believed to be victims of an adoption scam, killed for profit and never able to be properly memorialized by their families as no formal records had been made, leaving their spirits to reside at the park until a memorial was erected.[12] This leads Numata to search for more corpses, intending to find their next client. Instead, he uncovers a key which in turn leads the group to the body of a baby in a duffle bag stuffed inside a coin locker. As with the ear in *Waltz*, Karatsu is unable to hear the voice of the dead baby, as they died too young to speak,[13] but a picture reveals the face of the murderer, as Makino notes that the baby did not die of natural causes because "[the] bruises around the mouth and nose suggest suffocation" (Ōtsuka 2015 vol. 4, 126). They wonder why the baby's final wish would be to return to the woman who abandoned them without proper rites, trapping them from being able to move on. Despite Makino being concerned the mother will be difficult to find and that they also will not get paid by the client, Karatsu decides to help. With Sasaki's help, they find the murderer and follow her home, but not before they are confronted by a private investigator who reveals the truth of what is going on. He reveals that his client is the baby's real mother, who has possessed the woman who murdered her in order to provide care for the child. The mother, Shizuka, became a hybrid *onryō /ubume*, murdered by her former friend, Yukie, out of jealousy. However, as the *ubume* utilizes so much energy to care for the child "there's a limit to how long a spirit can ride the boy of the living" (Ōtsuka 2015 vol. 4, 147); once Yukie regained control she killed the child and hid the baby in the locker. With the baby in hand, Karatsu and the investigator enter the apartment. Inside, they find that Shizuka is still in control; she pulls herself across the floor, calling loudly for the return of her baby. Shizuka/Yukie presents immediately to the reader as a typical *onryō*, dressed fully in white with long black hair, one face emerging from the other. With the baby returned, though dead, Karatsu and the P.I., manage to quiet Shizuka before she can become a further danger, reuniting her spirit with that of her dead child so that they may both find peace. They leave Yukie and alert the authorities to the fact that there is a murderer to be arrested.

Surprisingly the baby's spirit, historically known as *mizuko*,[14] who experienced a deeply traumatic death and was not granted the proper funerary rites to ensure that the baby could find rest, does not manifest as a dangerous spirit in their own right. The spirits of children have been used in Japanese horror with great effect; Sadako in *Ringu* (The Ring, Hideo Nakata, 1998) Mimiko in *Chakushin Ari* (One Missed Call, Takashi Miike, 2003), and Mitsuko in *Honogurai Mizu no Soko Kara* (Dark Water, Hideo Nakata, 2002) are all children who were abandoned by their mothers and suffered tragic deaths, but whose mothers actively chose to abandon them. In Japanese horror, the spirits of young children tend to be unguided by typical patterns of *yūrei* behavior, and unconcerned about whom they harm on a scale even more destructive than the *muenbotoke* in *Waltz*. Daisetz Suzuki, a novelist and essayist who was seminal in the dissemination of Buddhism and Zen into the West, asserts that "all forms of evil must be said somehow to be embodying what is true and good and beautiful" (Suzuki 1993, 33). Perhaps then, instead of utilizing the possibility of the *mizuko* to bring further horror, Ōtsuka has graced the reader with a rare tale in which the dead, who so often cause harm to the living, are also capable of great acts of compassion at great cost to themselves. By possessing her murderer, Shizuka actively fights to care for her child, showing it love and keeping it from later becoming yet another vengeful spirit. For a time Shizuka is able to fulfill her maternal obligation and allay her rage; her wrath only becomes potentially dangerous to others when she learns that her child has been killed.

Furthermore, *The Look I Had 'til Yesterday* highlights how the horrors that the living perpetrate against each other are far more nefarious than the revenge brought against them by the dead. While Shizuka's *onryō* could have lingered further, had she not been reunited with her child, Karatsu and the private investigator ensure that the proper rites are observed and that order is restored and put an end to any further horror or misfortune. They also go a step further, ensuring Yukie will be brought to real justice in a court of law for her crimes.

ANSWERING THE RESTLESS GHOSTS

While *Kurosagi* is characterized as a horror manga, very rarely does the horror persist beyond the end of a given story. In *If You Should Die, Waltz*, and *The Look I Had 'til Yesterday*, the *yūrei* are able to be put to rest once their final wishes are fulfilled. They act according to codified behaviors and patterns, and are put to rest through Karatsu's right action, right resolve, and right effort. When the dead request help fulfilling their final wishes Karatsu takes up the task without hesitation, even at great risk to himself. It is through Karatsu that Ōtsuka ensures his tales of horror can truly be read as orthodox ghost stories, and serve as didactic tools as well as entertainment. By characterizing Karatsu as a young Buddhist monk, Ōtsuka is following a long tradition of Japanese tales of the supernatural, where often a religious individual would encounter the supernatural on their journey. While normally it is considered dangerous to handle the dead as "the corpses' impurity" can inflict harm on the living if one either touches the decomposing body or draws near to the raging and undisciplined spirit," (Suzuki 2000, 27) Karatsu never hesitates to communicate with the spirits of the dead through direct contact with their corpse or any part that may have been separated from the whole, no matter the state of dismemberment or decay. Through this direct contact, Ōtsuka is repeatedly subjecting Karatsu to the possible dangers that the *yūrei* pose to the living. Though not a full Buddhist monk, Karatsu is charged with the dangerous, and noble task of communicating with the dead and helping them find peace, acting as caretaker for the spirits of the dead. He must constantly come to terms with the fear and pain which keeps the spirits attached to this world, while also dealing with the horrors and dangers which led to their deaths: in *If You Should Die* Karatsu risks his life to travel to China and confront a sadistic murderer; in *Waltz* he seeks out the very sounds driving individuals to commit suicide; in *The Look I Had 'til Yesterday* he places himself in the path of a spirit who could kill him in her attempt to get her baby back. He prays for the release of these *yūrei* from their suffering and helps them have their last wishes granted, allowing them to release their anger and become *hotoke* (enlightening spirits), or beneficial spirits who can no longer bring harm to the living. Ōtsuka uses Karatsu as the voice of hope in the darkness. Much like the Buddhist priests who wander the forest at Aokigahara-jukai and pray for those who committed suicide so that their spirits may have peace,[15] or the ones who answered the call to come and pacify the many spirits of the dead who could not be recovered and laid properly to rest and let go of their resentment of the living after the Great Tohoku Earthquake and Tsunami in 2011 (Davisson 2015), Karatsu seeks out the spirits of those who have died as a result of tragedy and violence to help them move on, to bring closure and rest to the horror that exists in the real world, and bring to light societal and cultural anxieties and fears that shape the experience of horror in contemporary popular culture including, but not limited to, manga.

Where so many modern horror manga are characterized by their brutal sense of hopelessness, such as Junji Itō's *Gyo* or *Uzumaki*, where there is no recognizable world left to return to after the story has run its course, Ōtsuka's return to orthodox horror is a striking commentary on the modern world as he sees it. His horror is the horror of the everyday, ripped from history books and headlines, and imbued with *yūrei*. Horror and death are around every corner, and it is only when individuals like Karatsu step up to deal with and acknowledge the source of the horror rather than only the result, that things can be changed and cycles of suffering can be stopped. Additionally, by eschewing the more supernatural use of *youkai* and focusing on very human *yūrei*, Ōtsuka creates a horror experience more capable of acting as a tool to educate his audience, not only about proper moral behaviors, but about the darkness that exists in history and everyday life that if ignored could result in further suffering or an insidious return of behaviors leading to wanton violence and future atrocities. By utilizing history, artistic and literary traditions deeply shaped by Japanese Buddhist didactic traditions Ōtsuka's *The Kurosagi Delivery Service* successfully meets the criteria set out for a successful horror manga and creates a compelling series of stories that capture the spirit of the original Japanese *kaidan* tradition.

REFERENCES

Balmain, Colette. 2008. *Introduction to Japanese Horror Film*. Edinburgh: Edinburgh University Press.
Barrett, Gregory. 1989. *Archetypes in Japanese Film: The Sociopolitical and Religious Significance of the Principal Heroes and Heroines*. Selinsgrove: Susquehanna University Press.
Cook, Haruko and Theodore Cook. 2000. *Japan at War: An Oral History*. London: Phoenix Press.
Davisson, Zack. 2015. *Yūrei: The Japanese Ghost*. Seattle: Chin Music Press. Kindle.
Gilhooly, Rob. 2011. "Inside Japan's 'Suicide Forest'." *The Japanese Times Online*. Jan 26, 2011. Accessed May 12, 2021. https://www.japantimes.co.jp/life/2011/06/26/general/inside-japans-suicide-forest/.
Hearn, Lafcadio. 1971. *In Ghostly Japan.* Rutland: Charles E. Tuttle Company.
____. *Japan: An Attempt at Translation*. 2004. Project Gutenberg. Accesssed May 10, 2021. www.gutenberg.org/cache/5979/pg5979.html.
Iwasaka, Michio and Barre Toelken. 1994. *Ghosts and the Japanese: Cultural Experience in Japanese Death Legends.* Utah: Utah State University Press.
"Japan's Harvest of Death. 2004." *The Independent*. Tuesday, Oct 24, 2004. Accessed May 12, 2021. https://www.independent.co.uk/news/world/asia/japan-s-harvest-death-5368465.html
Kristof, Nicholas D. 1995. "Unmasking Horror: A Special Report. Japan Confronting Gruesome War Atrocity." *New York Times*. March 17, 1995. Accessed May 10, 2021. https://www.nytimes.com/1995/03/17/world/unmasking-horror-a-special-report-japan-confronting-gruesome-war-atrocity.html.
Ōtsuka, Eiji. 2015. "Afterward from the Author." *The Kurosagi Corpse Delivery Service Omnibus 1*, Vol. 2. Translated by Toshifumi Yoshida, 214-5. Milwaukie: Dark Horse Manga.
Ōtsuka, Eiji. 2015. "Waltz." *The Kurosagi Corpse Delivery Service Omnibus 1*, Vol.3. Translated byToshifumi Yoshida, 141-190. Milwaukee: Dark Horse Manga.
Ōtsuka, Eiji. 2015. "If You Should Die." *The Kurosagi Corpse Delivery Service Omnibus 2*, Vol.4. Translated by Toshifumi Yoshida, 53-108. Milwaukee: Dark Horse Manga.
Ōtsuka, Eiji. 2015. "The Look I Had Til Yesterday." *The Kurosagi Corpse Delivery Service Omnibus 2*, Vol. 4. Translated By Toshifumi Yoshida, 109-158. Milwaukee: Dark Horse Manga.
Reichert, Jim. 2011. "Deviance and Social Darwinism in Edogawa Ranpo's Erotic Grotesque Thriller *Koto no Ōni*." *Journal of Japanese Studies*, Vol. 27, No. 1 (Winter): 113–141. JSTOR.
Suzuki, Daisetz T. 1993. *Zen and Japanese Culture*. Princeton: University of Princeton Press.
Suzuki, Hikaru. 2000. *The Price of Death: The Funeral Industry in Contemporary Japan*. California: University of California Press.
Tamura, Yoshiro. 2000. *Japanese Buddhism: A Cultural History*. Translated by Jeffry Hunter. Tokyo: Kosei Publishing Co.

Tinsley, Elizabeth. 2017. "The Composition of Decomposition: The *Kusōzu* Images of Matsui Fuyuko and Itō Seiu and Buddhism in Erotic Grotesque Modernity." *Journal of Asian Humanities at Kyushu University*, Vol. 2 (March): 15–45.

Yoshida, Toshifume. 2015. "Disjecta Membra." In *The Kurosagi Corpse Delivery Service Omnibus 2*, vol. 4. Milwaukie: Dark Horse Comics.

NOTES

1. "Strange Recited Narrative" is a direct translation, but these stories are generally considered to consist of the supernatural and the strange and often called ghost stories.

2. *The Kurosagi Corpse Delivery Service* will be referred to as *Kurosagi*.

3. The English language editor also notes that *The Devil's Gluttony* was published by Kadokawa, the same publisher who originally distributed *The Kurosagi Corpse Delivery Service* in Japan. (Yoshida 2015, 217).

4. We never discover Woman Holding Her Head's name. Further reference will be made to her as "the woman."

5. The Daruma Woman is a very well-known urban legend, with many different tellings. Sometimes the woman is the wife of the man that comes into the bar, other times she is a student that says she is just like the man who has come to see her and that she wants to go home. Sometimes she can speak, other times she cannot because her tongue has been removed. The constant element between retellings is always that all four of her limbs have been amputated on display in a seedy location, and referred to only as "Daruma" on the sign.

6. Originally published in 1904, this quote has nothing to do with the atrocities of World War II, but the sentiment holds true for modern ghost stories.

7. In 1997 there was a campaign to remove mention of Unit 731 from history textbooks, and it was not until August of 2002 that a Tokyo District Court ruled that Japan has, in fact, engaged in biological warfare in China during the war.

8. This included the purposeful exposure and infection of Chinese civilians to anthrax, gangrene, syphilis, bubonic plague, and hemorrhagic fever in order to weaponize these diseases for use against the "enemy." (Cook and Theodore 2000, 158).

9. There are also accounts of the vivisection of test subjects who had been infected, often without the use of anesthetics. (Kristof 1995).

10. In regards to a vivisection conducted on a healthy Chinese Civilian, Japanese Army doctor Yuasa Ken remembers a nurse who was "even prouder than me. She giggled. The demon's face is not a fearful face. It's a face wreathed in smiles." (Cook and Cook 2000, 147–148).

11. It is important to note that while suicide is considered a violent or untimely death, it does not carry the same religious connotations as it does in the West. In Japan, suicide is not considered illegal or taboo, by religious or moral standards. (Gilhooly 2001, 2).

12. The author could not find any supporting evidence that these events took place, but Ōtsuka's use of such historical cases in the past to inform his manga leads the author to think that somewhere there may be a grain of truth. All of his stories tend to

incorporate elements of real history, urban legend, folklore, and current affairs, so it would seem odd if he completely invented this particular element of the story.

13. A note in the Disjecta Membra for this volume states that since the author never specifically revealed the gender of the child, they also chose not to give it gendered pronouns in translation. (Yoshida 2015, 218).

14. A *mizuko* is archaically the spirit or ghost of a child who died before birth or in early infancy, and can be quite dangerous. In the modern day they are more commonly miscarried, stillborn or aborted fetuses. Entire rituals have been created to pacify the souls of these young ones, referred to as *mizuko kuyo,* in which the spirit of the child is pacified, and the parent(s) can grieve.

15.A Buddhist priest conducts rites in the forest to pray for the repose of the thousands of people who have died there over the years. "We conduct these rites in order to ponder how we might help make a world that is free of such suffering" (Gilhooly 2011, 2).

PART 2

Posthuman Monsters and Grotesque Bodies

Chapter 6

"Love in a Chair"

Industrialization and Exploitation Edogawa Rampo's "The Human Chair" and Junji Ito's Manga Adaptation

Leonie Rowland

It is unconventional to find love in the folds of a chair, but capitalism, which constantly adapts to the needs of the consumer, cares little for convention. This chapter argues that Edogawa Rampo's short story "The Human Chair" (1925), originally published in the Japanese magazine *Kuraku*, engages with an early form of commodity animism, pre-empting the transgressive human–object relations that are rife in neoliberal times.[1]

Neoliberal Japan is often discussed in Gothic terms, with Charles Shirō Inouye arguing that Japanese culture is profoundly Gothic (2012). More specifically, this chapter suggests that the Gothic is embedded in Japan's consumer culture, which vocalizes (and capitalizes on) the "frustrations of life in the global economy" (Cross 2006, xvii) in an eruption of animated commodities. This eruption is also present in Gothic literature and film, making it a source of horror in fact and fiction alike. In *Millennial Monsters: Japanese Toys and the Global Imagination*, Anne Allison defines commodity animism as the "infusing [of] the material world with a life," leading to objects becoming "the conduit for various forms of communication, intimate relationships, and arousals" (2006, 86). These objects are sinister because they foster emotional dependence on something with no emotional capacity, prioritizing capital over connection. They are the result of neoliberalism making people lonely and then using their loneliness to sell them the illusion of companionship through cunningly Shintoesque marketing techniques.

The conflation of the spiritual with the commercial is expressed in "The Human Chair" through the literal and symbolic animation of the inanimate, generating horror in its insistence that human–object relations have become stronger than interpersonal ties. The story follows a man as he designs, builds and climbs into a chair, which is subsequently used to furnish the lobby of a foreign hotel. He is sexually gratified by the chair itself, as well as the knowledge that women are sitting "on [his] knees" (Rampo 2012, 29). The chair is eventually transferred into a private home where the man falls in love with a famous writer named Yoshiko. He reveals himself to her in a letter, and she is shaken by the "horrible ordeal" she has unknowingly undergone, but a second letter follows, assuring Yoshiko that the man is in fact an "admirer" of her writing and the entire story a work of fiction (Rampo 2012, 46). Junji Ito's manga adaptation of "The Human Chair" (2007), originally released as a one-shot and recently published in his collection *Venus in the Blind Spot* (2020), begins where Rampo ends, imagining a scenario where Yoshiko's admirer, far from being fictional, actually resides within the chair.

For Rampo, the narrator's connection to the chair is multifaceted—it is his creation, his accomplice, his lover—but it ultimately boils down to an expression of the desire to create a partner for himself. This desire is inseparable from a desire to join the bourgeoisie, since he believes that wealth will counterbalance his ugliness and solve his isolation. Thus, the chair becomes a vessel for his fantasies of human connection and material abundance, and he loves it for its promise of a better life. It is this mentality, particularly the demand for artificially designed companionship, that commodity animism taps into sixty years later, at the height of Japan's economic success in the 1980s. The chair is also a cypher for the socioeconomic changes that occurred in Japan following the Meiji Restoration[2] of 1868, which sparked rapid industrialization and the adoption of Western economic models. If, as Christopher Harding insists in *Japan Story*, "Edogawa drew his cast of characters from the rotten heart of modern Tokyo—and of modernity itself" (Harding 2018, 132), then the chair literalizes the depravity spawning at the heart of things, foreshadowing the unstable selfhoods and longing for connection that would become cultural signifiers by the end of the twentieth century. As such, connection in this story is always exploitative, suggesting that the simultaneous transformation of Japan into "a relation-less society" (Allison 2006, 5) and "the most advanced consumer culture in the world" had already begun in the 1920s (Allison 2006, 8).

So, first, this chapter reads the chair as a metaphor for the disregard for human wellbeing that became a defining feature of Japan after contact with the West forced it to industrialize (Harding 2018). Then, it analyzes the narrator's relationship with the chair as a forerunner to commodity animism. From here, it argues that "The Human Chair" ultimately reasserts conservative ideologies when the framed narrative is revealed as an elaborate sales pitch designed by the narrator, who is trying to promote himself as an author. Finally, it compares Rampo's text to Ito's manga adaptation of the same name in order to demonstrate that, by the twenty-first century, commodity animism has become the dominant narrative in this story.

GOING BACKWARDS

The image of a luxurious chair concealing a criminal is a metaphor for the rapid industrialization that took place in early-twentieth-century Japan, which prioritized economic prosperity over personal security. Since the chair is built by a Japanese craftsman to furnish the lobby of a foreign hotel, it is also a cypher for contact with the West. With industrialization and westernization in mind, Harding assesses 1920s Japan as follows: "For critics tempted to read a great deal into what a society does with its leisure time, all this was a clear sign that Japan was going backwards. Not long ago, the country's driving slogan had been *bunmei kaika*: 'civilization and enlightenment.' Now there was critical acclaim for a story about a man groping a woman through a chair" (2018, 133). The words "civilization and enlightenment," stamped across the cultural consciousness like a brand, signify a stark refusal to acknowledge the "deep, creeping" (Harding 2018, 116) shadow of industrialization that characterized this "era of uncertainty" (Harding 2018, 123). For many, the opportunities offered by expanding cities, growing population and thriving factories came at the cost of personal security, with Tokyo in particular teetering on the brink of "extreme poverty" (Harding 2018, 118). The image of a man groping a woman through a chair embodies this discrepancy between surface and interior: whereas the chair "immeasurably" surpasses the narrator's previous creations like the blossoming economy, its interior is hollow and "the cavity inside large enough to accommodate a man without any danger of exposure" (Rampo 2012, 34). The chair is, in other words, a vehicle for economically orientated deceit and corruption, posing as an expression of industrial skill and craftsmanship. It is no coincidence that the hotel it furnishes is located in Yokohama, where the "Treaty of Peace and Amity" was signed between America and the Tokugawa shogunate in 1854, forcing Japan to end two-hundred and twenty years of national seclusion (Harding 2018). Both hotel and chair are "luxurious" (Rampo 2012, 41) spaces that the narrator longs to be a part of, framing Western influence as desirable and lucrative. However, soon after the chair is stationed in the hotel lobby, the manager is "forced to leave for his homeland" and the building is "transferred to

Japanese hands," leading to the abolishment of unnecessary luxuries because they do not "increase profit" (Ibid). This policy of profit over pomp suggests not only that the Japanese have adopted Western economic models with great enthusiasm, but that they are able to generate capital more efficiently in their early days of industrialization than more advanced industrial societies. This can be read as the prologue to the "Japan Problem," a term used in the 1980s to articulate anxiety that Japan was more successful as a capitalist nation than its Western counterparts (Allison, 2006). It can also be read as a warning against rapid modernization, which, in this case, drives a man into the lining of a chair because he cannot cope with financial precarity. The narrator's relationship with his creation is an early form of commodity animism because it compensates for his lack of emotional ties and suggests that, in industrial Japan, expensive objects are necessary to human happiness.

The narrator is starved of human connection by his "humble" financial situation and his physical "ugliness," both of which are beyond his control and "torture" his soul (Rampo 2012, 31). Consequently, he compensates by indulging in fantasies of material abundance, which leave him unfulfilled. If, as Harding writes, the rapid industrialization of Japan exacerbated "the homelessness at the heart of the human condition" (2018, 135), then Rampo locates this homelessness in the valuing, on a national scale, of things other than the innate self, such as money, beauty and sex. It is this diagnosis of what it means to be human that Allison gestures to in *Precarious Japan* when she defines precarity under neoliberalism "not only [as] a condition of precarious labor but a more general existential state—a state where one's human condition has become precarious as well" (2013, 9). By this, she means that people's lives have become unfamiliar and unpredictable, resulting in a similar "search for orientation" (2018, 123) that Harding identifies in 1920s Tokyo. As such, the narrator presents himself as a victim of fate who is punished for his natural circumstances, suggesting that his problems are systemic rather than personal—however, as would become customary of neoliberal thought, he is held responsible for his facial and financial troubles and shunned by society. His dream of joining the bourgeoisie is ultimately a desire for acceptance since he believes that money and power will sooth his ugliness and solve his isolation. Here is an early iteration of commodity animism, where possessing objects coded with social acceptance is preferable to liberation from damaging social structures: by coveting expensive items, the narrator consents that he would rather be accepted into a broken society than not accepted at all. Consequently, upon finishing a chair, he "used to imagine the types of people who would eventually curl up in [it], certain people of nobility, living in palatial residences, with exquisite, priceless paintings hanging on walls, glittering crystal chandeliers hanging from ceilings, expensive rugs on the floor, etc." (Rampo 2012, 32). The "etc." suggests that the objects listed are important only as symbols of the lifestyle they represent, and the emphasis on their pricelessness over their peculiarities equates to a frivolous yearning for material abundance. However, linguistic signifiers of wealth such as "exquisite" and "expensive" are also attached to these objects to emphasize their inaccessibility (Rampo 2012, 32). Since the narrator's chairs will presumably sit among them, such fantasies highlight his skill as a craftsman whilst also alienating him from his produce. The gulf between his ability to create beautiful things and his physical ugliness demonstrates his aesthetic inferiority to his chairs, which are more complementary to luxurious surroundings than he is. As such, they serve in part as his Gothic double, allowing him to symbolically infiltrate bourgeoisie interiors through his creations, which stand as representatives of him. However, he is "haunted by feelings of utter despair" (Rampo 2012, 33) every time he completes a chair, framing his craft as a codification of what he cannot afford and a reaffirmation of his unsatisfactory place in the world. Considering that the chairs are valued more than he is by his bourgeois buyers, becoming a part of one is the logical solution to his perceived inadequacy.

However, connection in this story—be it between the narrator and the chair, the narrator and the hotel guests, or the narrator and Yoshiko—is always exploitative. Although the narrator attempts to form (primarily sexual) human bonds using the chair, his efforts ultimately equate to self-pleasure and sexual assault, reaffirming his isolation and undermining his dreams of joining the bourgeoisie. His string of "love affairs" begins with the chair itself, which "not only supported the person who sat in it, but it also seemed to embrace and to hug [. . .] I let my body sink deeply into the chair and, caressing the two arm-rests with my hands, gasped with genuine satisfaction and pleasure" (Rampo 2012, 33). Starved of human connection, he meets the chair's "embrace" with an eruption of desire for the comfort and caress of a lover. The object, endowed with human qualities, surpasses its most basic purpose to support the sitter physically, assisting him emotionally and erotically too. The "alluring touch" (Ibid) of leather repurposes language used to describe contact between human beings, just as gasps akin to sexual climax are brought on by the fondling of armrests, framing the object as a site of transgression. Their embrace is symbolic of sexual union, and the narrator's pleasure at his body sinking deep inside the chair foreshadows his eventual retreat into it, through which they become one being. Here, the narrator is sexually gratified by his own craftsmanship, which could not have "expressed with greater eloquence the definition of the word comfort" (Ibid). On one hand, he has succeeded so completely in his role as a chairmaker that his body derives physical pleasure from its successful service of capitalism. On the other, he is gratified by the action of using an object he has designed and built himself. If, as Harding argues, 1920s Tokyo was a place "crawling with 3 million people who live without making their own rice" (2018, 121), the narrator's symbolic intercourse with the chair is momentarily gratifying because it connotes self-sufficiency. However, his desire for the chair is quickly replaced by a desire for flesh, suggesting his self-gratification is ultimately unfulfilling. Thus, the story once again reasserts conservative narratives by suggesting that craftsmanship does not sate the desire to consume.

With this in mind, it is no coincidence that the narrator compares the women he assaults to non-human entities such as snakes, statues and, in one case, a rubber ball. He objectifies women and anthropomorphizes the chair, leaving both in a liminal state where they are alive enough to gratify his wishes and submissive enough to do so without complaint. This also suggests that, since he has presumably never been with a woman, he is processing the situation the only way he knows how—through the language of commodity. In this way, his objectophilia serves to emphasize his loneliness whilst also attempting to compensate for it. This is clear when, despite facilitating the narrator's "weird world of sensuous pleasure" (Rampo 2012, 40), the chair ultimately acts as a barrier between him and the women he desires, making him long to "remove [the] layer of leather" that divides them (Rampo 2012, 39). As such, the women's obliviousness to his presence, which makes it impossible for them to consent to or partake in the enjoyment he is feeling, reaffirms his isolation and suggests that all attempts to resolve his emotional and economic precarity in this way are ultimately futile.

MARKETING FEAR

The narrator dwells on his "months of unsanitary living" and "humble" (Rampo 2012, 31) profession for the same reason that he reveals his "weird world of sensuous pleasure" (Rampo 2012, 39)—to generate emotion, be it pathos or revulsion, in his object of desire: Yoshiko. Following the twist that exposes him as a competitive writer, the story of the human chair is transformed into a sales pitch designed to exhibit his artistic ability. Thus, since the narrator's true intention is to sell his story, the sympathy and horror generated by his situation are designed to reaffirm rather than challenge the capitalist system. The story is constructed to ensure Yoshiko keeps reading: the narrator builds rapport by apologizing for the "presumptuous letter from a complete stranger" and then promises to "shock [her] to no end" with his "confession," suggesting that he is imparting a secret to her and her alone (Rampo 2012, 30). By implying that Yoshiko is the sole witness to his confession, he establishes a bond between them based on the fact that he trusts her with "the strange workings of [his] mind," which he is certain she will "understand" (Ibid). This marketing tactic is an early version of the logic used by brands in neoliberal advertising—particularly in the case of commodity animism, which relies on the consumer loving and understanding the product in question, which then promises to love and understand them in return. In *No Logo*, Naomi Klein argues that "brands must 'establish emotional ties' with their consumers" (2000, 20), fostering loyalty by convincing the subject that they are being personally cared for. However, this "psychological intimacy" (Allison, 2006, 18) is subverted in "The Human Chair" when the potential for emotional connection created by the narrator's confession is undercut by the "horror of horrors" Yoshiko experiences by reading his tale (Rampo 2012, 46). Here, instead of establishing positive emotional ties, the narrator turns to another marketing strategy that, according to Klein, finds success in the production of "the most powerful images" (Klein 2000, 4), creating an "opportunity for emotional leverage" on the part of the brand (Klein 2000, 21). This is evident in the graphic descriptions of the narrator's objectophilia, which makes him gasp with "satisfaction and pleasure" (Rampo 2012, 33), and his subsequent assault on a string of women, of whom Yoshiko is the last. Despite (or perhaps because of) its capacity for horror, the story entices Yoshiko with "magnetic force" (Rampo 2012, 30) and rouses her curiosity "to the bursting point" (Rampo 2012, 45), conforming to Fred Botting's assertion that a successful Gothic story should "provoke repugnance, disgust and recoil, but also engage readers' interest, fascinating and attracting them" (Botting 1996, 6). Yoshiko admits that "it had been her intention to stop reading and tear up the eerie message; but somehow, she had read on" (Rampo 2012, 46), suggesting that even though she wishes to extract herself from its grasp, she is unable to. As a Gothic story, this is evidence of the "amusing" and "entertaining" effect that the author wishes to achieve (Rampo 2012, 47). However, as a sales pitch, the tailor-made narrative, designed to override the consumer's better judgement with the goal of persuading them to buy into a product or service, equates to what Jean Baudrillard, in his Marxist-leaning *The System of Objects*, calls "a totalitarian conditioning of man and his needs" (2005, 179). In this way, Yoshiko (who represents the consumer) is manipulated into consuming a narrative she believes she is emotionally involved in, despite the negative effects it has on her, so that its author (who represents the market) can benefit.

Likewise, Ito's adaptation of "The Human Chair" is explicit in its use of Rampo's story as a sales pitch. The antagonist, like Rampo's narrator, is a chair seller, binding him to the capitalist system, which will profit from the success of his trade. It also frames him as a double of the original chair maker, who is revealed to be his relative. In Ito's adaptation, the seller uses Rampo's story, which doubles as his family history, to convince Yuzuho—a customer, famous writer and double of Yoshiko—that purchasing a chair is necessary to her wellbeing. The story begins soon after Rampo's ends, with Yoshiko receiving news that a manuscript entitled "The Human Chair" won first prize in a competition on her recommendation. The implication, of course, is that Rampo's narrator successfully sold himself to her as a writer. However, it quickly becomes clear that his story is far from fiction—he has indeed been living in Yoshiko's chair, and proceeds to murder her jealous husband. Yoshiko is consumed by horror and disappears, only to be discovered years later inside the chair, perched on the lap of her husband's murderer, naked and screaming. The chair seller shows Yuzuho their mummified corpses, which still reside within the chair, and explains that they loved each other "so deeply" (Ito 71). Although the sales pitch pivots on Yuzuho requiring a new chair to solve her writers' block, the implication is that, on purchase, she will experience a similar love to Yoshiko.

In "Carlos Ruiz Zafron and the Gothic Marketplace," Glennis Byron argues that the Gothic has "beg[u]n to function very much like a brand," finding purchase in a mainstream culture where "we buy not the product but the story that is offered with the product" (2012, 72–73), suggesting that Gothic images—in this case, a human chair—are successful marketing tools because of the way of life they signify. When faced with a story of transgressive "love" facilitated by a chair, the consumer buys into the narrative attached to the chair rather than the chair itself. The Gothic is successful in this regard because of its easily recognized, highly image-based set of tropes (the image of Yoshiko inside the chair connotes transgressive sexuality, for example), which, as Botting (1996) suggests, repel and entice in equal measure, triggering intense passion in the consumer. In keeping with the sale of Gothic as a lifestyle, the seller frames his chairs as quasi-supernatural objects capable of "chang[ing] a person's life" (Ito 2019, 48), emphazising the power objects have over people and suggesting that Yuzuho's future happiness rests on her acquisition of the product. He equates the choosing of a chair with "destiny" (Ibid), tapping into advertising techniques that, according to Klein, are "not just scientific [but] also spiritual" in their appeal to emotional as well as material needs (Klein 2000, 6). In this way, the seller draws parallels between Yoshiko and Yuzuho, suggesting that if the chair was able to solve the former's private struggles, it can do the same for the latter. Since Yuzuho has been "having some trouble" (Ito 2019, 72) with her work, the lifestyle imposed on her by the chair seller capitalises on her desperation and functions like a Faustian bargain. Her ability to write may be restored, but first she must accept the chair's companionship. Here, Ito demonstrates the conservative nature of Gothic as a marketing technique: despite the chair's associations with transgression, its ultimate service is to the capitalist system.

The Faustian nature of this marketing technique implies a level of desperation in Yuzuho, and the chair seller bases his pitch on the fact that she has "writer's block" (Ito 2019, 72). However, since he emphasizes Yoshiko's "eternal comfort" (Ito 2019, 71) as his product's unique selling point, his methods are also based on the assumption that Yuzuho is lonely. Sure enough, Yuzuho and Yoshiko are both coded with symbols of loneliness in Ito's adaptation: the opening panels show Yuzuho walking down a deserted street, alone on a public holiday, and Yoshiko is often drawn sitting quietly in her armchair. Both women are successful writers—a solitary vocation—and whereas Yuzuho lives on her own, Yoshiko's "work as a writer is more important to [her] than [her] husband" (Ito 2019, 62), suggesting that she values success above her relationship. As such, the professional difficulties faced by both women are attributed to the absence of a chair—and, implicitly, the absence of a man—in their lives. The marketing techniques used to convince Yuzuho of this are exploitative and invasive: the seller identifies her by name and occupation, disclosing, in the style of personalized marketing, that he knows who she is and has structured his pitch accordingly.[3] According to Baudrillard, advertising of this kind seeks to make the consumer "aware that the industrial revolution took place for his benefit, that today all the structures of society are embodied in the qualities of this armchair, qualities which themselves come together in his own individual personality" (2005, 183). As such, the meeting of person and product takes on connotations of fate. The chair, it seems, has been made just for Yuzuho—to fulfil her needs, fit her body and remind her that the market is working to her benefit. The seller's knowledge of his audience allows him to target Yuzuho personally, assuring that her writer's block will cease when she purchases his chair. In other words, Yuzuho is promised success because of the chair's companionship, implying that she could not have sustained her career alone. This is confirmed when the bulging chair arrives with a person inside. Thus, the chair being marketed as a solution to her writer's block is a foil for what the seller believes she truly needs: a man as a solution to her loneliness. This duality is established earlier in the narrative when Yoshiko receives a letter declaring that the chair is "indispensable to your creation [. . .] you must sink down deep into me and be held gently by my body. Otherwise, you cannot make full use of your true creative power [. . .] you are such that you simply cannot live without me. And I too cannot live without you" (Ito 2019, 62). Here, man and chair are interchangeable. The passage suggests not only that both are "essential" to Yoshiko's work but that they are necessary to her biological survival, since her body "cannot live" without them (Ibid). The repeated insistence that a man is necessary to the economic and emotional wellbeing of (already successful) women reveals an ulterior motive in chair human and chair seller alike: both assume the form of a neutrally gendered object to restore traditional patriarchal values in women who defy them, suggesting that it is the female vocation to sooth and share in the loneliness of men. The seductiveness of shared warmth and romance is noted by Howard Schultz, CEO of Starbucks, for whom "the romance of the coffee experience, the feeling of warmth and community people get in Starbucks stores" (1997, 5) is central to his brand. The human desire for comfort, companionship and community that Schultz capitalises on is the driving force behind the chair seller's pitch, down to the language used by both. The imposition of this desire onto both women, which culminates in the chair being delivered to Yuzuho despite the fact that she does not want it, demonstrates the sheer pervasiveness and complete disregard for human autonomy that has come to define marketing in the twenty-first century.

So, where Rampo withdraws the immediate threat to Yoshiko by revealing the human chair to be a work of fiction, Ito doubles down on the horror experienced by Yuzuho when a bulging chair arrives, unwanted, at her doorstep. Whereas both women are subject to invasive marketing techniques that threaten their safety and disturb their emotional wellbeing, Yoshiko retains a level of agency that Yuzuho does not since, despite the obvious manipulation she has undergone, it is still ultimately her choice whether to promote the story or not. In Yuzuho's case, however, her efforts to reject the marketing campaign are meaningless, and the chair is delivered to her regardless, suggesting that her autonomy is in dispute from the moment she makes contact with the chair seller. Thus, if the hollow center of Rampo's chair reveals a shadow side to the global economy, Ito's adaptation suggests that this side is no longer concealed in neoliberal times. To this end, where Rampo's chair maker is permanently concealed, Ito's chair seller addresses Yuzuho in the broad light of day, suggesting that there is no need for him to hide his identity. Likewise, where the chair maker's ugliness codifies him as a symbol of moral backwardness, Ito's chair seller is conventionally attractive, implying that corruption and deceit are made pretty under neoliberalism. Exploitation is, in other words, etched on the surface of things. It is in this climate that commodity animism, marketed as a balm to the human condition, thrives.

REFERENCES

Allison, Anne. 2006. *Millennial Monsters: Japanese Toys and the Global Imagination*. Los Angeles: University of California Press.

———. *Precarious Japan*. 2013. Durham: Duke University Press.

Baudrillard, Jean. 2005. *The System of Objects*. Translated by James Benedict. London: Verso.

Botting, Fred. 1996. *Gothic*. London: Routledge.

Byron, Glennis. 2012. "Gothic, Grabbit and Run: Carlos Ruiz Zafron and the Gothic Marketplace." In *The Gothic in Contemporary Literature and Culture: Pop Culture*, edited by Justin Edwards and Agnieszka Soltysik Monnet, 71–83. London: Routledge.

Cross, Gary. 2006. "Foreword." *Millennial Monsters: Japanese Toys and the Global Imagination* by Anne Allison, xv–xviii. Los Angeles: University of California Press.

Harding, Christopher. 2018. *Japan Story: In Search of a Nation, 1950 to the Present*. London: Penguin Random House UK.

Harvey, David. 2005. *A Brief History of Neoliberalism*. Oxford: Oxford University Press.

Inouye, Charles Shirō. 2012. "Japanese Gothic." In *A New Companion to the Gothic*, edited by David Punter, 442–454. Chichester: Wiley-Blackwell.

Ito, Junji. 2019. "The Human Chair." In *Venus in the Blind Spot*. Translated by Jocelyne Allen, 45-74. San Francisco: Viz Media.

Klein, Naomi. 2000. *No Logo*. London: HarperCollins.

Rampo, Edogawa. 2012. "The Human Chair." *Japanese Tales of Mystery and Imagination*. Translated by James B. Harris, 29–47. North Clarendon: Tuttle Publishing.

Shultz, Howard. 1997. *Pour Your Heart into It*. New York: Hyperion.

NOTES

1. Broadly, neoliberalism describes social systems that favor *laissez-faire* capitalism, deregulating markets to allow for a free and competitive international trade (see Harvey). In this chapter, "transgressive" describes human–object relations that are considered illegal, immoral or outside of social norms but that ultimately reaffirm neoliberal beliefs.

2. The Meiji Restoration reinstated practical imperial rule in Japan, meaning that the political system was carried out under the rule of an Emperor.

3. Incidentally, a similarly invasive sales technique is present in Rampo's original text, when the narrator confesses that his tale was constructed based on "the knowledge that [Yoshiko] had recently bought that chair" (2012, 46), pre-empting the personalized marketing that would come to define the way audiences are targeted in the twenty-first century.

Chapter 7

The Monstrous Feminine in Mari Asato J-Horror films

Mariana Soledad Zárate and Canela Rodríguez Fontao

INTRODUCTION

Japanese horror has given viewers worldwide a panorama of vernacular social, cultural, and political anxieties. However, Japanese cinema is almost entirely male-run, male-directed, and male-produced. Japan is a deeply patriarchal culture and, although the interest in capturing the lives of women in films is undeniable, there is no correlation behind the camera. Adam Bringhman dedicates a chapter of his book *Contemporary Japanese Cinema Since Hana-Bito* (2015) to female filmmakers in modern Japan. According the author, immediately after Second World War, the Japanese movement for gender equality was reflected through cultural practices. However, family life and the private space were the norm for women.

Bingham states that "there have traditionally been few opportunities for female filmmakers to work within Japan's studio system, and prior to the 1990s there had been only a small number of women working as directors" (2015, 241). The number of women working on horror films is even smaller. This chapter will analyze part of Mari Asato's horror cinema through the typology of the female monstrous and the abject as analyzed by scholars Julia Kristeva and Barbara Creed. The chapter will discuss not only the ideological and theoretical apparatuses that make possible the female monster, but also how this monster is constructed as a correlate of the cultural anxieties generated by the new roles of women in contemporary Japan. The "complexity of such changes in gender roles has relegated the modern female as the demonic other in Japanese cinema," (Shana 2016, 5) a trope that Asato uses with subversive impetus.

The representation of women as monstrous beings has been systematic throughout the history of horror cinema and Japanese genre filmmaking is no exception. In her book *The Monstruos-Feminine. Film, Feminism, Psychoanalysis* (2003) Barbara Creed argues that culture is disrupted by the abject, for instance, what transgress boundaries, either cultural/social or corporeal. Yet, people feels fascination and are drawn to the abject and its ruptures to the point of desire, even if self-destruction is close.

Creed takes the term "abjection" from Julia Kristeva to expose that the concept of female monstrosity falls directly on the woman's body, specifically, on her reproductive capacity, an area that escapes patriarchal norms. Kristeva argues that there are two types of bodies: symbolic, for example, under the logic of culture, and the abject one (1982, 102–3). The abject body is quintessentially female: unlike the male body, the female body changes shape, swells, produces milk, monthly blood, gives life. Paradoxically, this "production" makes the female body, through the lens of culture, repulsive. Camille Paglia argued that, while the male body is Apollonian (geometrically perfect, closed), female bodies are Dionysian (ever-changing, open) and, as such, monstrous (1991).

Asato's cinema adapts the monstrous feminine as a countercultural force of defiant/deviant feminism. Her female monstrosity is not explicit and/or literal. In most cases the monstrous shapes the behavioral via a body that is not subjected to any social or cultural norm. In other examples, the body is capable of fragmenting or dividing itself, constructing an alternative reality in which the characters live, materializing desires, hatreds and perversities. In all examples, the woman, the bearer of a body that yields, disturbs or shatters into fragments, is torn between different realities, one that asks her to comply with the traditional role Japan asks for women, other pushing her towards modernity. The construction of the monstrous in Asato's cinema is always mediated by the tension between a symbolic order, (represented by the traditional ideals of patriarchal Japan where women are wives, mothers and submissive creatures) and threatening elements with the capacity to disrupt stability: the woman's body and identity.

Asato is a woman involved in the big industry of filmmaking working for big horror film franchises such as *Ju-On*. But she is also responsible of personal horror productions showcasing her particular view on the role of women in contemporary society. Yet, her personal films and her franchise-based productions share may narrative devices and tropes. By analyzing her horror films, it is possible to find two recurring motifs in her filmography: the curse and the double.

This double motif is extensively developed in her film *Bilocation* (Bairokêshon, 2013). The internal debate between traditionalism and modernity generates a bilocation in Asato's women and the subsequent resistance generates a curse. *Bilocation* and *Fatal Frame* (Gekijoban Rei Zero, 2014) are representatives of this double motif, even if multiple references are scattered throughout her filmography. *Bilocation* and *Fatal Frame* are specifically interested in patriarchal cultural contexts, wherein men are assumed to be classical representative of the (hetero)normative, universal subject which codes as monster any woman who rejects the compulsory submissive role. The recurrence to the double is a painful ritual through which the Japanese patriarchal culture begins to break into itself.

TWICE ONE

Julia Kristeva identifies that we first experience abjection in the point of separation from the mother when the child (a being without any borders and non-separated from mother) enters the symbolic realm and is threatened by the outside, the marking of borders and differences. From that point on, the self strongly rejects any issue that can disrupt the ideal of a tightly closed identity and sense of individuality. In this scenario, the anus, urine, mucus, blood (especially menstrual blood), excrements or rotting are expelled out from our construction of identity (Kristeva 1982). This phenomenon that can best be described as abjection is the movement of throwing away all the things with the power of potentially disrupting our construction of "closed" identity. As Barbara Creed, following Kristeva, argues, the monstrous feminine marks the encounter between the symbolic order and that which threatens its stability, its borders.

In her book *The Monstrous-Feminine in Contemporary Japanese Popular Culture*, Raechel Dumas establishes a series of narrative devices useful to address the phenomenon of feminine monsters within Mari Asato's cinema: the female body in relation to monstrosity, the place of men and the tension between the public and private sphere. The ubiquity of the monstrous feminine facilitate the reading of the motif in specific terms, historically and culturally situated, with "the female body as a site for mapping shifting configurations of Japanese subjectivity and nationhood" (2018, 3).

Dumas exposes the importance of the Japanese postwar period as a decisive moment for the configuration of the female monster. The period brought the disruption of traditional gender and sexual norms (2018, 94). Asato's cinema works on this shift towards the potentialities of female agency, coding said possibilities as a "curse." Asato plays out the tensions between tradition and progress by constructing dynamic relationships within women, building dualities that fragments both, reality and female bodies. Only this duality shapes spaces women can legitimately inhabit.

Asato shots *Bilocation* (based on Hojo Haruka's book, published in 2010 and awarded as the best horror novel of the year) after years laboring on widely recognized horror franchises. Among these "impersonal" films are the episode *The Boy from Hell* (Jigoku kozo, 2004) for Hideshi Hino's *House of Horror* and five years later *Ju-On: Black Ghost* (Ju-on: Kuroi Shoujo, 2009) based on the story created by Takashi Shimizu in homage to the franchise's ten years. *Bilocation* turns out to be her most personal film to date, the one that begins a small corpus, including *Fatal Frame* and *Under your Bed* (Anda Yua Beddo, 2019), which attempt to build a general panorama of the situation of women in contemporary Japan and the internal battles they must face every day.

The first minutes of *Bilocation* (2014) leave the viewer puzzled. There is a sharp contrast generated between the initial images (spoken in Russian, without subtitles and with two looking-alike women reciting a passage from the Bible) with those that follow: the panoramic view of a small town in contemporary Japan which is being painted by Shinobu (Asami Mizukawa), a young woman who smokes non-stop. Over the sound of charcoal scratching canvas, the woman's voice-over repeats in frustration: "it's my last chance." She paints in a rush, with quick strokes. The sound of her doorbell snaps her out of her trance. She hesitates to open the door. When she does so, she meets a young man on the other side who offers her a welcome gift (she has just moved upstairs in her building). The image of both facing each other is mirrored on the pool of water that comes out of her apartment. The voice-over, now without the familiar tone of frustration informs viewers: "That meeting changed my life."

Cut to the apartment's interiors, where things look different. The light illuminates an intimate space that denotes the harmonious coexistence of a couple. Shinobu now lives with Masaru (Yosuke Asari), the young neighbor from the previous sequence. Time has passed, old habits (smoking) have disappeared and her art is now perfectly integrated into this new family life. The bliss is not perfect, however; Masaru has a visual disability which prevents him from distinguishing details, seeing faces and measuring the distance between his body and objects. He relies on Shinobu for his daily chores.

A key scene stages the conflict, one that links Shinobu with the asphyxiating reality of patriarchal Japan. In the laundry, Shinobu hesitates between putting Kirimura (her maiden name) and Takamura (her married name) when signing a form. The woman attending the place observes her with unusual surprise. Viewers are left in darkness regarding the nature of her surprise: is the owner judging her for denying her married status? Is there something else going on? In the next scene, when Shinobu tries to pay the supermarket bill, an employee takes her to a small office where she meets Detective Kano

(Kenichi Takito). He shows Shinobu a video from the security camera where she is seen paying the same bill to the same cashier earlier that day. Scared, she tries to convince the detective that the woman recorded earlier is not her. Surprisingly, the detective believes her and takes Shinobu in his car to a meeting place for victims of bilocation. Shinobu not only has just discovered that there is someone who looks exactly like her, but there is also a group of people who share her condition of having been "doubled."

Iizuka (Kosuke Toyohara), the leader of the group, is in charge of providing information to Shinobu and, by extension, to viewers. Through the film, the existence of a double is not defined in terms of doppelgänger, but as bilocation. The difference between the two concepts lies, according to Iizuka, in the fact that the bilocation produces a being exactly the same as the original, who has an existence of its own and it preserves the memories of the originals. This means the bilocated subjects can live two completely different lives, in the same space, without either of them noticing the existence of the other. Yet, being false, the human copies eventually disappear. The reason why they cease to exist has no explanation. To prevent their disappearance, the doubles sometimes try to eliminate the originals.

In *Japanese Horror and the Transnational Cinema of Sensations*, Steven Brown analyzes the motive of the double and its use in Japanese horror cinema. Brown argues that the term doppelgänger (literally, "double goer") was first coined in 1796 by German Romantic author Jean Paul (1763–1825) and was used as a term for "people who see themselves in person." (2018, 87). The brothers Grimm cite Jean Paul's usage but expands the definition for someone able to manifest in the same time in two different places. This last definition is topological in nature, since it emphasizes spatiality. According to Brown, the way in which the double is conceived and situated differs around the world, depending on the author, the culture and the socio-historical period. We are particularly interested in Baryon Tensor Posadas's analysis in relation to the way in which the doppelgänger motif is articulated in Japan since this trope subsumes a constellation of interlinked images "all of which involve the idea of an interplay between identity and difference" (2018, 1), returning thus the analysis again to the concept of abjection. The novelty of Asato's approach lies in the fact that, unlike the long tradition of cultural productions working with the motif of the doppelgänger, *Bilocation* offers multiple originals with their respective copies. The issue of bilocation, or the existence of a double is not explained in terms of "mental illness," as something that only happens to a subject, but rather as a social and cultural issue. Asato cuts out the doppelgänger from its psychological roots and turns the trope into a sociological problem. In the film, all the characters that have being "bilocated" experience similar problems related to gender roles. In all the cases the bilocations appear for the first time when the originals are experiencing a moment of existential crisis. The originals will have to unravel a personal mystery to understand why the bilocation exists and what these doubles want to try to steal from them. In the case of Shinobu, the answer is Masaru.

Kagami (Sho Takada), one of the most mysterious members of the bilocation group, tells Shinobu the secret story of Iizuka, whose relationship with the group comes from having fallen in love with a double who disappeared in front of his eyes the moment the original killed herself. After Shinobu's leaves the house, her double appears. She does not recognize Kagami. The scene is saturated with ambiguity: who is the real Shinobu? The one that appears now and does not recognize Kagami or the one that audiences followed through the narrative right up to this point? Everything becomes a game of mirrors and reflections and, ultimately, of dislocation taking place inside women under patriarchal power. There is a Shinobu who, after falling in love with a man, abandoned her job as an artist to embrace the domestic space. The real Shinobu, however, never left her dark and gloomy apartment, never opened the door or met Masaru. She continues to dedicate her days and her savings to her works of art that she considers her last chance of personal triumph. The first meeting between both versions of Shinobu takes place in her maiden's apartment. The double watches her chain-smoking double while she talks on the phone with art dealers. The original Shinobu learns that her work has been selected to being exhibited on an art gallery. This event represents the final crisis; on the day of the exhibition, she discovers that she has been disqualified and that the winning work is that of her double.

Unlike the rest of the bilocations shown through the film, who decide to eliminate the originals in order to establish a real existence, Shinobu's double chooses to disappear, to give her life, her husband, and also her art to the original. The film's final sequences evoke the first scene, with Shinobu painting alone in her apartment. Her doorbell rings, but her intensity is not strong enough to bring her out of the artistic trance she is in. It rings and, as the sound of the doorbell continues, the room darkens. Slowly the bilocation begins to take shape and, once complete, it opens the door. "If you had opened the door, instead of your double [. . .] a loving husband would have changed your life and your art." The real Shinobu listens those words coming from Iizuka, while trying to convince him that there is no difference between the two since her double is part of her. Both are faces of the same socio-cultural context, of the same desires. Yet, the real Shinobu cannot help but being jealous of her copy. It is her double who won the prize for her work. In the film's climax, one Shinobu offers her ring and Masaru's love to the other one. "I have never been with a man. For a long time, art was the only thing I have known," the original states. Shinobu Takamura has accepted her fate. Disappearing. Suddenly, the body of the real Shinobu is seen falling through the window. Before Masaru could ask his wife Shinobu to explain what happened she had already disappeared. With the death of the original the copy has nothing to do but vanish. As such, the existence of both women is simple impossible; the two parts (domestic life and marital bliss in one hand, and a job on the other) are incompatible. Joel Gwynne notes that the modern Japanese woman is fragmentary, divided between the traditional and the modern to the point that varied identities are necessary, for the "female subject is required to perpetually negotiate and reconstruct the terms of her empowerment in the context of a backlash culture that aims to inhibit and deride women's progress" (2016, 57). *Bilocation* filters this negotiation through horror lens, staging a woman divided between two antagonistic desires (being a working woman/a wife) incompatible in traditional, patriarchal Japanese culture.

Bilocation is built on the motif of the double. Almost each character has a copy, an other that highlights the original's fears or miseries. Although the film ends with the physical disappearance of the two Shinobu (one due to suicide, the other due to the absence of the original), an epilogue at the end of the credits adds an unexpected twist. In this new ending the real Shinobu also kills herself, but the copy does not disappear. What has saved her from her tragic destiny was her ability to engender a new life, an existence of her own. This new ending offers an alternative, a moment of agency; rather than create a daughter/son, the offspring expected on women, Shinobu is able to recreates herself into a double, a woman capable of getting it all.

Women as complex beings, full of internal debates and contradictions, are a common trope in Asato's cinema, the duplicity working in different ways. The motif of the double manifests the internal conflict of the protagonist between being an artist (what she wants to be) or becoming a married woman (the role society compulsorily asks for women) capable of renouncing her true passion. Another take on the double is offered by *The Boy from Hell* where the presence of a double (child/monster) takes place in the body of the protagonist's son. This split serves to highlight the moral dilemma that the mother faces. When her son dies in a traffic accident, she must decide between accepting the fatality (as a good woman of science) and bearing the burden of not having been able of save her son, or resort to black magic and bring him back to life. The monster appears when she decides to revive her child in a ritual. In *Under your Bed*, Chihiro Sasaki (Kanako Nishikawa), the object of desire of Mitsui (Kengo Kora), is represented in a dual way from the perspective of whoever is in love with her. She is the girl to whom he has fallen in love in his youth, but she is also the wife of an abusive man and the mother of a small child whom she is unable to protect from the violence around her. This confrontation between being single/being married is the obsession of Mitsui; even if time has passed, he refuses to accept the incompatibility between his youthful love and the married woman who now lives close to him. To further reinforce this divide, the man recreates their first encounter by building a mannequin that is dressed and smells like she did when she was a single woman. Like in *Bilocation*, women are divided between single/married and normal/non-human, both cultural patriarchal constructions.

In these duplicities/confrontations, gender roles play a determining role. The motif of the double manifests a struggle between being (or wanting to be) and the duty imposed by patriarchal society. The single, artist and self-sufficient Shinobu cannot coexist with the married version of herself, submissive and dependent on a man's love. Despite having had the chance to choose that other life, Shinobu chooses suicide. Steven Brown points out that "it is at this moment that the gender politics of bilocation become particularly heightened as Shinobu forcefully questions why she should feel compelled to adopt the heteronormative model of marriage that is being forced upon her by her bilocation" (2018, 210). Destroying her body seems to be the only act of independence left to her, the only thing she could actually choose.

In the case of Japanese society, singleness is viewed in a pejorative way and marriage necessarily implies the submission of the woman to the husband, father and eldest son. As Akiko Yoshida explains, "never-married women have been objects of criticism and ridicule, particularly since the late 1980s when the number of unmarried women began to surge" (2016, 1). The rupture between who these women are and who they have to be is decisive since it enables the appearance of the monster. This dilemma not only highlights the complexity of women, their "monstrosity" in the eyes of the patriarchal system of which they are part, but also makes visible the fears they generate in society and the lack of understanding of the processes women are forced to go through. The female monstrosity is embodied through the corporeal: through its ability to give it up love or motherhood, to destroy, outrage, submit. To have the decision to be able to finish the body off.

Asato uses this motif to express the contradictions that exist in contemporary Japanese society between tradition and modernity. Any decision against being a wife, being a mother or being heterosexual is understood as a monstrosity, as something that generates rejection for being on the edge of what is socially accepted. This contradiction becomes visible in the relationship established between the two Shinobu. However, the conflict that originates the bilocation is not only due to Shinobu's deep identity crisis in response to the social mandates of the patriarchal order but also to the changes taking place in the status of women within patriarchal societies and that, inevitably, translate into cultural anxiety. The only thing left for women who dare to break the norm is to abort the system in a suicidal act. There is no place in society for them.

Despite the fact that the film is provocative because it highlights disjunctions at the heart of Japanese society, the elimination of difference may be read as a conservative act. For everything to return to "normal" it is necessary that these women cease to exist. However, suicide appears as an act of freedom, the only one that cannot be controlled by the system in which they live, the only thing that they can choose without pressure.

This division does not manifest itself only through the figure of the double; as mentioned in the introduction, this cultural divide also takes the form of the curse. Live a divided existence, torn between two desires, generates a curse that spreads and kill, turning the woman responsible a literal monster. Divided women are, thus, monstrous metaphors of the tensions taking place between the socially expected and the deviant.

THE UNNAMED CURSE

Through the aftermath of World War II, Japan was swayed by capitalist logic via a complex and rushed process of modernization. Japan's economy had been left prostrate after the war due to significant territorial loss, restrictions in the fishing areas and the loss of more than two million civilian homes. Rebirth, however, came soon after a strong agrarian reform and constitutional changes. Japan was reborn to generate a high per capita income in just a generation, becoming one of the most prominent financial structures in the global scenario (Tsuru, 1995). This capitalist wave threatened to drag the much-valued traditional Japanese way of life into oblivion, and in the face of this tangible threat, the Japanese reacted by significantly clinging to their traditional culture. Japan, still torn between the modern and the traditional, found itself in a symbolic limbo, within a crack dividing the traditional from the modern. Along this ontological crack the role of women is widely discussed in regard to modernity and tradition.

This discussion is clearly visible in Japanese horror cinema, which presents viewers with female figures who carry a lifelong curse as symbolic punishment for being torn between accepting a traditional role or opening up to modernization. If the question of the double in Mari Asato's cinema alludes to the inner world of women and to the continuous debate between two possible realities, the question of the curse is located immediately after the crystallization of the dilemma of bilocation. Purification from the curse many times comes with death and suicide, as the perverse Mother Superior (Jun Miho) states in *Fatal Frame*.

The most representative example of how the curse plays within Asato's filmography is *Fatal Frame*, basically a rewriting of the successful horror video game created by Makoto Shibata. Although the game's central ideas are present, the story itself has been modified by Asato at her convenience and with a clear need to account for the female situation.

The film, set in a contemporary rural Japanese village, focuses on a group of girls who study in a Catholic school presided over by a mother superior who is the embodiment of stubborn tradition. The pupils are revolutionized by an atypical situation: one of her classmates, Aya (Ayami Nakajô), has locked herself in her room one month ago and refuse to come out. Simultaneously, the students have strange vivid dreams or fantasies that involve Aya asking them to release her from a curse. The dreams also include a photograph of who appears to be Aya and a request to kiss the photo. Rumor has it at school that whoever kisses the photograph will be cursed by Aya and die. Many of the girls will kiss the photo in these vivid dreams and end up disappearing in real life; all of them are eventually found dead at a nearby river. When Aya finally leaves her room, it is revealed that it is not her who appears in those fantasies, but her twin sister, Maya, who died in a strange childhood episode that involves mother superior. The story basically gravitates around a female ghost who claims for her freedom but, at the same time, cannot stop killing innocent people, thus becoming monstrous.

When asked by one of the pupils about Aya's confinement, the institute's director states that Aya was suffering a curse that *only affects girls*. This will be repeated several times through. The phrase resonates as the camera pans over old paintings on the walls, but one stands out above the others, a portrait that represents Ophelia, Hamlet's love interest in the Shakespearean classic. Ophelia, a woman cursed by her desire, is symbolically brought back to the *Fatal Frame* universe over and over again as a warning sign, as a premonition of death, especially visible on the girl floating dead in the river.

The phrase "a curse that only affects girls" alludes to both, menstrual blood and, linked with the latter, sexual awakening. There is a homoerotic bond between the girls and specifically with Aya to whom all are attracted to. The girls' nightmares with Aya start terrifying, but veer towards the erotic. The girls are erotically attached to the "closeted" character, the kiss in the photo the confirmation of homosexual desire circulating through the institution. Thus, Aya suffers a double process of monstrosity; she is a monster who shows herself in dreams and kills girls and, also, the conduit of lesbian desire.

Female desire, especially of the homoerotic kind, is systematically oppressed in most cultures; in the Japanese context, in addition to being repressed, it has a destabilizing tinge that is anxiety-generating. This desire crystallizes the inner feminine struggle that has come to be assumed but is systematically denied by the status quo. In *Fatal Frame*, the bearer of the curse, Maya, has been killed and forgotten. The twins Aya and Maya (both played by Ayami Nakajô) enter the school as pupils. There, Maya is killed by the abbess, the latter haunted by the ghost of her lesbian lover. The headmistress reveals that to keep her lover from haunting her, she murdered Maya so the latter could accompany her in the afterlife. In consequence, Maya is killed and suppressed from school life and repressed in Aya's mind.

The ghost marks a double return of the repressed. Not only she comes back from the dead to accuse the culprits, but she is also the bearer of repressed sexual desire. She is the return of the deviant female. Maya's purpose is not the systematic killing of young girls (the real culprit is a man, the brother of a school nun), but to be found, to be named again. This reclamation of identity involves the homosexual rite of kissing the photo, the recognition of a sisterhood and same-sex desire. The denial of lesbian identity is the root of the curse. Maya was thrown dead into a water reservoir at the school and is destined to return a thousand times in search of her own existence. The woman who leans to modernity will be homologated with evil, with the embodiment of the monstrous, in this case represented in part by lesbian tendencies. In *Fatal Frame* Maya's existence is reenacted in Aya, her double, both corporeal (she looks like Maya) and symbolic: both are girls at the brink of disappearing; one is a forgotten ghost, the other one lives "closeted." The presence of water (where one of the girls in found drown) refers to fluidity, the passage from death to life. *Fatal Frame* connects with what society and culture has repressed but somehow always finds the way back.

THE SPRING OF DEATH AND REBIRTH

Water will be key in Mari Asato's cinema. Following Creed, the monstrous woman is linked with fluidity, with destabilizing factors, beginning with that stage of maternal presence in which the child's body is ordered by laws rooted in fluids and humidity. The mother, immediately after birth, becomes rejected by the creature in order to constitute herself/himself as an individual differentiated from the maternal body. The overbearing mother, the one who denies this difference, marks the birth of the female monster. Remaining attached to the female body, open to fluctuations and watery imagery, is monstrous (1993, 18–20). In *Fatal Frame*, the river will be a central trope, not only in linkage with the many allusions to Ophelia, but also as the space of haunting and suicidal pacts between lesbian lovers. Humidity is where ghosts are shown, especially the type of specter that Asato's cinema privileges.

Fatal Frame belongs to the Japanese *kaidan* genre (weird tale). The figure of the *onryō*, a Japanese ghost (*yūrei*) believed to be capable of causing harm in the world of the living, leads the film. Women finding death in water is common in Japanese horror mythology and imaginary. Water, bathtubs and bathrooms are particularly important spaces in Japanese genre cinema (Eljaiek-Rodríguez 2018, 120). Further, water is related to the amniotic fluid, feeding viewers with the dreary reality of the undifferentiated being.

The *onryō* is related to a central character of the Japanese Shinto religion: the *miko*. Working as shrine maidens, the *miko* begin their training within the religious temples at a very young age, most of them starting as young as thirteen. For centuries, *miko* have performed *kagura* (sacred dances for entertaining and satisfying the Shinto deities), practiced divinations and acted as oracles. The *miko* are educated in relation with the divine through multiple rituals linked to water. *Yutati*, literally "immersion in hot water" (Reader 1991, 67), for example, is a purifying ritual that involves fire, cauldrons containing water and *mikomai* (ancient ritual dances performed by the miko). Further, in Shinto religion, the guardian deities residing in water were all female (Kramarae and Spender 2000, 1847).

Water has the symbolic power to erase the "feminine" part of women to turn them into "pure," asexual beings. As such, water codes death (of the feminine) in Asato's *Fatal Frame*. Maya marks the return of the repressed; the asexual female teenager who must choose between killing her feminine part or become a woman. Further, the adult woman must choose between the modern or the traditional role. Adolescents at their moment of becoming adults end up being trapped in this borderline passage between the two, a priori, irreconcilable possible worlds. Maya returns not only for vengeful ends but rather as a way of rebellion against the denial of her existence.

The theme of the double is further developed in *Ju-On: Black Ghost*. The film, told through anachronistic order, tells the story of a girl named Fukie (Hana Matsumoto), who grows a kind of cyst on her ovaries that is actually her twin sister developing late into her. Fukie, in addition of being possessed by her unborn twin, also spreads the curse to those around her. Mariko, Fukie's sister, concludes that the twin is a ghostly parasite; she performs an exorcism to expel the evil spirit, but the spirit tricks Mariko to expel Fukie's spirit instead.

The curse of the unborn twin can be homologated with the unsaid, the silenced voice that returns with a scream similar to Maya in *Fatal Frame*. A key scene in *Black Ghost* reconnects the topic of death with the fluidity of water: when Fukie is hypnotized (suspecting that her illness may be psychological), the hypnotist asks her to imagine her existence floating on the amniotic fluid on her mother's womb. In the end of *Ju-On: Black Ghost*, Fukie's mother kills herself to end the conflict with her self-sacrifice. Yet, the ghost of the unborn continues to cry out to exist and kill, including people who tried to remove her from the body of her now-dead sister. The ghost is Fukie's double, deformed and shapeless, asking for identity, even if that purpose turns her a monster. The difference between Fukie and Maya is that the former is anchored in denial while Maya integrates with her sister Aya, her double, generating a synthesis.

Mari Asato also gives a fundamental role to the cursed woman in *Ring of Curse* (Gomennasai, 2011). Kurohane (Miyabi Natsuyaki) is an unpopular girl, likely due to her morbid appearance. Completely rejected by her family, she is also hated by her schoolmates. In a way to antagonize her, the girls in the school decide to torment her by having her write a script for a school production. Kurohane is actually very glad to do this because it allows her to experiment with the power of words to kill people. After weeks of bullying, Kurohane writes a play and circulates it at school. Everyone who reads it dies. In the film's climax, the girl confess that she killed her younger sister using this method.

Her rivalry with her outspoken and annoying sister (again the duality between two female behavioral models that fail to integrate) is what leads her to conclude that the only way to live forever and gain notoriety is to be (literally) a curse. With the nickname "Curse," she kills her schoolmates even after one of the girls kills her. It is not by chance that Kurohane's curse is contained into words, as she only can express herself within culture through a fictional play: basically, the same action that Asato does with her films. The latent danger of the proliferation of curse-bearing monsters is the fear of the dynamic, of contaminating other people with the power to speak, to write, to find identity.

In the three films analyzed in this section, audiences were witnesses of the passage of women through adolescence, a significant moment for development and identity. The key word here is passage. The passage of becoming a woman, of integrating the female desire with society and face the backlash or hiding into traditional roles, such as Maya does.

CONCLUSIONS

Asato's horror films work with female characters who become monstrous by the act of embodying a duality. This duality is manifested, in bodily or psychological terms, through the figure of the double and the curse as an intrinsic condition of female subjectivity. In symbolic terms, female duality functions as a reflection of the tensions that exist in contemporary Japan between what women want to be and what patriarchal society requires them to be. The monstrous woman is the one who wonders about the place she should occupy and the one who chooses something different.

In Asato's cinema the female body becomes "increasingly other, unreachable, even demonic" (Dumas 2018, 9). It is a cursed body, capable of dividing and multiplying, a body that destabilizes order and, to resume the status quo, must be destroyed. Monstrosity emerges not only in the weird figure of the double, but also in the desire *to being in another way*. In all the films here analyzed, men are either absent or have some type of physical or psychological disability. In all cases they are dependent on women. They require female help, their love, or approval. Faced with these handicapped men, women are complex, dual creatures. In *Bilocation*, Masaru cannot even distinguish his wife from the original. He is unable not only of observing his wife's suicide, but also the disappearance of his wife's double. In *Fatal Frame*, the only male character with some relevance is a killer while the father figure in *Ju-On: Black Ghost* is completely passive, all of the decisions to the mother.

The female monstrosity as showcased in Asato's cinema works by stirring up old anxieties which not only jeopardizes established gender roles but also the social function of the family and, with it, the realm of the domestic. The threat to patriarchal order results in an inevitable reading of women as the source of the evils that afflict society. Male anxiety is what allows the existence of the monstrous feminine. Women who get out of control have no choice but to be destroyed. However, faced with a society that fills them with obstacles and limits their freedom, these women choose to expel themselves from the system. It is better to cease to exist than to live to calm the fears of others. The female monster in Asato's cinema should be read as an act of resistance.

REFERENCES

Brown. Steven. 2018. *Japanese Horror and the Transnational Cinema of Sensations* New York: Palgrave Macmillan, 2018.
Creed, Barbara. 1995. *The Monstrous-Feminine. Film, feminism, Psychoanalysis*. New York: Routledge.
Raechel, Dumas. 2018. *The Monstrous-Feminine in Contemporary Japanese Popular Culture*. New York: Palgrave Macmillan.
Eljaiek-Rodríguez, Gabriel. 2018. *The Migration and Politics of Monsters in Latin American Cinema*. New York: Palgrave Macmillan.
Joel Gwynne. 2016. "Warrior of Love: Japanese Girlhood's Postfeminist Asian Body in Cutie Honey (Hideaki Anno, 2004)." In *International Cinema and the Girl*, edited by Fiona Handyside and Kate Taylor-Jones, 49–60. New York: Palgrave Macmillan.
Kramarae, Cheris and Dale Spender, eds. 2000. *Routledge International Encyclopedia of Women: Global Women's Issues and* Knowledge. New York: Routledge, 2000.
Kristeva. Julia. 1982. *Powers of Horror: An Essay on Abjection*. Translated by Leon Roudiez. New York: Columbia University Press, 1982.
Paglia, Camille. 1991. *Sexual Personae: Art and Decadence from Nefertiti to Emily Dickinson*. New York: Vintage Books.

Posadas, Baryon. 2018. *Double Visions, Double Fictions. The Doppelgänger in Japanese Film and Literature*. Minneapolis: University of Minnesota.
Reader, Ian. 1991. *Religion in Contemporary Japan*. Honolulu: University of Hawaii Press, 1991.
Sanusi, Shana. 2016. "The Ghostly Double: The Crisis of (Gendered) Subjectivity and the Self in Asato Mari's *Bairokêshon*." *The Asian Conference on Arts & Humanities*. Accessed May 1, 2021. http://25qt511nswfi49iayd31ch80-wpengine.netdna-ssl.com/wp-content/uploads/papers/acah2016/ACAH2016_22692.pdf
Tsuru. Shigeto. 1995. *Japan's Capitalism: Creative Defeat and Beyond*. Cambridge: Cambridge University Press.
Yoshida, Akiko. 2016. *Unmarried Women in Japan: The Drift into Singlehood*. New York: Routledge.

Chapter 8

Composite Corpses and Viruses of Viewing

J-Horror as Film and Media Theory

William Carroll

In Aoyama Shinji's 1999 J-horror film *EM: Embalming*, the protagonist, Miyako (Takashima Reiko), conventionally embalms corpses for open-casket funerals of wealthy and famous people. Embalming is the practice of preserving the remains of a dead person so that they do not decay as quickly; it is, in effect, the practice of mummification. Legitimate embalmers like Miyako preserve human bodies intact, and only intervene in the corpse to prevent it from further decay or, at most, restore it to something closer to what it had looked like before death. However, when the head of one of Miyako's patients disappears, she learns of a secret black market using an illicit practice of embalming: one that does not preserve human bodies whole, but instead takes body parts from multiple bodies and stitches them into new composite mummified corpses.

   In this film, Aoyama is both developing a grotesque horror plot and commenting on Bazinian film theory. André Bazin famously wrote of "the mummy complex" in relation to photography, claiming that the photographic image could preserve a fleeting moment from decay (2005, 9). Cinema, which was moving photographs, went further, by preserving not only an individual instant, but movements and transformations as they happened, hence Bazin's famous declaration that film was "change mummified" (2005, 15). But in fact, most films, and certainly most feature-length theatrical films, are not simply preservations of continuous movements as they took place. Through editing, filmmakers take tiny fragments of mummified change and reconstruct them into a new whole. In other words, cinema is less like the idealized Egyptian mummies in Bazin's essay and actually closer to mummies that piece together body parts from a multiple corpses and restitch them together into a composite corpse, a mummy of someone who never existed. This also describes Aoyama's film itself, which flaunts the composite nature of the filmmaking process with techniques such as poorly disguised rear-projection.

Aoyama's play with film theory in *Embalming* does not exist in a vacuum; it is part of a larger trend in 1990s, and post-1990s, J-horror film to play with and develop film theories alongside their own written theory and criticism. This trend has a longer legacy dating back to the cinephilic turn in Japanese film discourse. Like preeminent J-horror directors Kurosawa Kiyoshi and Nakata Hideo, Aoyama had studied film under Professor Hasumi Shigehiko, one of the central figures of this cinephilic turn in the 1970s and 1980s (Kurosawa, Kunitoshi, and Shinji 2017). Through the 1970s, Hasumi developed a critical approach that eschewed narrative and social interpretation, and instead prized films that challenged the act of looking. At the same time, he rose to prominence as an academic first by translating the work of poststructuralist theorists. By the mid-1980s, Hasumi was both a celebrity of "*Nyū Akademizumu*" (*New Academism*),[1] and the figure at the center of Japan's cinephile culture; he remained in the latter position for several decades.

As he began writing his own criticism, Hasumi developed a method that celebrated self-reflexivity in film form: films that articulated the inherent contradictions between the superficial appearance of depth within the cinematic image and its inherent flatness, or films that revealed the underlying absurdity of the conventions of continuity editing. Returning to the mummification metaphor, while most critics might judge the aesthetic value of the embalmed composite corpse by how well-preserved it is, or how convincingly it looks like a singular, preserved body, Hasumi was more interested in observing the awkward stitching job between disparate body parts. Early on, one of the key filmmakers that Hasumi began writing about these techniques was Suzuki Seijun, whose films he celebrated for their use of techniques that would have been considered simply poorly executed by other critical standards, such as rear-projection sequences that fail to create the sensation of a realistic, continuous space. It is no coincidence that Seijun himself appears as the embalmer who first informs Miyako of the secret, illicit embalming practice in Aoyama's film.

This chapter analyzes Hasumi Shigehiko as one of the formative figures of J-horror. It may seem counterintuitive to claim that a film critic and theorist who never made a film, and indeed, never showed any particular interest in the horror genre *per se* in his own writing, is a formative figure for a set of internationally popular horror films. However, many figures who contributed to the J-horror cycle studied in Hasumi's film seminars at Rikkyo University or Tokyo University: not just Kurosawa, Nakata, and Aoyama, but also Shiota Akihiko,[2] Manda Kunitoshi,[3] and Shinozaki Makoto.[4] Beyond merely studying under Hasumi,[5] many of these filmmakers have remained closely tied to Hasumi in a variety of ways: many have published books and essays together with Hasumi or participated together in public film events and roundtable discussions. Moreover, in spite of having made films that were enormously internationally popular, or that opened at prestigious international film festivals, these filmmakers still defer to Hasumi's judgment, and find him to be an awe-inspiring, even frightening, figure.

Thus, I analyze the relationship between Hasumi's discourse on film and the horror films of his students to enrich our understanding of both Hasumi as a thinker and the J-horror films themselves. I focus on four films—Nakata's *Ringu* (1998), Kurosawa's *The Serpent's Path* (1998) and *Pulse* (2001), in addition to Aoyama's *EM: Embalming*. Many other films made by these filmmakers would benefit from analysis alongside Hasumi's writings, but these most straightforwardly address the themes I explore regarding the material properties of images and the difficulties of seeing them, both keys to Hasumi's film theories and to J-horror. Hasumi's theories will help uncover and understand the origins of these thematic concerns in the films. In the end, though, I will be treating the films as primary sources in applied film theory—not just Hasumi's theory itself, but their own theory of visual media and spectatorship that has been shaped both by the influence of Hasumi and by the experiences of the filmmakers.

HASUMI AND J-HORROR

Hasumi's primary contributions to film theory and criticism in Japan are not themselves directly related to the horror genre, and further, Hasumi has generally tended to be dismissive of genre taxonomies that would distinguish horror films from any other type of film. Why, then, would Hasumi's progeny become horror filmmakers when horror was not a matter of particular concern for him? The answer lies in the films themselves. By closely examining the horror films made by these directors, and others made in their wake, I show affinities with Hasumi's own writings about the nature of film and spectatorship in a broad sense. Nakata's and Kurosawa's most famous horror films are about *looking* at media. Further, Hasumi's celebration of films that visually articulate the inherent contradictions in the cinematic image, like the tension between its apparent depth and its inherent flatness, lend themselves naturally to the cinematic uncanny in the way that his students apply them in their films.

At the same time, in one crucial respect, these films would seem to present a challenge to Hasumi's writings on film, or at least to the conventional wisdom surrounding them. A common critique leveled at Hasumi is that his conception of film and the film experience is rooted too deeply in the past, to a conception of cinema as the material of film and the film experience as the theatrical viewing experience, both of which seemed dated by the 1990s, let alone today. In his history of Japanese schools of film theory and criticism, Aaron Gerow has called Hasumi "ill prepared for a different media world that, with the rise of television, video, and then the digital [. . .] increasingly seemed to need neither cinema nor criticism" (Gerow 2014, 74). Likewise, Yomota Inuhiko has written that "the overwhelming spread of video transformed these experiences into something common and ordinary," turning cinephilia into "a kind of '*otaku*-ism'" that had "lost its way as serious intellectual discourse" (Inuhiko 2019, 181).[6] However, these J-horror filmmakers all began film production at this precise moment: they films for television or direct-to-video release early in their careers and are of the generation that oversaw the transition from 35mm to digital filmmaking. Because of the moment at which they entered the film industry, these filmmakers had to work through ways that shifts between different types of visual media and the conditions of the viewing experience present new challenges to the ways they can think about the relationship between visual media and spectatorship.

HASUMI ON FILM SPECTATORSHIP

Hasumi first rose to prominence as a film critic in the journal *Cinema 69* (later *Cinema 70* and *Cinema 71*), where he took part in an important turn in Japanese film criticism and theory. In the self-description of Ueno Kōshi, another *Cinema 69* critic regularly associated with Hasumi, film criticism up to that point had tended to summarize a film's narrative and analyze it in terms of humanistic, social, or political meaning. What had been missing was any attention to the moving image itself: the thing that made cinema cinema, or to the experience of encountering these moving images. This new generation of film critics focused not only on the techniques of film, but also the devices by which films could attract and engage spectators. In Ueno's words, "while criticism had once aimed to seek out a hidden meaning, it now began to try instead to grasp the lively movement of the image itself" (1986, 12–13). At the risk of oversimplification, I will summarize their approach to cinema with two key terms: *omoshirosa* and *dōtai shiryoku*. *Omoshirosa* translates most literally as "interestingness," but is perhaps better understood as the "source of interest." In this school of criticism, the *omoshirosa* refers to whatever element(s) of the film arouse the viewer's interest and leave the most lasting impression from the film.[7] Inasmuch as *omoshirosa* emphasizes the significance of individual moments or stylistic choices over reading the film, it can be seen as an anti-narrative gesture, and bears some resemblance to concepts such as *photogenie*, or to what Christian Keathley refers to as "cinephiliac moments." *Dōtai shiryoku* literally refers to "the skill of seeing movement," and refers to the ability to see, deduce, and infer from a moving object.[8] The idea that viewing properly is itself a difficult task that needs to be actively performed and can be done improperly is one that differentiates Hasumi's theory and criticism from other brands of cinephilia: cinephilia in this conception is a skill rather than a simple fetishization.

Hasumi's theory of film and spectatorship does not evaluate film along conventional narrative lines. He typically eschews genre classifications of films, as well as conventional hierarchies of prestige.[9] Ryan Cook has argued that Hasumi's ideal process of watching a film is "to attempt to surrender one's thoughts to the system of a film, to submit to the movement at a film's surface" (Cook 2012, 139). In their place, he prizes films that break down "systems," (*seido*) which Cook has defines "scheme[s] establishing order and ultimately meaning" that creates the illusion of greater freedom while actually imposing greater *limitations* on cinematic form (Cook 2012, 132).[10] Frequently, this means Hasumi self-reflexivity in film form: films that articulate the inherent contradictions between, for example, the superficial appearance of depth within the cinematic image in spite of the fact that it is, in fact, a flat surface, or films that revealed the underlying absurdity of the conventions of continuity editing. In his writings on Suzuki Seijun at *Cinema 69*, he celebrated the director's creation of "depth without depth": a moment in *Youth of the Beast* where a character tries to escape into the depth but is blocked by a matte painting, in the recurring use of fields of abstract color in *Kanto Wanderer* (1963), *Gate of Flesh* (1964), *Tokyo Drifter* (1966), and other films, and in his use of rear-projection sequences that create impossible spaces, such as a sequence in *Our Blood Will Not Forgive* (1964) where a car is shown in front of a rear-projected ocean background. These moments, in Hasumi's view, tease the illusion of depth but ultimately force viewers into confrontation with flatness, and further, foreground the material process by which the film was made in the form of matte paintings, studio set walls, or rear projection.[11]

At the same time, Hasumi also admires films that place demands on spectators' viewing process and that reward viewers who observe closely. For example, in a review of Theo Angelopoulos *Alexander the Great* from 1982, Hasumi praises Angelopoulos for his choreographed long-take style, writing that it "overcomes the habit by which films too easily narrate to audiences through montage" (1990, 321).[12] By refusing to cut to foreground narrative elements in his films and combining disparate spaces and timeframes within single long takes, Angelopoulos forces viewers to observe the frame more carefully. Though Angelopoulos' long-take style would seem to be the antithesis of Seijun's strange compositing or Ozu's breakdown of the continuity system, but what is consistent to Hasumi's method across these films is the veneration of techniques that challenge viewers by forcing them to view the image more closely, either through artifice that challenges the diegetic illusions of the cinema or through the use of techniques or visual motifs that are difficult to observe. They bring viewers closer to the field of pure movement, and to the tangible properties of the cinematic image itself, which is why Hasumi cherishes such techniques.

ANXIOUSLY ATTENTIVE VIEWING

According to testimonies by his students, Hasumi's critical tendencies informed the way that he taught his film seminars. Nakata writes that Hasumi stressed three points: (1) to overcome the tendency to immediately narrativize or interpret films in a literary way by observing images directly, (2) to observe the way that films disguise their limitations to viewers, such as simulating depth to disguise flatness, or using images and sound to simulate senses that cinema cannot depict, and (3) to have a relationship of friendly rivalry among fellow students, trying to "outview" each other (2017, 137–138). In a roundtable discussion, Kurosawa, Aoyama, and Manda echo this second point in particular, claiming that Hasumi would regularly ask the question, "What could you see?" to students after showing them a sequence or image from a film, and would praise answers that best described the precise images without interpretation or contextualization in narrative terms (Kurosawa, Manda and Aoyama, 2017, 110–111). In so doing, Hasumi bestowed his unique practice of viewing and criticism onto his students, which influenced the ways that they have written about and made films.

In his essay "Horā eiga to wa nanika?" ("What is horror film?"), Kurosawa explores the tension between his investment in the horror genre and the discomfort with genre taxonomies passed down from Hasumi (2018). Initially, Kurosawa begins with the tautological definition: a horror film is a movie that is frightening. From there, he distinguishes the genre from science-fiction and disaster films where scientists are able to overcome the threat, as well as serial killer films where the killer can ultimately be apprehended. These can both be frightening, but not in the way that he means. He describes the feeling of fear in a horror film in this way:

An enshrouded figure is standing on the other side of the fence. If you look closely, it's your friend who has died. You're startled. Then the figure disappears. How can you overcome this fear? There is no way to escape from it, at least as long as you are alive. Your life has completely changed. Even if it goes away, and even if it never returns, the shadow of the dead will stay with you even if you flee to the end of the universe. (Kurosawa 2018, 24–25)

Kurosawa's emphasis here is not on the typology of monsters, but the way that the film *haunts* viewers, which he associates with the act of *looking closely*.

It is easy enough to think of moments such as the one he describes here in his own films: a figure somewhere in a composition seems slightly *off*, and compels viewers to inspect it more closely. It may turn out to be a ghost or a person under the spell of a hypnotist or viral internet video, or it may not be on screen long enough to know for certain who or what it is. However, the very existence of these mysterious figures or objects that are difficult to see, and buried somewhere in the recesses of the frame, lead to a kind of paranoia: viewers begin looking for them even in moments when they are *not* on screen. This both leads viewers to a more careful and attentive viewing process, and associates with a specific emotional response. Kurosawa thus reorients the definition of "horror" as a type of relationship that a viewer can have with a film. Where Hasumi and his peers at *Cinema 69* had offered *omoshirosa* as a concept to explore the ways that certain images or movements from a film could leave an impression in viewers, Kurosawa offers *osoroshisa* (terrifyingness, or the source of terror) as the key to understanding the way that this works in the horror genre: the images or movements that continue to haunt viewers after the film is over.

Looking at Kurosawa's writings and his own horror films, we can also see how he incorporates Hasumi's prizing of films that challenge viewers to observe closely into the way that he creates horror in cinema. Consider, for example, Hasumi's praise of Theo Angelopoulos for his challenging long-take style, a filmmaker whom Kurosawa also deeply admires. Kurosawa writes that he discovered Angelopoulos' films while he was beginning as an independent filmmaker, and learned from them the power of refusing to edit: the typical method of connecting shots together "only produces an easy-to-understand explanation," Kurosawa writes, while Angelopoulos' long take method "allows things to reveal themselves, sometimes very slowly and sometimes very suddenly" (2008, 163). But this technique is also something that Kurosawa observed as an effective technique for producing horror, as he discusses regarding a scene in William Peter Blatty's *The Exorcist III* (1990). The scene is set in a hospital corridor that the camera observes from a distance as a nurse and some night guards making their rounds from a fixed distant camera position, going into and emerging from different corridors and doorways on the sides of the hall. As with the long takes of Angelopoulos and other long take auteurs, viewers have to observe the composition more carefully precisely because they do not know what they are looking for. But in the context of a horror film, Kurosawa associates this need to look more carefully with a rising sense of anxiety: it gives viewers the sense that they "don't know when or how someone will be killed, but just know that someone will be killed" (Kurosawa and Shinozaki 2003, 274).

Kurosawa cites this scene from *The Exorcist III* as the inspiration for the final long-take in his own film, *Cure* (1997) (Kurosawa and Shinozaki 2003, 275), but this approach can also be seen in numerous long takes in Kurosawa's own horror films that challenge viewers to observe the frame more carefully by either creating anxiety so that viewers will scan the frame more carefully to uncover a possible source of danger (or place that it might emerge from), or instances where an important detail is buried in the recesses of the frame, visible only to observers viewing the most closely, before it eventually presents itself as a source of danger, rewarding those who were paying most close attention (who have prepared themselves) and taunting those who were not paying attention (who have not prepared themselves). This tendency can be seen in *Pulse*, most famously in a long take where a woman who had previously been seen putting red tape around a doorway is visible in the distance of a long take climbing a water tower before she jumps to her death. The strategy is also at work throughout the film in its use of the red tape motif, which is often visible in the background of shots without drawing attention to itself to alert the possibility of danger to viewers who are looking.[13] As a result of this process, attentive viewing and the feeling of fear become mutually reinforcing: seeing something frightening compels viewers to look more closely, in the manner that Hasumi advocated, and this act of close viewing leads to more anxiety and the noticing of gradually more and more buried details that, in turn, contribute to producing the feeling of dread.

VISUAL MEDIA AS VECTOR FOR INFECTION

Cinema, and the viewing of it, is the central preoccupation of Hasumi's film criticism; accordingly, new media, and the viewing of it, is a central preoccupation of J-horror.[14] In J-horror's earliest stages, new media was its means of both production and distribution. Its roots date back to small budget projects in the early 1990s, such as the V-Cinema *Hontō ni atta kowai hanashi* (*Scary True Stories*) series (1991–1992) and the television series *Gakkō no kaidan* (1995–1999). Even later films that were shot on 35mm and distributed theatrically, such as the ones that I consider in this chapter, were made with the knowledge that they would eventually be encountered on home video and television.[15]

Many of these films feature visual media that compels characters in the film to watch them, and whose lasting impression *haunts* viewers who watch them (either supernaturally or psychologically). At the same time, they also emphasize the specific relationship between media and viewer that each media type engenders. Some films even deal explicitly with haunting by media spectatorship as both the crux of their narratives and the source of their horror. *Ringu*'s videotape curses anyone who views it, and the curse can only be lifted by copying it and spreading it to others. *The Serpent's Path* is about two men exacting vengeance against a criminal outfit that produces VHS snuff videos, and analog video is also used as a torture technique. In *Pulse*, viral web videos induce viewers to perform a ghost summoning ritual before killing themselves; even the ghosts, when they appear, kill their victims by looking at them straight in the eye, conceiving the relationship between ghosts and people itself as a form of media spectatorship. This focus on *haunting* (either supernatural or psychological) by media can be traced from Hasumi's theoretical concerns analyzing cinema through its images that arouse the viewer's interest leave the most lasting impression (*omoshirosa*), or, perhaps more accurately, Kurosawa's modification of that as the way the film produces fear and continues to haunt viewers after they have seen it (*osoroshisa*).

However, by invoking new media, these narrate the encounter between spectator and media object with careful attention to the different modes of spectatorship that each media type produces. For example, *Ringu* catalogues the different possible spectatorship methods presented by home video. Reiko (Matsushima Nanako) watches the video on her own from start to finish without stopping, she and Ryūji (Sanada Hiroyuki) watch it again, pausing it and going over it multiple times, scrutinizing the image moment-by-moment in a way that is not possible in the theatrical experience. Further emphasis is placed on the fact that the viewing location is private: in a domestic space, either alone or among a small group of acquaintances.

Kurosawa's *The Serpent's Path* has its own curious hybrid media history of being shot on 16mm film to be transferred to video and released as V-Cinema, only to be changed at the last minute and blown up to 35mm film for theatrical distribution. Home video also plays a prominent role in the narrative: while torturing members of Hiyama's gang, Miyashita (Kagawa Teruyuki) repeatedly plays a home video of his daughter on a television screen in front of them before reading out the details of her death. It is an ineffective torture technique on these gang members since none of the gang members either admit responsibility or seem the least bit troubled by either the video or his description of it. However, in the film's climax, Miyashita's supposed partner,

Nijima (Aikawa Shō), plays replays the video on loop over multiple television screens in front of Miyashita while playing a recording of himself reading out the same description that Miyashita had, and it creates an immediate psychological response in Miyashita, who attempts to touch the various television screens that surround him in order to get closer to his daughter. In short order, it is revealed that Nijima's own daughter was murdered by the same gang, and that he holds Miyashita responsible for her death, so Nijima chains Miyashita to a wall and plays the snuff video of his (Miyashita's) daughter's death on the same television that Miyashita had previously, unsuccessfully, attempted to use to torture the other gang members. In its invocation of video spectatorship, the film plays heavily on individual intimate reactions to specific videos that are not widely shared: Miyashita incorrectly assumes that his home videos of his daughter will have the same psychological effect on her killers that they do on him. The video's power over viewers is not universal, but is contingent on the viewer's own direct connection to the contents of the video. Kurosawa is thus revising Hasumi's model of spectatorship from one of theatrical, where films are viewed publicly and the experience is assumed, in Hasumi's and many other theorists' conception, is assumed to be universally shared, to home videomaking, where intimacy to the subject matter is paramount.

Kurosawa's later *Pulse*, working with digital rather than analog video, distributed over the internet rather than through home video tapes, takes the isolated viewing experience and the replication of the videos to an even further extreme. Whereas in *Ringu*, the spread of the video was still limited by the need to replicate it and circulate it with VHS tapes, the digital videos in *Pulse* spread to viewers uncontrollably over the internet, with viewers apparently unaware that they are taking part in replicating and spreading them. The experience of viewing the video itself is as isolated as it is with the VHS tapes in *Ringu* and *The Serpent's Path*, but strangely impersonal, and the viewers have no direct connection to the images they see nor any awareness of where they have come from or their own roles in continuing their circulation.

In their treatment of the media within their films (analog video on VHS tapes for *Ringu* and *The Serpent's Path* and digital video contained on the internet for *Pulse*), all three films foreground the relationship between media and spectator, and specifically the way that the media capture the viewer's attention, produce curiosity, and linger in viewers' minds. In so doing, they refashion the aspects of the relationship between cinema and spectator that Hasumi emphasized for a new media environment. In each of these cases, we might observe, the practices of spectatorship that these new media engender are not conceived of in a positive light: in spite of their apparent convenience from the ability to watch video in a domestic space and to be able to repeat the act of spectatorship endlessly, this ultimately turns into a threat: while in cinema, powerful images were fleeting and only left traces in the memories of their most attentive viewers, the powerful images in home video continue to be present, and can emerge from the television, or simply repeat endlessly to the point that no experience outside the video is longer possible.

MEDIA MATERIALISM

As previously mentioned, Hasumi frequently praises moments in films that might have otherwise been dismissed as technical mistakes, such as uses of rear-projection that do not produce a sense of continuous space. These moments, Hasumi has argued, bring viewers closer to the awareness of film as a flat surface by overcoming the illusion of depth. J-horror films frequently feature these kinds of technological mistakes or breakdowns and incorporate them into the way that they produce horror. However, while 35mm film, digital video, and analog video within mainstream narrative films are frequently designed to make viewers as unaware as possible of the material properties of each individual medium so that they instead focus on the mediated images, when the media break down, the material differences between each of these becomes visible.

There are a variety of possible responses audiences can have to technical breakdowns in cinema: they may find it to be comical evidence of the filmmaker's ineptitude, or as a source of cinephilic pleasure of the kind that Hasumi finds in these moments. However, this can also provide a source for the cinematic uncanny: the faith that most viewers place in the photograph's (and by extension, cinema's) reliability as an index means that they may interpret a breakdown in its resemblance as an occult phenomenon rather than simply a technical malfunction or the result of image manipulation. Discussing the uncanny in spirit photography, Tom Gunning has pointed out that the practice of spirit photography often combines superimpositions or other photographic tricks with banal and familiar figures and spaces. On the one hand, to a viewer familiar with the technical processes at work, "this collision of separate orientations betrays the technical means by which the photographs were produced," but on the other hand, "their incongruous juxtaposition yields an eerie image of the encounter between two ontologically separate worlds" (Gunning 2007, 99–100). It is here that Hasumi's critical methodology finds an unlikely companionship with the cinematic uncanny: drawing viewers closer to the technical processes at work through technical breakdowns can simulate a breakdown of natural sight that causes discomfort and simulate how viewers may expect to feel when they encounter a ghost. From the opposite perspective, one could take the view that Hasumi's students making J-horror films are taking advantage of the eerie effects of these technical breakdowns to explore the visual possibilities of cinema outlined by their teacher within a conventional, popular cinematic context.

We can see techniques like this at work in many J-horror films. Kurosawa in particular frequently uses deliberately artificial rear-projection or green-screen driving sequences (most visibly in *Cure* and *Creepy* [2016]). The films that take up media objects as the objects of their horror, *Ringu*, *The Serpent's Path*, and *Pulse*, each find ways to articulate the unique visual structure of their media types as well. To address this issue, however, we should start by distinguishing the properties of the three media concerned here: analog video, digital video, and film. What distinguishes analog video from digital video is that digital can be broken down into absolute, discreet units of equal value, while digital cannot. Film is often referred to as an analog medium, but in fact it's a hybrid: its photographic images cannot be broken down into individual units like pixels, but its movement can be broken into individual still frames. This distinguishes it from analog video on the one hand, which does not have frames, but in which visual information comes in waves, and from digital video on the other hand, which has frames of still images like film, but whose images can also be broken down to the basic unit of the pixel.

Both *Ringu* and *Pulse* carefully incorporate evocations of the structures of their media into their visual design as motifs. *Ringu*'s opening title is set against crashing waves, possibly the sea near the fishing village on the remote island that we eventually learn Sadako comes from. However, if we observe closely during this sequence, we can see the intermittent breaking down of the image into analog video noise, and the sequence culminates with a dissolve between the crashing waves and analog video noise, which gradually turns into an analog video image of a baseball game seen up closely enough that the signals look like abstract patterns, before a zoom out reveals the image in its entirety. Both the video as it is first seen and the culminating video, from which Sadako emerges a week after the first video is seen, play with properties that are unique to analog video representation, and these could either be evidence of a degradation in image quality as the result of successive copying or traces of some phenomenon that is beyond the representational capacity of video. In particular, there is noticeable analog video jitter and noise throughout both videos. Additionally, these make it more difficult to notice and trace Sadako's movement in the film's climax as she first begins to emerge from the well. *Pulse* likewise draws on the properties of digital imaging: there are prominent motion blocks in the videos that circulate, and, ultimately, the movement of one of the ghosts in a "forbidden room" near the end of the film. But the act of turning people into digital data also transforms into a broader visual motif: a graduate student in computer science builds a model of the world using simple digital imaging, showing representations of people as tiny dots moving on a computer image. This central image is repeated throughout the film, particularly in a number of long takes showing characters moving around the frame from a slightly elevated angle, so that we can see underneath them checkerboard tiles that resemble discrete units like pixels. In each case, the media's inability to render supernatural phenomena lays bare their material properties by allowing us to see them break down into their component parts, and the visual structures of their component parts are echoed in other sequences in the films. These help us to see past the apparent reality effect of moving images to the underlying material properties that produce the images, much like observing the stitching on the reconstructed corpses of Aoyama's *Embalming*.

CONCLUSION

In this chapter, I have focused on three common techniques and motifs of a small number of J-horror films that resonate with the critical and theoretical tendencies of post-1970s Japanese cinephilia, in which each of these filmmakers was educated. First, by staging horror scenes so that sources of danger often first appear within the deep recesses of the frame, J-horror filmmakers use fear and anxiety to provoke the kind of attentive spectatorship for which Hasumi advocated in his writings. Second, many J-horror films foreground the act of media spectatorship, and depict it as one where viewers become so enraptured by the experience of viewing that it either hypnotizes or infects them; this, too, closely resembles Hasumi's conception of the experience of viewing films. And finally, J-horror films frequently provoke the cinematic uncanny by drawing attention to the material properties of the cinematic image (as well as other media images contained within it), which I argue derives from Hasumi's fixation on the physical properties of the cinematic image itself in his critical method. As the filmmakers themselves not only studied under Hasumi, but have also discussed the way that he emphasized these aspects of his critical methodology in the classes they took with him, I argue that Hasumi's film theory and criticism have played a formative role in the J-horror cycle that emerged in the late 1990s, which continues to influence Japanese and international horror films to this day.

In addition to the arguments that I have made here, I believe that it would be productive to consider this framework more broadly in future studies. By not emphasizing the connections between these filmmakers and Hasumi, English language scholarship on J-horror to date has largely overlooked a critical connection between film theory and film production in contemporary Japan, and as a result has overlooked the theoretical underpinnings of many of the canonical J-horror films. There are numerous former Hasumi students mentioned in this chapter, such as Manda and Shinozaki, whose work has been almost entirely overlooked by both distributors and scholars in the West, even though they are among the most interesting filmmakers working in J-horror today. Further, looking at this collective of filmmakers, their frequent collaborations, and their shared educational heritage can help bring to light connections between J-horror and Japanese art house filmmaking since the 1990s.

ACKNOWLEDGEMENTS

I would like to thank the audience of my 2019 Society for Cinema & Media Studies Conference presentation for their helpful feedback. I am also grateful to Mikki Kressbach, Nicole Morse, and Jordan Schonig for their constructive criticism.

REFERENCES

Bazin, André. 2005. *What is Cinema?: Volume 1*. Translated by Hugh Gray. Berkeley: University of California Press.

Cook, Ryan. 2010. "An Impaired Eye: Hasumi Shigehiko on Cinema and Stupidity." *Review of Japanese Culture and Society* 22 (December): 130–143.

Crandol, Michael. 2020. "Horror: The Ghosts of *Kaiki eiga*." In *The Japanese Cinema Book*, edited by Hideaki Fujiki and Alastair Phillips, 630–652. London: B.F.I.

Gerow, Aaron. 2014. "Critical Reception: Historical Conceptions of Japanese Film Criticism." In *The Oxford Handbook of Japanese Cinema*, edited by Daisuke Miyao, 61–78. Oxford: Oxford University Press.

Gunning, Tom. 2007. "To Scan a Ghost: The Ontology of Mediated Vision." *Grey Room* 26 (Winter): 94–127.

Hasumi, Shigehiko. 1990. *Eiga yūwaku no ekurichūru* (*Cinema: The écriture of Temptation*). Tokyo: Chikuma Shobō.

____.1969. "Suzuki Seijun to sono chinmoku no naritachi." *Shinema 69*, 2 (1969): 49–57.

Kinoshita, Chika. 2009. "The Mummy Complex: Kurosawa Kiyoshi's *Loft* and J-Horror." In *Horror to the Extreme: Changing Boundaries in Asian Cinema*, edited by Jinhee Choi and Mitsuyo Wada-Marciano, 103–22. Hong Kong: Hong Kong University Press.

Kurosawa Kiyoshi. 2008. "Angeroporosu to no taiwa" ("Dialogue with Angelopoulos"). *Kyōfu no taidan: Eiga no motto kowai hanashi*. Tokyo: Seidosha, 2008, 161–173.

Kurosawa, Kiyoshi. 2018. *Eiga wa osoroshii* (*Cinema is Terrifying*). Tokyo: Seido-sha.

____. 1992. *Eizō no karisuma* (*The Charisma of the Cinematic Image*). Tokyo: Firumu aato-sha.

———. 2008. *Kyōfu no taidan: Eiga no motto kowai hanashi* (*Discussions of Terror: Even More Frightening Conversations About Movies*). Tokyo: Seidosha.

Kurosawa, Kiyoshi, Manda Kunitoshi, and Aoyama Shinji. 2017. "Hasumi Shigehiko to Eiga no yūwaku" ("Hasumi Shigehiko and the Temptation of Cinema"). *Yūrika* 49-17, no. 710 (October): 106–123.

Kurosawa, Kiyoshi, and Shinozaki Makoto. 2003. *Kurosawa Kiyoshi no kyōfu eigashi* (*Kurosawa Kiyoshi's History of Terrifying Cinema*). Tokyo: Seido-sha.

Nakata Hideo. 2017. "'Eiga gentaiken' toshite no Hasumi zemi" ("Hasumi's Seminar as the Origin of Film Experience"). *Yūrika* 49-17, No. 710 (October): 135–138.

Scahill, Andrew. 2010. "Happy, Empty: On Authorship and Influence in the Horror Cinema of Kiyoshi Kurosawa." *Asian Journal of Literature, Culture, and Society* 4, no. 2 (September): 59–78.

Suga, Hidemi, ed. 2005. *1968*. Tokyo: Sakuhinsha.

Ueno, Kōshi, ed. 1986. *Suzuki Seijun Zen'eiga*. Tokyo: Rippū Shobō.

Wada-Marciano, Mitsuyo. 2009. "J-Horror: New Media's Impact on Contemporary Japanese Horror Cinema." In *Horror to the Extreme: Changing Boundaries in Asian Cinema*, edited by Jinhee Choi and Mitsuyo Wada-Marciano, 15–38. Hong Kong: Hong Kong University Press.

Yomota, Inuhiko. 2019. *What is Japanese Cinema?: A History*, translated by Phil Kaffen. New York: Columbia University Press.

Zahlten, Alexander. 2017. "1980s Nyū Aka: (Non)Media Theory as Romantic Performance." In *Media Theory in Japan*, edited by Marc Steinberg and Alexander Zahlten, 200–220. Durham: Duke University Press.

NOTES

1. For a more complete discussion of *nyū akademizumu* and Hasumi's place within it, see Alexander Zahlten, "1980s Nyū Aka: (Non)Media Theory as Romantic Performance" in *Media Theory in Japan*, ed. Marc Steinberg and Alexander Zahlten (Durham: Duke University Press, 2017), 200–220.

2. Though best known internationally for critically celebrated dramatic films like *Harmful Insect* (2001) or *Canary* (2005), Shiota wrote the screenplay for an entry in the *Scary True Stories* V-Cinema series in the early 1990s.

3. Though little-known outside of Japan, Manda's J-horror films include *The Tunnel* (2004), *Seppun* (2007), and *Synchronizer* (2017).

4. Shinozaki is the co-author of *Kurosawa Kiyoshi no kyōfu eigashi*. Though likely best-known for his early dramatic work such as *Okaeri* (1995) and *Not Forgotten* (2000), his more recent films *Kai-ki: Tales of Terror from Tokyo* (2010), *Shine! Shine! Shinema!* (2011), and *Sharing* (2014) play on motifs from J-horror films.

5. Hasumi has numerous other students who became prominent filmmakers who have not worked in the horror genre, including Suo Masayuki (*Abnormal Family, Shall We Dance?*) and Funahashi Atsushi (*Nuclear Nation*).

6. Here, as elsewhere in Yomota's writing, Yomota (who was once one of Hasumi's students himself) is implicitly directing a critique at Hasumi without mentioning Hasumi's name.

7. Ueno developed this concept in a series of articles on the *yakuza* genre at *Cinema 69*, and fleshed out the idea in an essay, "Eiga no omoshirosa to iu koto" ("What is called a film's *omoshirosa*"). The concept has been used not only by Hasumi, Kurosawa, and other Hasumi students, in their criticism.

8. See interview: Ueno Kōshi and Hasumi Shigehiko, "1968 nen wa nan da/nan deatta?" (What is/was 1968) in *1968*, ed. Suga Hidemi (Tokyo: Sakuhinsha, 2005).

9. A telling anecdote: in a recent roundtable discussion between Kurosawa, Manda, and Aoyama, the three filmmakers discussed their experiences taking Hasumi's film seminar at Rikkyō (Kurosawa and Manda at different points in the 1970s and Aoyama in the 1980s), and each filmmaker shared the first film that Hasumi had them watch for the class: for Kurosawa, it was *The Black Windmill* (Don Siegel, 1974), for Manda, it was *Watashi no SEX hakusho: zecchōdo* (*Nurse's Sex Journal*, Sone Chūsei, 1976), and for Aoyama, it was *Nostalgia* (Andrei Tarkovsky, 1983) (Kurosawa, Kiyoshi, Manda Kunitoshi, and Aoyama Shinji. "Hasumi Shigehiko to Eiga no yūwaku" in *Yūrika* 49–17, no. 710 (October 2017): 108–109.

10. The simplest example of a "system" that Cook discusses in Hasumi is the "eyeline match" of Classical Hollywood filmmaking. Eyeline matches are an editing technique in which a shot of one set of eyes looking off-screen is followed by a shot of another set of eyes, looking off-screen in the opposite direction, with the implication that the two pairs of eyes are looking at each other. This is "a systemic effect in that it forgets the impossibility of filming two sets of eyes looking at each other" (Cook, 133), but for this "forgetting" to work the eyeline match must be repeated in the same way, in fact limiting the possibilities of cinema while seeming to expand them. Only when a director "breaks" the system, as Ozu does with his "false eyeline matches," do most viewers remember them.

11. Hasumi first wrote of this tendency in Suzuki Seijun's films in the essay "Suzuki Seijun to sono chinmoku no naritachi" for *Cinema 69* in 1969; however, it is a recurring theme in his writings about the filmmaker.

12. Section on Angelopoulos is 318–322. Originally published in *Mainichi shinbun* on June 6, 1982.

13. The same could be said of Kurosawa's use of the 'X' motif in *Cure*. Andrew Scahill discusses this tendency in Kurosawa's work more extensively. See: Andrew Scahill, "Happy, Empty: On Authorship and Influence in the Horror Cinema of Kiyoshi Kurosawa." *Asian Journal of Literature, Culture, and Society* 4, No. 2 (Sept. 2010).

14. I should note here that I use "J-horror" to refer not to all Japanese horror, but to the specific strand of Japanese horror film that gained international prominence in the 1990s. The best definition of this cycle of films has been given by Chika Kinoshita (who calls J-horror a "movement" rather than a "genre"): "J-horror specifically refers to a group of relatively low-budget horror films made in Japan during the late 1990s, such as the *Ringu* cycle. A closely knit group of filmmakers and critics, including Kurosawa, has been involved in the production of those films. Aesthetically, J-horror

films concentrate on the low-key production of atmospheric and psychological fear, rather than graphic gore, capitalizing on urban legends proliferated through mass media and popular culture" (Chika Kinoshita, "The Mummy Comples: Kurosawa Kiyoshi's *Loft* and J-horror," in *Horror to the Extreme: Changing Boundaries in Asian Cinema*, ed. Jinhee Choi and Mitsuyo Wada-Marciano (Hong Kong: Hong Kong University Press, 2009, 104). Significantly, this designation excludes not only Japanese horror films made prior to the 1990s, but also many Japanese horror films and filmmakers that are sometimes grouped together with Kurosawa, Nakata, and the others under the "J-horror" banner. The most notable exclusion in this regard is Miike Takashi, whose approach to horror is fundamentally different than the filmmakers I consider here. For a broader lineage of the horror genre in Japan, see: Michael Crandol, "Horror: The Ghosts of *Kaiki eiga*" in *The Japanese Cinema Book*, ed. Hideaki Fujiki and Alistair Philips (London: BFI, 2020).

15. Mitsuyo Wada-Marciano has compellingly argued that the prominence of omnibus films and films with episodic narrative structures in J-horror are designed for interrupted viewing patterns, either in television syndication, where commercials would be placed between the episodes, or allowing viewers on home video to watch single sections at a time. See: Mitsuyo Wada-Marciano, "J-Horror: New Media's Impact on Contemporary Japanese Horror Cinema," in *Horror to the Extreme: Changing Boundaries in Asian Cinema*, ed. Jinhee Choi and Mitsuyo Wada-Marciano (Hong Kong: Hong Kong University Press, 2009, 26).

Chapter 9

Spiral into Samsara in Junji Ito's J-Horror Masterpiece *Uzumaki*

Wayne Stein

Within the hypnotic vortex, people are drawn into its very center of death. Though the pattern persists in a variety of creative manners, the *Uzumaki* effect is often fatal. As one of the greatest showcases of J-Horror in Japan, Junji Ito's *Uzumaki* trilogy challenges us to die a thousand different ways as we follow his meta-analysis into demented realms of a creative curse. From the very start, the narrative becomes less about the fate of doomed individuals and more about the interconnectivity that suffering creates as it destroys an entire town on the coast of Japan: Kurozu-cho. One way to approach the narrative is to look at the recurring spiral as a symbolic mandala of the wheel of Samara that defines Buddhism. This wheel of life and rebirth is actually the predominate recurring theme of all narratives of J-horror. Everyone is stuck within this death spiral of samsara, for we all live a life of suffering and die one day, only to return again back into this life of suffering. This is what separates the Judeo-Christian narratives from Asian tales. From a Christian point of view, one of the miracles performed by Christ is that he was reborn, for he was able to rise up after he died. From an Asian perspective, that remains an old tale, for we have all been reborn countless times. That act seems to be no miracle but the natural cycle of life and death and rebirth. Instead, if Jesus had never been born again, that would have been a real miracle. Therefore, in Japan, Christianity made no sense and has never been very popular there. Instead, this cycle of samsara repeats itself as the main journey in life. Our life trajectory is like a spiral, going around and around in circles. Heaven and

Hell are not in some afterworld, just temporary states of being available to all in this life. Hell is a state of mind or a state of horror. By decoding the system of samsara, this chapter can uncover deeper meanings in *Uzumaki*.

Deeper Meanings to the Spiral of Insanity

The first volume of Junji Ito's *Uzumaki* was published in 1998 which stood at a precarious time in Japanese history where the early economic miracle years had quickly spiraled into a living nightmare. "Japan was not over-regulated but underregulated and its capacity to formulate good policies and implement them was undercut by political factors [. . .]. Japan's subsequent failure to undertake serious reforms during the 1990s was not caused by the economic bureaucracy's intervention in the economy but by the economic bureaucracy's loss of autonomy to implement policies in the face of vested interests" (Johnson 2001). Chapter 1, "The Spiral Obsession," beautifully sets up the samsara cycle of suffering of the series. Indeed, we see the narrator—Kirie Goshima, a young high school student—looking at her hometown, Kurozu-cho. Immediately, we can see spirals in the clouds above the town. The opening four colorful splash pages has vortexes upon each page. The fourth page even shows vortexes in the grass. While circles are natural in the world and seemingly harmless and beneficial, Junji Ito skillfully reconstructs these symbols of benevolence into symbols of terror. Kirie is late, for she always goes to school with her boyfriend, Shuichi.

While running to meet him, she notices Shuichi's father in an alley looking at the shell of a snail which contains a spiral shape. Over time, the father becomes obsessed, more and more with spirals. In Buddhist terms, this obsession is causing mental anguish. "Mental confusion is a veil that prevents us from seeing reality clearly and clouds are understanding of the true nature of things" (Ricard 2006, 80). Finally, the father manages to contort his body into a snail like vortex, crushing his own bones and life as he dies happily.

To further understand samsara, it is important to understand its causes. Three basic poisons or *klesha* cause samsara: 1) *Moha*, the phantasmagoric delusion of a confused life, 2) *Raga*, the lustful nature of being, full of greed, addictions, and seductions of life, and 3) *Dvesha*, the hateful, vengeful, and negative attachments of life. The father was confused and suffered from *Moha* as he became obsessed with the various shapes of spirals. He also suffered from *Raga* because he was seduced by this obsession as he tortures and kills himself. The spirals seduced him. In chapter 3, Azami, a student, suffers from *Raga*, for she wants to seduce all the boys and enjoyed being the center of their attention. When Shuichi does not seem to notice her, she becomes more obsessed with him. On pg. 100, there is one of the most famous images of Junji Ito's career, for the spiral becomes half the size of Azami's head as it starts to grown and to pull her left eye into its center vortex. This image remains one of the most haunting ever created in the history of manga horror. The readers start to also suffer from *Raga,* and become addicted to the narrative. Indeed, this image is often copied in the Internet and has even become an animated gif.

Illusionary Attachments to the Spiral of Samsara

Another classmate has fallen in love with Azami. His name is Okada, and he will do anything for her. Azami asks Okada to bring Shuichi, her greatest desire, to meet her. She promises that she will then go out with Okada. He keeps his promise and brings Shuichi to her. Instead of keeping her promise, she proceeds to dump him. This act turns him insane as he strikes her which demonstrates that he suffers from *Dveshi*. Azami is then pulled into his *Dvesha*. We witness that her scar which starts as a small vortex opens up and grows bigger and bigger as her anger grows consuming her and sucking Okada into the vortex-like meat grinder. He dies as she dissipates too melting into the *Dveshi* of pain. Both dissipate into puddle of nothingness.

The manga was also made into a live action film, *Uzumaki* (□□□□, Higuchinsky, 2000). In the opening scene, Kirie (Eriko Hatsune) is looking down upon her home of Kurouzu-cho (black vortex township), which parallels the original splash pages of the first volume of the trilogy (1998). Directed by Higuchinski, one particular symbolic scene was added that differs than the manga: Kirie quickly walks by the six statues of Jizo. When I visited Japan, I noticed that Jizo is everywhere. Uniquely, Jizo stands as a boy Bodhisattva. In all of Asia, I do not know of another child bodhisattva, and this boy has become my favorite. Often in parks, he stands to protect travelers. In a larger context, since life remains an arduous journey, we need safeguards. Though I never saw six Jizo statues in a row, his presence is of great value to all Japanese. Some Japanese may no longer value Shintoism, Confucianism, or Buddhism; however, the meaning of the symbolism is not lost on the Japanese consciousness.

Entering into Neo-Confucianism and the Spiral of Respect and Tradition

In Neo-Confucian context, *"Kasa Jizō"* (笠地蔵) is a famous child's story that every Japanese knows about. The story is about an elderly man who is walking home during a freezing winter storm. Compassionately, when he sees a Jizo statue, he stops and puts some warm clothes on the "cold" child. Though he is a poor grandfather without much to eat, he seems content with his life of suffering. He goes to sleep hungry only to wake up the next morning and find food left at his door. In the distance, he sees the boy "Jizo" walking away. Basically, he knows that Jizo returned a favor for a favor. Symbolically, the story occurs during the new lunar new year, usually around February. So with a new year, begins a new life with new possibilities. Therefore, the tale becomes a filial piety narrative of Jizo returning kindness with kindness.

The origins of Jizo's Neo-Confucian symbolism actually began from the Buddhist Mulian tale of filial piety associated appropriately with the annual summer ghost month, the O-bon festival in Japan. Mulian's mother had died and is suffering in hell. Out of love, the monk does the impossible and enters hell to liberate his mother. He manages to pull her out and back into this realm of the living. Originally, Buddhism was not popular in Asia because of the main narrative of Shakyamuni Buddha leaving his parents to seek liberation. What good son would abandon his parents? This filial piety narrative is well appreciated by all Asians, even Christians there. In Japan, the Jizo tale reconstructs the gender and is about a girl who for maternal love she enters hell and manages to save her mother. She is later reborn as a boy: Jizo. The pain of hell can function as "a training tool" (Bays 2002, 175). To sacrifice in order to ultimately help someone is significant in life. Jizo has become a model of how to be compassionate to the Japanese during these difficult times.

While the manga trilogy is a series of individual tales of nineteen chapters, often about different individuals, the film itself is structured differently where the narratives concurrently overlap with a shared chronology. The movie was not able to explore the complexities of all the characters and narratives in ninety minutes. The ending of the manga is left out. Finally, the curse ends in the town, but returns in the form of a newly discovered galaxy in the shape of the spiral as seen through telescopes by inhabitants of the town, which unleashes a new curse. Thus, the curse, the spiral of samsara, returns.

Therefore, this might have made the film even more suspenseful. Often, less becomes more which allows for the imagination to fill in the psychic emptiness. The music by Keiichi Suzuki and Tetsuro Kashibuchi helps to guide the cadence of tension in the chaotic spiraling of the horror of existence. Music always enhances moments of suspense, especially as we visit and revisit the vortex of pain and punishment.

In Chapter 4 of the manga, "The Firing Effect," Kirie's father becomes obsessed with producing spirals in his pottery. This obsession parallels an obsession that many fathers have with their work. In Japan, many people die of *karoshi* (過労死). They, basically while dedicating themselves to being useful, work themselves to death. The fire used to create pottery parallels the flames of hell that the father is tormented by through his obsession. "Hell does not exist outside of your actions" (Bays 2002, 172). The building that he worked in burns to the ground as her father himself nearly dies because of his unhealthy obsession. The chapter ends as a warning. "Thus we distance ourselves from reality and are dragged into the machinery of attraction and repulsion that is kept relentlessly in motion by our mental projections" (Ricard 2006, 81). In a Buddhist sense, all is projections. We see what we think we see.

BREAKING FROM THE SPIRAL AND ENTERING LIBERATION FROM THE CURSE

Toward the end of the series, chapter 18 is called "the Labyrinth." Now the entire town replicates the design of the spiral. In the opening chapters of the series, the houses are more rectangular with the road fitting between the houses, the basic structure of modern municipalities, towns, and cities. Perhaps there is a way out of the labyrinth of samsara or these spirals of doom? Indeed, there is. Three anti-poisons or forms of liberations can act as positive mental states within the narrative: 1) *Prajna* an overarching awareness about life in general; 2) *Albha*, a genuine bounteousness and goodness about life; 3) *Advesa*, a loving-kindness about the quality of life. Both Kirei and Shuichi seem to possess a bit of *Prajna*, for they seem the most balanced characters in the series. In addition, *Kirei* with her higher state of harmony possesses *Albha* which she uses to guide Shuichi in his daily battles to stay sane.

In final chapter 19 called "The Completion," both Kirei and Shuichi seem to agree to a solution to end the suffering from the spiral into Samsara. Perhaps, this then becomes a way to exit the maze of suffering. With a sense of loving-kindness in mind and conjoining and becoming one, they break their bones, break down any barriers between themselves, and finally, break the curse. Both Kirei and Shuichi seem to possess a bit of *Prajna*. They seem the most balanced characters in the series. Kirei has a higher state of harmony though as she guides Shuichi in his daily battles to stay sane. Though the curse seems to end, we sense that all will return one day and the curse will be reborn. A true sense of *Advesa* or loving-kindness is missing. Reaching nirvana and exiting the eternal wheel or spiral of samsara is not transpiring.

There remains one extra chapter: the "Lost Chapter, Galaxies." One of the important influences on Junji Ito was through H.P. Lovecraft. In an interview with Winsby, Ito explained, "The different stages of the spiral (in "Uzumaki") were definitely inspired from the mysterious novels of H.P. Lovecraft. His expressionism with regard to atmosphere greatly inspires my creative impulse." Furthermore, Sean Moreland explains, "Ito's interest in the epistemological and aesthetic roots of Lovecraft's spiral obsession is most evident in the 'lost' chapter of *Uzumaki*, making it an effective bridge between the early twentieth century astronomical context of Lovecraft's cosmic horror and the turbulent transfigurations of *Uzumaki* as a whole." Certainly, there will always remain haunted individuals, haunted spaces, and haunted paths, yet Junji Ito's *Uzumaki* trilogy seems to be more about the artistic design of horror conduits and the aesthetic constructions and instructions of being damned.

A Deeper New Meaning of the Curse Applied to Our Daily Struggles

Finally, the series of mishaps becomes less and less about the actual people who are cursed or the specific places that are haunted because in the end, the readers find themselves becoming haunted by the tales of *Uzumaki*. We, the cursed, are pulled back into the gravity of Junji Ito's creativity into the very center of the vortex, again and again trying to decode its meaning. Indeed, the legacy of this curse is that we have become addicted to this deconstructive narrative of J-horror as it spirals out of control. Indeed, we need this creative emancipation from our own daily insanities, sufferings, and chaos. Therefore, a new four-part animated series is being constructed for a 2021 release by Toonami to save us. To make sure that the crew of animators were not cursed, they visited a Shinto shrine so that the project will be blessed.

The blatant corruption of our politicians, the curse of another economic doom, and the hell of our current pandemic tells us that we desperately need something to resurrect our hopes. Oddly, horror can offer a new way to reconstruct meaning, for it takes horror to destroy horror. In Buddhism, meditation can become a way to allow these elements of horror to dissipate in power. According the esoteric traditions of Tibetan Buddhism called *Chöd* (Severance) developed centuries ago by Machik Labdrön, we can free ourselves from the effect of such horror, for she wrote, "Meditate on the harm-doers and so forth who prefer flesh eating the flesh, those who like blood drinking the blood, and those who like bones sucking the bones" (Kongtru Lodro Taye 2016, 191). Look upon Junji Ito's *Uzumaki* trilogy as a meditation of "severance." Finally, it is not that we understand completely the curse of the spiral or how to remove such a curse. Instead, the journey into the psychic unknown is always worth the gnosis earned through such inspections. We are enlightened by the worlds we have traveled through along the arduous paths protected by the six Jizo guides. Thank you, Junji Ito for understanding our struggles.

REFERENCES

Bays, Jan Chozen. 2002. *Jizo Bodhisattva: Modern Healing and Traditional Buddhist Practice*. Boston: Tuttle Publishing.

Ito, Junji. 2013. *Uzumaki*. Volume 1–3. Translated by Viz Media. Yuki Oniki.
Johnson, Chalmers. 2001. "Japanese 'Capitalism' Revisited." *Thesis Eleven*, 66(1): 57–78.
Kongtrul, Jamgon, ed. 2016. *Chöd: The Sacred Teaching on Severance*, translated by Sarah Harding. Bolder: Snow Lion.
Matthieu, Ricard. 2006. *A Guide to Developing Life's Most Important Skill: Happiness* Translated by Jesse Browner. Little Brown and Company.
Moreland, Sean. 2018. "The Downward Spiral: Thoughts and Lovecraftian Spirality and Ito's *Uzumaki*." *Postscripts to Darkness*. Accessed May 12, 2021. https://pstdarkness.com/2018/11/02/the-downward-spiral-lovecraftian-spirality-and-itos-uzumaki/
Winsby, Mira Bai. 2006. "Into the Spiral: A Conversation with Japanese Horror Maestro Junji Ito." Translated by Miyako Takano. *78 Magazine*. Accessed May 14, 2021. http://www.78magazine.com/issues/03-01/arts/junji.shtml

Chapter 10

Controlling the Inner Demon
Theological Approaches on Devilman

Fernando Gabriel Pagnoni Berns

Devilman (Debiruman) is a creation of manga artist Go Nagai. The manga revolves around Akira Fudo, a wimpish high school student who mixes his soul with that of a demon named Amon following the indications of his best friend Ryo Asuka. Ryo reveals to Akira that an underground race of demons hibernating for millennia in the ice of the Himalayas will invade Earth and destroy humankind. According Ryo, demons existed before humankind and now they want to take their world back. The only way to defeat them is if a noble human mixes his soul with a demon; taking control of the creature, the human will gain supernatural powers. Via a ritual, Akira merges with Amon, one of the most powerful creatures, and transforms himself into Devilman, a demon who battles other demons. Only Akira's pure spirit keeps his new acquired demonic personality at bay. At the end of the manga, published between 1972 and 1973 in *Weekly Shonen Magazine*, Akira learns that Ryo is Satan in disguise, and that humankind, which has devolved into forms of fascism, may be exterminated for good. The manga ends after Armageddon, with Akira killed by Ryo/Satan and God invading Earth.

Devilman was adapted into anime by Toei Animation only a month after the manga was published. Broadcasted through 1972 to 1973, the anime consisted of 39 episodes that took some of the manga's dark themes. In the TV show, Devilman is one of the most powerful demons, and as such, he is sent to Earth to create chaos among the humans. To fulfill his purposes, Devilman takes the body of Akira, a teenager who was killed with his father during their archaeological visit to frozen caverns. In home of friends of Akira's parents, Devilman falls in love with Miki Makimura, the young daughter of their adoptive parents. Now in love with a human girl, Devilman breaks liaisons with their former race and starts a war against the demons led by the Great Zenon. *Devilman* the anime is, ultimately, a monster-of-the-week show where the titular (anti)hero battles each episode a different demon. In the last episode, Devilman reveals himself to Miki, confessing that he is a demon in disguise. Yet, she is still in love with him and both remain together to battle future new threats.

The anime follows some ideas from the manga—the demon acting for the forces of good and protecting Earth, Devilman falling in love with Miki, the mixing of human identity with that of a demon—but simplifies the darker aspects offered by the comic book. Yet, both stories share the "taming of the demon" as a central aspect of Devilman's mythology. However, the taming and conquest of evil impulses manifest differently in each case. While the manga offers a posthumanist approach to understand life on Earth, the anime follows the Buddhist doctrines of cleansing and purifying. Both versions, even if temporally taking place at basically the same time (1972–73), offer distinctive approaches to the problem of evil in a society as Japan, informed by "logic of relative contrasts" that displaces "the absolute dichotomies of good and evil" (Winston 1992, 60) in favor of nuanced versions of this binary.

TWO TAKES ON JAPANESE RELIGION: ADAPTING DEVILMAN

As Eduardo Grüner argues, when we find resonances, inspirations, or echoes of other works in an artistic text—such as a TV show—we cannot just turn our heads and look the other way as if that relationship were not there due to a principle of "intellectual honesty" and scholarly rigor (2006, 113). The author of a concrete cultural artifact has willingly connected his or her work to another time/nation/aesthetic/philosophy, inviting us to read it from our socially and culturally located point of view. Thus, the practice of adaptation is both a strategy of hermeneutic intervention and a form of "political reading" (Grüner 2006, 114) that affects the production, circulation, and reception of the work in question.

In this framework, there is *no original source*, only interpretations. The anime Devilman is not merely a passive illustration of the manga, but a work with its own internal logic. One of the most striking aspects in the adaptation of this particular work is its religious approach. In both versions of the myth of Devilman, religion, the human being and the problem of evil are central, but both versions produce its own theological framework.

Before beginning my analysis, however, I should point to the difficulties inherent in the term "devils" or "demons" as presented by Japanese culture and Devilman in particular. Both the manga and the anime are not populated by demons as understood by Judeo-Christian philosophy, but by "oni." Noriko Reider argues that, if certainly the *onis* have a relationship with Western demonology and the history and development of the representation of demons, the truth is that this comparison "falls short of capturing the full idea of these creatures [*onis*]." (2010, 1). Reider describes the *oni* as

> dreadful supernatural beings emerging from the abyss of Buddhist hell to terrify wicked mortals; their grotesque and savage demeanor and form instill instant fear; and their omnipresence in the sociohistorical and cultural archive of Japan is directly attributable to the moral, social, and religious edification. (Ibid)

Yet, the *oni* differentiates from the common demon as understood by Judeo-Christian eschatology. Oni's etymology and formation have evolved from Chinese, Buddhist, Japanese and Onmyōdō theological lines. Some ideas are shared, however: *oni* is informed by negative forces against humanity. Rather than evil, however, they represent fright of harm. Fear in humanity is not only instilled by evil, but also by "the destructive power of phenomenological occurrences such as thunder and lighting, storms and earthquakes" (Reider 2010, 2). As such, *oni*'s imagery is associated with nature and the fear nesting within the human soul in reference to the frailty of human life. One of the most powerful forces of nature, lighting, is heavily associated with the *oni*, highlighting "the threat of potential, instantaneous destruction" (Reider 2010, 23).

It is not coincidence, then, that many of the monsters battling Devilman in the anime are linked with natural phenomena. The demon Gondroma uses its brainwave powers to control animals and push them to attack humans ("Brainwave Demon Gondroma"), Demon Dodo uses avalanches and snow as its main weapons ("Demon of the Snow, Lala"), Kilskey symbolizes the power of meteors ("Demon Kilskey, the Crimson Tornado"), Magdora the burning power of volcanoes and lava ("Demon Magdora, the Flying Lava"), Demon Dremoon personifies the unruly tides ("Demon Dremoon, the Moon is Hell"), while Demon Weather has all the powers of different climates in its arsenal ("Demon Weathers, the Sun's Revolt"). Even the boreal aurora is represented by a demon ("Demon Aurora, the Sparkling Prison"). Further, each episode of Devilman starts with shots of the Himalayas, frozen landscapes barren with cold weather and swept by icy winds. No life, except demons, can live in these frozen spots.

However, it is not so much that *oni* represent nature but the negative forces of destruction that can harm the human sphere. These forces are integral to human existence, but not friendly yet not completely antagonist. The *oni* is best described as indifferent to the human, its "evilness" more a manifestation of this disinterest than a desire to kill and destroy the human. They are gigantic and shapeless, thus reinforcing their association with phenomena of nature such as tornadoes or tsunamis. As such, the *onis* are posthuman in essence, as they basically steal from the human their superior entitlement regarding all other beings in the world. The anime, with its emphasis on animals, natural phenomena and even cruel vegetation ("Demon Woodddou, the Entaged Greenery"; "The Bewitching Scarlet Flower Lafleur") hints at a posthumanist ethos and theology. Yet, the *Devilman* anime firmly follows the Buddhist line of *onis*' imagery: as beings close to Judeo-Christian demons. To the Buddhist theology, the *onis* are creatures habiting Hell and in charge of terrifying sinners (Reider 2010, 10). Further, they are portrayed in some traditions as cannibalistic beings with a huge appetite for human flesh (Reider 2010, 14) and with transformative powers (Reider 2010, 16). Both characteristics are presented in the anime. The different monsters the titular hero battles are able to transform from one shape to another in just seconds. Beautiful women hiding behind a monstrous and evil nature is a recurrent motif within the anime ("Demon Sirène"; "Demon Alron, the Terryfying Maxi Dress"; "Demon General Zannin"). Even Demon Lala, who will turn her back to the Demon Tribe to help Devilman in several episodes, shifts from a beautiful woman to a horrifying hag after a little sneezing.

One of the episodes, "The Silver Mayako," seems directly inspired by a specific *oni*'s myth. In the episode, Mayako, a beautiful young woman, begins to work at a Café attended by Miki and Akira's friends. Her alluring beauty draws male clientele. Soon, young men start killing each other over Mayako. Behind her appearance, the girl is a demon sent by the Demon Tribe to lure humans into doom. One classical tale of *onis*' powers of transformation refers to a monster disguised as a beautiful woman waiting at a bridge. A hero looking for a fable monster which has been terrorizing the area gets trapped into the alluring aspect of the woman who soon reveals its true form: a green monster with disheveled hair.[1]

Yet, encapsulating the *onis* within the sphere of the evil is not completely adequate. It is clear these creatures share many traits with the Western demons, such as the ability (and desire) to harm humans. This belonging, however, is ambiguous, as the *onis* are closer to being troublemakers than evil. Katarzyna Marak, in her study about the differences between American and Japanese horror, establishes an important dichotomy: "In American horror fiction, defined by Christian mythology, demons are generally associated with evil, regardless of their portrayed origin; in contrast, Japanese horror fiction depicts its native demons as amoral –if ever" (Marak 2015, 198). Reider

Noriko addresses the fact that the evil side of the *onis* have been emphasized through history and culture; yet, *onis* "can also be supernatural entities that bring good fortune and wealth" (2010, 25). *Onis* defy definitive categorization—they are ambiguously positioned beyond (or maybe between) Manichean conceptions of good and evil.

At first, it seems that the anime *Devilman* positions the *onis* as unmistakably evil. All the monsters attacking Devilman also provoke great destruction in the city, supposedly killing thousands of innocent people in the process. Even Devilman participates in the destruction, especially in the first episodes. In the series' second episode ("Demon Sirène"), the titular creature battles Devilman within underground tunnels. At one point through the fight, both Sirène and Devilman increase their size to skyscraper level, destroying many buildings, all them presumably occupied with people. In another moment of the fight, Devilman attacks Sirène using an electricity tower as his weapon (tearing it off from the ground), other action that, arguably, affects the lives of the Japanese. In this scenario, it is clear that the anime depicts the *onis* as destructive evil creatures. Yet, as mentioned, forces of nature also sometimes provoke the same level of wreckage as depicted through the series. Further, Devilman is an ambiguous creature that highlights the non-Manichean character of the *onis*. Unlike as told by the manga, Akira is not the combination of man and devil. In the anime, Akira and his father are killed while mountain climbing the Himalayas. After defeating other demons for the "honor" of possessing a human body, Devilman chooses Akira's corpse as his surrogate form. There is no mixing of souls, as Akira is an *oni* using (not possessing) a dead human body. Devilman is purely an *oni*, the human part just a façade. Yet, Devilman, after moving with the Makimuras, falls in love with Miki and abandons his mission of terrorism. Even if he is an *oni*, Devilman is capable of feeling love and empathy for the humans and, in consequence, becomes a force of good. The manga differs from this story, presenting Akira controlling a demon soul as a way to access new levels of power that he will eventually use to put the demon invasion to a halt. Akira sometimes controls and sometimes is controlled by his demonic half, but the human part prevails even in the end, when Akira unleashes a battle he knows he will lose.

These differences between manga and anime do not only affect Akira/Devilman but also the whole cosmology of the stories. Both theological perspectives are encapsulated in the climax of the stories; while in the anime Devilman has saved humanity after becoming too-much-human, the manga's last pages indicate that the human world has came to its definitive end. In brief, humanity prevails in the anime, while the manga discards the human. These differences involve, in turn, different theological approaches: the anime tells its story within a traditional and humanist Buddhist worldview, while the manga favors a posthumanist approach to religion. As we will see in the next section, both theological worldviews share common ground but presents interesting differences regarding how to understand the human in religion.

A WORLD WITHOUT HUMANS, A DEMON TOO-HUMAN: TWO WORLDVIEWS

The manga begins separating the human from the non-human via Manichean imagery of light and dark, normal and monstrous. The story starts with a cosmic battle between the forces of God against demonic forces. While the angels are depicted having anthropocentric features, the demons are deformed beings, monstrous forms with bat wings, sharp teeth and long tentacles. The angels are killed in spectacular and gory detail, their entrails ripped apart by the demons. At the end, calm remains but it is hard to say who has won the battle. This Manichean view that distinguishes between ugly, deformed demons and angelic beings with human appearance is, however, informed by a posthumanist ethos. The angelic beings are hermaphrodite, having female breasts but male genitalia as well. In this scenario, the privilege of the anthropocentric is complicated by the destruction of the binary that sustains most of civilization: the "essential" separation between the sexes. Even Satan is hermaphrodite. At the end of the manga, Ryo acknowledges the fact that he/she/it has fallen in love with Akira.

This flux of gender categories clashes heavily with the first pages of *Devilman*: Akira Fudo is too shy to step up and protects his friend Miki from a gang of bullies. Miki is baffled at Akira's lack of bravado. Miki's attitude is rooted in conservative gender dichotomies that accommodate "essential" traits according the genre: bravado and competitiveness to men, shyness in women. Akira's anti-violent approach to life, however, serves Go Nagai's purpose: to voice an anti-war message.[2] At first, it seems that Akira will become the ultimate warrior after blending with the Demon Amon. Nagai, however, prefers to keep Akira struggling for control rather than falling into violence. *Devilman* stages a battle for humanity embodied in Akira himself, a young man possessed by a demon: if he is able to keep his demonic impulses under control, anyone can. Akira's peaceful philosophy is the mold that will turn him into a hero rather than the other way around, having the shy boy gaining superpowers and smashing everything and everyone around him. The manga is not so much around humanity fighting supernatural demons as humanity fighting (and losing) against inner demons. When fascism starts dominating Japan and obscurantism gains weight, with hordes of humans hunting down and killing anyone suspected of being a demon, humanity fails and falls. The hero's path is not toward sophisticate forms of violence but its reverse, keeping calm and empathy in a world devoid of it.

The pages of *Devilman* follows some precepts from Buddhist doctrines. As explained by Vladimir Tikhonov and Torkel Brekke in their introduction for their edited volume *Buddhism and Violence: Militarism and Buddhism in Modern Asia* (2012), "violence is seen as an endemic evil of the profane world bound by ignorance of truth, attachments and cravings" (2012, 6). A communal social contract is necessary, one that appoints a ruler who will take the burden of punishing wrongdoers as his responsibility. The rest of the community should avoid violence "in action, thought and word" (2012, 7) because violent attitudes led to karmic consequences. Yet, Tikhonov and Brekke warn against the stereotypical Western myth of Buddhist as essentially anti-violence. Indeed, Buddhism eschews violence but also knows that it is part of society and, as such, sometimes "permissible" (2012, 10). Rules and those holding the Law must resort to violence occasionally to keep kinship and internal security.

Buddhism is informed by the logic of the "taming of the demons." Like Akira Fudo, people must struggle with inner demons to keep themselves free from impurity. Yet, as Jacob Dalton argues in *The Taming of the Demons: Violence and Liberation in Tibetan Buddhism*, this taming is mostly only doable through violence (2011, 3). The logic of "taming the inner demons" is central to the anime. As mentioned, Akira is a demon occupying a human body. As such, he starts the TV series as an irascible young man always looking for a good fight. There is little told about the real Akira before his murder, but it is implied he was a nice, peaceful young man. Now, nobody seems to understand his transformation, except as a psychological reaction to his father's death. Miki takes charge of keeping Akira's behavior under control, even if she needs to resort to violence sometimes. In many episodes (especially in the first ones), Miki slaps Akira's face when the young man misbehaves. In the series' first episode ("Resurrection of The Demon Tribe"), Akira hits one of his teachers with his motorcycle. Miki climbs down from Akira's bike and slaps his face, an action she will repeat later in the episode, when she finds that Akira is fighting his classmates. Interestingly, one of the classmates that Akira brutally hits with his belt is a young man who acts like the manga's Akira does. The classmate keeps a peaceful attitude towards Akira, even if the latter is threatening him with violence. Thus, Nagai is able to introduce, briefly, a character that strongly resembles the Akira from the manga's pages.

Miki works as a form of moral conscious, even if she needs resort to violence to keep Akira calm. Following Buddhist's doctrines, there is a Law (Miki) who sometimes needs to exert violence to keep the continuity of peace. Still, she is not the only one "taming the beast." As the episodes unfold and Akira/Devilman becomes more empathic with humans, he is the one trying to keep control. This need for control is not so much to keep his evil from emerging, but to remain calm in situations where his foes are winning the battle. Devilman reaches calm through the use of violence, but now directed to himself. When Devilman feels he is losing concentration due his enemies' powers, as happens in "Brainwave Demon Gondroma," Akira wounds himself with a sharp object or a piece of glass (in gory detail) to keep his senses alert.

After a careful chronological review of the anime, it is clear that Nagai constructed a story that goes from Devilman/Akira as a violent boy to someone not only taking care of humans and other living beings, but also willing to sacrifice himself for the welfare of humans. At first, he only wants to protect Miki, but already in episode 1 Devilman risks his life to save Tare, Miki's little brother. Yet, Devilman battles his foe destroying, in part, the Makimuras' house. In episode two, "Demon Sirène," Devilman destroys part of the city without giving a second thought. In episode three, "Demon General Zannin," Devilman battles Demon Vetra in the middle of the city. While Vetra provokes some damage, Devilman does not use (like he did previously in "Demon Sirène") parts of the city—like houses or electric towers—as weapons. The end of the episode depicts Devilman battling Vetra at the ocean floor and at the skies, leaving the cities untouched. The episode shows explicitly that the battle is taking place far from the city, as the latter is seen disappearing in size as the monsters take their battle away.

Learning to calm is the path to control the body and the mind. Buddish teaching makes emphasis on

> cultivating wholesome mental states and avoiding all unwholesome actions of body, speech and mind. As traditionally conceived, a person practices to purify all mental defilements and accumulate all virtues. In the process, one's self-cherishing and self-grasping attitude becomes transformed from a limited awareness to a universal awareness, from self-centered concern to concern for the welfare of all living beings. (Tsomo 2020, 136)

While the first episodes depict a Devilman only interested on Miki and with little patience for other humans, later episodes showcase a deeper engagement with the human. However, even in later episodes, Akira falls into fits of rage when some situations escalate beyond his control, as when his enemies make Miki a target or when he becomes jealous of men competing for Miki's affections. Iwao Himura, a demon adopting human form, arrives at Nakado Academy and becomes a rival to Akira regarding Miki's love. While Devilman tries to keep his inner monstrosity at bay, Iwao pushes him to the limits. The first time he shows in the series, "The Sleeping Beauty, Zoldova,"

Iwao challenges Akira to a race, a test that Akira foolishly accepts. In "The Terrifying Puppeter Zulu," Akira gets increasingly jealous of Iwao, as the latter paints a portrait of Miki that the girl loves. Akira keeps his fury at bay, even when Iwao kicks him. But when Miki and Iwao leave the art studio, Akira smashes the place, unable to remain calm. He only stops when a demon attacks both Miki and Iwao, and, as such, Devilman is needed.

Yet, as mentioned, violence is integral to the taming of demons and Buddhist theology. As Jacob Dalton explains, the history of violence in Tibet is rooted in a fundamental pairing of myth about demons threatening the cosmos in one hand and the ritual of liberation, binding the demon with compassionate violence, in the other. The "painful irresolvability of violence" (Dalton 2011, 17) lies at the heart of Buddhist doctrines, as killing is sometimes necessary to ensure peace. At the end of each episode, and faithful to the "monster of the week" formula, Devilman kills a demon, but he does so to protect humanity and peace. In this scenario, *Devilman* does not spare blood. In the first episode, the demon sent to kill Miki, an elephantine creature, brutally injures the girl (the level of damage inflicted on Miki remains uncertain, but the blood loss, as exhibited, is profuse). In "The Terrifying Puppeteer Zulu," one of the goriest episodes, the titular demon explicitly addresses how pleasurable is to kill humans in horrifying fashion. A famed sportsman is vertically cut into two halves and an airplane's pilot starts to burn while driving a plane (all the passengers are killed in the process). All this violence is impure and demonic, produced by *onis* with the only goal of torturing Devilman and coercing him to return to the Demon Tribe. It is killing for the pleasure of killing.

The origins of Buddhism lie in rites of coercion and violence, as the great Demon Rudra, married to the Goddess of desire, Krodhvar, and surrounded by terrifying minions, reigns with great power. Rudra wants to plunge the universe into unimaginable suffering. To bring peace, he must be defeated through coercion and violence. Coercion, as told by the myth, is closer to "purification" than compulsion and intimidation, but subjugation is also present in the story: only through the slow replacing of Rudra's demons with buddhas the demon is weakened enough to be defeated via violence (Dalton 2011, 24). Rudra is finally overpowered when a trident is plunged into his chest. Rudra is then revived "as a worldly god bound by powerful oaths to protect the Buddhist teachings" (Dalton 2011, 12).

Like Rudra, Devilman is coerced and tamed in the anime. Miki's recurring slapping of Akira's face functions as a coercive way to keep the boy from taking the path of rage and evil. This is the path that Go Nagai traces for the boy, thus evoking one of the most complex themes from the manga: the control of demons. At the end of the TV series, Devilman has reached a point of empathy that leads him into self-sacrifice. In the episode "Demon Wooddou, the Enraged Greenery" (episode 37 of the thirty-nine-episode-anime), when

Akira transforms in Devilman to protect his friends, he unknowingly reveals his status as *oni* to Tare. After defeating Wooddou, Devilman decides to leave Miki and his family behind, as Tare now knows he is a monster. Rather than coercing or threatening Tare, Devilman takes the path of the hero and chooses self-sacrifice. When Tare wakes up, however, the little kid believes everything has been a dream; thus, Devilman's identity is safe, at least until the last episode, "Demon God, the Miracles of God." Demon God warns Akira not to interfere in its plans of world's domination; otherwise, the creature will reveal Akira's identity to Miki. At first, Devilman accepts and leaves the city plunging into chaos. When Demon God increases his cruel attack on humanity, beginning a massacre, Devilman chooses to interfere, even if this action implies losing Miki's love. Certainly, Devilman reveals himself to Miki, who remains in love with him at the end of the episode. The anime ends in an optimistic note: the Demon Tribe is still active, but the most important aspect of the anime was not so much the "monster of the week" formula as Devilman's path to inner enlightenment.

The main topic in both anime and manga, even with differences in their approach, is the Buddhist philosophy of the taming of the demons and a complex relationship with violence. This engagement with pious forms of violence and self-control informs the anime because both themes were central in the manga. Still, there are differences: in the anime, Devilman follows a path of enlightenment that takes him closer to the human. The manga's theological thinking, in contrast, discards the human completely, privileging instead a posthuman stance.

POSTHUMANIST RHETORIC IN THE MANGA

Every discussion on posthumanism must begin with references to the way in which Western thought has constructed life through the politics of humanism and the anthropocene, both theoretical constructions that try to describe reality in terms of human superiority. Our comprehension of common reality (the world we live in) had been shaped through history by social and cultural institutions and discourses. The entire Western thought was dominated by humanist conceptions of the individual through a negotiation of sameness and difference. In other words, humanity and human beings were socially and cultural "constructed" via negative difference and politics of exclusion. Humanist ontology established that human characteristics were built on the difference against all that was not human: the environment, animals, plants, and machines, all of them coded as objects to serve humans. There is a radical alterity that presents humanity as superior—via "essential" traits such as intelligence or souls—to all things no human (of course, these "essential" things were also naturalized cultural constructions). Thus, following this logic, animals and entire landscapes can be exploited due to their inferiority to humanity: all that is considered non-human must serve, as objects, the social progress of humanity. This shift to "nonhuman objects" implies the loss of inherent rights, thus becoming "the Other," more specifically, "things, no-things, or, simply, nothing." (Stalwood 2016, 195). Through the anthropocentric turn, man becomes the measure against any living thing must be measured.

Posthumanism offers a faultless illustration of Foucault's critique of humanism in *The Order of Things* in which "man" is just a discursive construction, "no more than a kind of rift in the order of things" and as such, doomed to disappear: man is "a recent invention, a figure not yet two centuries old, a wrinkle in our knowledge, and that he will disappear again as soon as that knowledge has discovered a new form" (1974, xxiii). To the politics of posthumanism, humans are just another species sharing the world with animals and plants. As Robert Pepperell explains: "Post-Humanism is not about the 'End of Man' but about the end of a 'man-centered' universe or, put less phallocentrically, a 'human-centered' universe" (1995, 176).

As told in the manga, the Demon Tribe was present during the Earth's Mesozoic Era and, as such, predated the coming of humans. They were those "ruling the Earth" centuries before the first human starts to take shape. This image is posthuman in nature, as it presumes that the human came later; the demons are not a figment of human imagination, but an important part of life in the planet.

As told by Ryo to a stunned Akira, the demons fought each other and acquired some traits that make them survive through millennia. One of these aspects involve another posthumanist turn: the ability to assimilate the aspect of any other living thing. As such, demons were able to pass as animals, vegetation and humans. As depicted by *Devilman*, demons are posthuman beings capable of shifting from one category to the next: they are non-anthropocentric, deformed beings with deep links with the animal and vegetal world. Rather than producing a great schism between the human and all other forms of life, the demons mix with the Otherness, becoming one. As such, they were able to survive, even if trapped in the ice of the Himalayas. Global warming has thwarted the ice and now the demons are free to conquer the planet. In brief, human disinterest for the environment has produced the demise of humanity, a sort of "dark ecology" as proposed by Timothy Morton (2016): the awareness that we are living in a dying world, slowly killed by our own hands.

The manga emphasizes the responsibility of humans on the deterioration of kinship and community. When humans learn about the presence of demons walking among them, suspicions and paranoia arise. Akira's fears of retaliation soon become reality when citizens from Japan starts a witch hunt looking for "suspicious" neighbors. At the end, humanity is revealed as the real monster. *Devilman*'s volume three opens with a classmate of Akira informing his friends about news on global famine, overpopulation and potential apocalypse. All these fears were easily recognizable for readers at the time, as the 1970s and first years of the 1980s were informed by fears of global overpopulation. There is a shift, both in popular culture as in society, from the concerns on nuclear bombing of the post-Second World War to "a growing concern with domestic, terrestrial issues—most of which are related to totalitarian government control of people's lives or over-population, food shortages, pollution, and ecology" (Sobchack 2007, 82). The change of subject from the previous two volumes seems abrupt at first, as the themes of environmental concerns are not mentioned earlier. However, these new anxieties about the fate of Earth are deeply connected with the posthuman opening of the first volume: humankind is only secondary to life on Earth. As such, humankind is a virus, a parasite that must be exterminated. The same classmate who voices his worries about human overpopulation also wonders on why humanity lacks its own depredator. He is mistaken: humans are the predators of humans.

Akira thinks that humanity must be protected since it has progressed through the centuries right up to the point of reaching new heights of civilization. Still, he acknowledges that non-human animals became extinct due human's actions (Nagai 2002 vol. 3, 19). As such, human's extinction is not an "evil" for the planet, the latter facing painful and slow ecocide. Yet, Akira feels his war against the Demon Tribe makes sense (Nagai 2002 vol. 3, 20). It is interesting that Akira does not offer any insightful reason about why humanity needs to be saved. Akira belongs to the human race and, as such, he finds reasons of privilege. Volume three ends, however, with Ryo predicting that humans will become the predator of other humans (Nagai 2002 vol. 3, 192).

Indeed, the last two volumes shift their focus from the *onis* as the main antagonists toward humans behaving as monsters, hunting and killing without giving much thought anyone suspected of being a demon. A parallelism with fascism is clear, especially in scenes of armed neighbors irrupting houses of people deemed suspect to take them away. In the last volume, Ryo reveals himself as Satan, the extermination of humanity via a new rise of fascism his plan all along. For Satan, humanity must be erased so Earth may see a new era with no humans behind the stars (Nagai 2002 vol. 5, 71). A planet predicated on the absolute absence of the human is what Timothy Morton calls "dark ecology" through a word play with deep ecology. Deep ecology was derived mainly from philosophical and social criticism and authors such as Henry David Thoreau, John Muir or Aldous Huxley. Theology was another source of inspiration as ecological consciousness of the Deep Ecology movement "can be traced to the ecocentric religions and ways of life of primal peoples around the world, and to Taoism, Saint Francis of Assisi, the Romantic Nature-oriented countercultural movement of the nineteenth century with its roots in Spinoza, and the Zen Buddhism [specially the principles of non violence against any living thing] of Alan Watts and Gary Snyder" (Sessions 1995, ix).

Deep Ecology is holistic in essence. It does not separate the human from other aspects of Nature such as vegetal/animal life or landscapes; neither establishes hierarchies enthroning the human as the measurement of all living things. Through care for the environment, theology "is thus reconciled not only with nature and with the cosmic world from which it was always distanced and to which it was blind, but is restated in ecological terms and in depth" (Vigil 2010, 183). This "new" ecotheology, born amidst the gloom-and-doom landscape of the 1960s, is concerned with spiritual attitudes of respect towards biodiversity.

Still, as Emmanouil Aretoulakis (2014) argues, Deep Ecology is still humanist insofar as it presupposes a harmonious mixing of humans and the no-human through a complete whole. Timothy Morton's "dark ecology," in the other hand, is interested in the ecosphere without the intermingling of the human. It is a kind of ecology predicated *upon the death of the human*. The nihilistic dark ecology sees humanity as a disease that should be eradicated since it destroys the fabric of life with wars and pollution. We might consider modes of deconstruction in which the future is not hospitable and affirmative since there "is no shortage of data regarding the possible or inevitable absence of humans" (Morton 2016, 44): terrorism, new sophisticate forms of war and climate change predict apocalyptic scenarios. Dark ecology, then, is the cohabitation of the human with the awareness that the planet is (due to human action), dying. Death becomes inextricably linked to life and the frailty of the ecosphere, all of them inseparable from each other. Dark ecology is a negative eco-philosophy/theology predicated upon a world where death is a grim companion to the everyday and, as such, oppositional to the Christian imaginary of man as the measurement of all things; "any puny human was an absurd contingency, not the godlike meaning of it all" (Garrard et al. 2019, 168). God will not come to save us, so we all are left living in a world reaching death.

Akira tries to save humanity but, in the anime's last volume, Miki is killed by enraged mobs, unleashing Devilman's hopeless onslaught against both humans and demons. At the end, the battle is won by Satan. Nagai dedicates the last pages to a tender scene of Ryo/Satan talking lovely to Akira's corpse. Akira was the only victim that Satan did not planned, as he fell in love with the young man. Further, Satan made his best attempts to make Akira realizes that humanity is the error in the world: only with the death of the human the planet can live in peace.

The end of Devilman is not a bleak one, if readers interpret it from the perspective of posthumanist, a philosophical framework that is inextricably linked with Buddhism. Everything having equal value is a doctrine that shares both, deep ecology and Buddhism. The difference in Devilman lies in the fact that Nagai, at the end, lends himself to dark ecology, the complete eradication of the human.

CONCLUSIONS

The doctrines of Buddhism are rooted in both versions of Devilman: manga and anime. Yet, both stories take different approaches. The anime lends more to the taming of inner demons, as Akira/Devilman learns to empathize with the human. The story is all about controlling inner rage and learning to free the mind (and, subsequently, the soul), from impurities as a way to avoid karma. With this approach, however, the series enthrones the human. As a *oni*, a being that represents the natural phenomena, Devilman is the non-human. Yet, he learns how to be human. This shift comes vis-à-vis with goodness: being human is being good and, as such, Devilman becomes both: human and a good being through acts of control and self-sacrifice.

Self-control, so important for the Buddhist religion, is central to the manga, as Akira must control the Demon Amon to defend the world. Still, as the series progresses, Nagai slowly peels the multiple layers, insinuating at first that the human is not the most important and, in the last volumes, unpacking his main posthumanist thesis: his heart sides with the non-human. The multiple mentions to animals being annihilated by the human open the path to a new speciesism: the planet, like the animals, is the victim of humans. As such, Nagai takes Buddhist rhetoric to the extremes: rather than the human having the same value that animals or plants, humanity is coded a virus, a sickness. Like a parasite, humanity must be destroyed. The end of the anime is not a bleak one, as humanity must fall so new forms of life can spring and start anew.

Both anime and manga presented worldviews that share many elements, while others oppose each other. Devilman is a rich case of adaptation where the source and the adapted works basically share the same time and yet, are works with their own logic.

REFERENCES

Aretoulakis, Emmanouil. 2014. "Towards a Posthumanist Ecology." *European Journal of English Studies*, 18:2 (2014):172–190.
Dalton, Jacob. 2011. *The Taming of the Demons: Violence and Liberation in Tibetan Buddhism*. New Haven: Yale University Press.
Davis, Winston. 1992. *Japanese Religion and Society*. New York: State University of New York Press.
Foucault, Michel. 1974. *The Order of Things: An Archeology of the Human Sciences*. Anonymous translation. New York: Random House.
Garrard, Greg, et al. 2019. *Climate Change Scepticism: A Transnational Ecocritical Analysis*. London: Bloomsbury.
Grüner, Eduardo. 2006. *El Sitio de la Mirada: Secretos de la Imagen y Silencios del Arte*. Buenos Aires: Norma.
"Entrevista de l'auteur." n/d. Accessed May 13, 2021. https://www.manga-news.com/index.php/auteur/interview/NAGAI-Go.
Marak, Katarzyna. 2015. *Japanese and American Horror: A Comparative Study of Film, Fiction, Graphic Novels and Video Games*. Jefferson, McFarland.
Morton, Timothy. 2016. *Dark Ecology: For a Logic of Future Coexistence*. New York: Columbia University Press.
Nagai, Go. 2002. *Devilman*. Tokio: Kōdansha.
Pepperell, Robert. 1995. *The Post-Human Condition*. Exeter: Intellect Books.
Reider, Noriko. 2010. *Japanese Demon Lore: Oni from Ancient Times to the Present*. Logan: Utah State University Press.
Sessions, Georges. 1995. "Preface." In *Deep Ecology for the Twenty-First Century*, edited by Georges Sessions, ix-xxviii. Colorado: Shambhala.
Sobchack, Vivian. 2007. "Cities on the Edge of Time: The Urban Science Fiction Film." In *Liquid Metal: The Science Fiction Film Reader*, edited by Sean Redmond, 78–87. New York: Wallflower Press.
Stalwood, Kim. 2016. "Utopian Visions and Pragmatic Politics Challenging the Foundations of Speciesism and Misothery." In *Animal Rights: The Changing Debate*, edited by Robert Garner, 194-208. New York: New York University Press.
Tikhonov, Vladimir and Torkel Brekke. 2012. "Introduction." In *Buddhism and Violence: Militarism and Buddhism in Modern Asia*, edited by Vladimir Tikhonov and Torkel Brekke. New York: Routledge.
Tsomo, Karma. 2020. *Women in Buddhist Traditions*. New York: New York University Press.
Vigil, José María. 2010. "The Seductive Future of Theology." In *Toward a Planetary Theology: Along the Many Paths of God*, edited by José María Vigil, 180–188. Montreal: Dunamis.

NOTES

1. There is a green monster with transformative powers (albeit with no hair) in the episode "Demon of the Snow, Lala." For more in this particular folk tale, see Reider, *Japanese Demon Lore*, 16.
2. See "Entrevista de l'auteur." n/d. https://www.manga-news.com/index.php/auteur/interview/NAGAI-Go.

PART 3

Cultural Flows

Chapter 11

The Transpacific Complicity of J-Horror and Hollywood

Seán Hudson

THE REMAKE ECONOMY: A DIVISION OF LABOR

It has been argued that the concept of globalization in film studies is sometimes just a more egalitarian-sounding way of describing what are essentially the transforming methods employed by Hollywood (the film industry of the USA) to maintain hegemony over global markets and cultures (Miller et al. 2001). In the case of the J-horror boom of the late 1990s and 2000s, one might argue that "global success" only became apparent once Hollywood became involved in remaking the original Japanese films, despite the fact that J-horror cinema first flourished by inspiring producers, creators, and distributors in the East Asian sphere, and then began making waves in European film festivals and finding distribution outlets there—all before Hollywood took note. For this reason, J-horror is often framed as an example of global flows working against traditional regional hierarchies of power; in other words, as a rare example of Japanese cinema invading both global markets and the workings of the American film industry (Wada-Marciano 2009).

However, once Hollywood did become involved, a fascinating collaborative process between Japan and America began which marked a new phase of the J-horror phenomenon, and which, far from being a one-sided appropriation of Japanese culture, was predicated on a system of exchange and a cultural division of labor, what one could call a remake economy. An investigation of this arrangement reveals power dynamics in the cultural and material processes of globalization which are rather different from those usually described in discussions of film and globalization. I find that the more usual term "remake industry" places too much emphasis on Hollywood's role of repetition and production, whereas "economy" implies not only a mutually agreed upon system of exchange, but also the attachment of specific yet arbitrary value to the units of exchange. In the case at hand, these units are not just films, but also aesthetics, images, and even national identities, as I will show.

Hollywood and East Asian genre cinema have a shared history of being inspired by (or purloining from) each other, such as in the back and forth borrowing between Hong Kong and Hollywood action films, as well as Kurosawa Akira's samurai *jidaigeki* films and American Westerns (not to mention the translation of *Kakushi Toride no San Akunin / The Hidden Fortress* [Akira Kurosawa 1958] into the international sci-fi hit *Star Wars* [George Lucas, 1977]). However, as copyright laws became stronger and international cinema more available to the public, these kinds of unofficial cultural exchanges became less easy. In this context we can retell J-horror's global success story as beginning with Roy Lee, an American film producer born to South Korean parents, who developed a method that would redefine Hollywood's role in East Asian cinema. Lee would travel to East Asia to approach filmmakers who had had a hit in their own countries, convince them that their film would not do well in the international market (due to the fact that audiences do not like reading subtitles, etc.), but that they could make a greater profit by selling him the rights to their film instead. His first hit using this tactic was the Hollywood remake *The Ring* (Gore Verbinski, 2002), which ensured the continuation of the method in the following years. On the Japanese side, the producer Ichise Takashige, who had invested heavily in the J-horror boom by financing much of its domestic output since the success of the original *Ringu/Ring* (Hideo Nakata, 1998), saw the opportunities of not only selling story rights but also becoming involved in the production of Hollywood remakes, and so began producing projects in Japan with the aim of eventually producing their more profitable remakes in America, too (Schilling 2004). Ichise's importance to the boom is such that one could even delineate the timeframe of J-horror according to the major dates in the history of Ichise's production company, Oz: launched in 1989; enjoyed great success in the late 1990s and early 2000s; and bankrupt in 2012. In 2006, though, Ichise made a three-year deal with the Hollywood studio 20th Century Fox, allowing Ichise to offer American financing for domestic Japanese film projects (La Porte et al. 2006).

While the actual number of Hollywood remakes of horror films from East Asia since then is relatively low (what qualifies as a remake is sometimes arguable, but at an estimate there are around fifteen such films), what is significant is the nature of this new model for transnational productions, which also impacted the production of domestic film industries. In general, for every film that is realized, there are countless negotiations and collaborations towards projects that never make it to the big screen: it is the development of this process of production that is our focus here. Effectively, through producers like Lee and Ichise, Hollywood was now putting a new financial pressure on East Asian and especially Japanese horror filmmakers: if they could provide fresh and original films, they could make a lot of money through selling the rights to Hollywood, or even better, through a Hollywood coproduction. Ironically, when Hollywood did make use of the story rights it had bought, it would engage in "cultural transposition" to try and make the films more accessible, while utilizing the label of "J-Horror remake" as a selling point. The remake economy thus demanded firstly Japanese creativity and national specificity, and secondly Hollywood homogenization for a domestic American audience and an international audience.

As other commentators have noticed, the audience for Hollywood films had already been primed for the atmospheric, supernatural horror that J-horror became renowned for. While the output of horror films at this time were mostly low quality, violent slasher films, the rare horror hits which gained both commercial and critical acclaim among Western audiences had a slower pace and a focus on ghosts or other invisible menaces, as seen in independent film *The Blair Witch Project* (Myrick and Sánchez, 1999), Hollywood's *The Sixth Sense* (Night Shyamalan, 1999), and the English-language Spanish film *The Others* (Alejandro Amenábar, 2001) (Rose 2002). The cultural climate of globally successful horror cinema was thus well-prepared for what Hollywood's producers might otherwise have branded "unsellable" Asian films due to their cultural specificity. Even so, this specificity, beginning with the language but extending to narrative, cinematography, casting, etc., all had to be reconfigured so as to appear less "Asian" or less "Japanese" and more "universal." This method is evidenced by the resulting films and how they compare to their Asian counterparts, which has been a point of interest in both fan discourse and academic research on J-horror (e.g., Lee 2011; Balmain 2008). Thus the conceptual framework of the remake economy has the effect of regionalizing images and styles of filmmaking into two categories, "the West and the rest," thereby contributing to, amongst other things, the conflation of Asia and Japan in filmic discourse on modern horror cinema. This dichotomy goes some way in explaining why, despite the relevance of the atmospheric horror made popular by the non-Asian contemporary supernatural hits listed above, that context was elided in most discourses (marketing and critical) surrounding the remakes of Japanese and later other Asian horror films.

While much has been written about the aesthetic and cultural impacts of the remake economy, very little has been said of the framing of Hollywood as culturally universalistic and Japan as culturally specific sites of production, nor of the regional divisions of labor between Japanese and American producers that took place. This is likely due to the dichotomy that frames discussions regarding the globalization of popular culture. The first half of the dichotomy focuses on the decentralization of power and the rise of either images produced by "peripheral regions" or images that have become non-regionalizable in their pervasive diffusion, such as those discussed in Vera Mackie's paper on the exportation of Japan's "gothic Lolita" fashion, a process she refers to as "transnational bricolage" (Mackie 2009). The second half of the dichotomy focuses on the ways in which the culturally dominant or "central region" of the West has had to make only minor concessions to further its hegemonic influence on the global stage (e.g., Miller et al. 2001). While both approaches are often interested in the weakening of bonds between images and their regions of origin, the conclusions they reach about how this modern transformation effects flows of power seem somewhat irreconcilable. Are the peripheries eroding the center, or is the center invading the peripheries? Writing about the rise of a global-Japanese cinema must be considered within the context of the tension between these two approaches. While I do not think there is a simple way to reconcile them, I believe that there is a danger in depicting globalized popular culture as primarily a boundary-effacing force, as both of these approaches do. That is to say that whether globalization is depicted as a democratizing process in which various cinemas can flourish or a strategic maneuver in which Hollywood effects its hegemony by losing its foreignness and becoming a global norm, both cases take the disintegration of national boundaries as a given. This is also the case when the cautious position of global flows of power "going both ways" is suggested (e.g., Lowenstein 2009). I believe that introducing the work of Naoki Sakai into the study of Japanese popular cinema is revelatory in its depiction of how globalization has the effect of consolidating old discourses of power between nations, thereby reinforcing rather than opposing the national.

TRANSPACIFIC COMPLICITY: A CULTURAL CONTINUITY WITH POSTWAR IDEOLOGY

To better understand how Sakai's work applies to J-horror, I will summarize his argument for "transpacific complicity" between the USA and Japan as an organizing framework for the production of regional knowledge. This framework traces back the formation of the contemporary power dynamic between the United States and Japan to the immediate postwar period. At this time, following the wartime form of Japanese imperialist ideology, the rewriting of that hierarchically multiculturalist, "Pan-Asia" narrative became an imperative for two groups: the USA, who needed Japan to function as a secure, self-sufficient satellite for the approaching Cold War, and Japanese nationalists who wanted to emphasize the authority of the Emperor, the uniqueness of the Japanese people, and, ironically, the oppressive colonialist attitude of America in Japan. As such, knowledge "was produced and reproduced to replace the integrationist logic of a multiethnic nationality by the exclusionary logic of ethnic singularity" (Sakai 2010 b, 247). This led to an "international division of labor" being instituted, in which the USA would continue "to legitimate its polity in terms of universalism," while Japan would give up this role in order to be a "particularistic counterpart" to the USA (Sakai 2010 b, 252–253). This binary relation positions Japanese culturalism (whether in the form of domestic nationalism, Orientalist discourse, assumptions of a clearly bounded "national cinema," and so on) as a supporting pillar of American hegemony in East Asia. Even anti-American nationalist sentiment in Japan argues for things such as cultural or militaristic "independence" from America, an aim which only furthers the particular-universal discourse of power and does nothing to challenge American hegemony in East Asia (Tanaka 2017). (Contrast this with the anti-American sentiment in Okinawa, which also targets the national government for their complicity in maintaining the bases.)

Under a simplistic postcolonial framework, the remake economy might be seen as an American exploitation of Japanese culture and creativity, which in some cases utilizes Orientalist prejudices and images of the country whose films it is profiting from. Roy Miller's concept of "self-Orientalism" goes some way in problematizing this framework (Iwabuchi 1994, 209), and might seem an ideal term to describe the Japanese producers and filmmakers who take part in these processes. However, reinscribing Japan as simultaneously Orientalized and self-Orientalizing only superficially challenges the problematic oppressor-oppressed binary, and retains its basic structure. On the other hand, when the relationship is viewed using the lens of transpacific complicity, one can see that the encouragement of Japanese creativity by Japanese and American producers is itself part of a wider, entrenched dynamic that values both nationalistic, culture-specific symbols of Japan and their status as currency within a universalist American hegemony.

For example, when the director Higuchinsky (the notably non-Japanese-sounding alias for Higuchi Akihiro) made the surreal J-Horror *Uzumaki* (2000), he reportedly said, "I wanted to make a film like *Star Wars*, but I realised that because I'm Japanese, I should do something different" (Kalat 2007, 87). His "realization" that Japanese horror films should be "different" as opposed to Hollywood's "sameness" must be understood in the context of transpacific complicity, especially given that *Uzumaki* was financially supported by Omega Project, a Japanese company focused on producing J-horror films for an international market (Kalat 2007, 91). Films like *Uzumaki*, based on the Ito Junji manga about a Japanese village cursed by recurring images of spirals, would then fuel the "weird Japan" stereotypes in marketing and critical writing, which figured J-horror not only as an exotic other to Hollywood (Dew 2007), but also Japan as the creative *source* of that difference. As well as Higuchinsky, various Japanese filmmakers have mentioned the new incentive towards originality after the success of Hollywood's *The Ring* (Zahlten and Kimata 2005). While Shimizu Takashi and Nakata Hideo were hired to direct Hollywood remakes of their own J-horror originals, in a domestic context there have been limited opportunities for Japanese horror directors like Higuchinsky to make their "films like *Star Wars*." When asked in an interview if he would like to make large-scale, action-oriented films in the style of Hollywood, J-horror auteur Kurosawa Kiyoshi responded, "Honestly, I would love to one day," but claimed he was simply unable to do so for lack of money (Kirkham 2016).

As mentioned, academic responses to the globalization of Japanese popular culture tend to emphasize the rise of regional cultures to the level of global culture, which is indeed an important effect of globalization. For example, Wada-Marciano frames the remake economy as a reversal of cultural flows (from Japan to America rather than from America to Japan), thereby figuring the remake economy as part of a process of the decentralization of power from the center of Hollywood to the periphery region of Japan (Wada-Marciano 2009, 32). While this is true, the image it creates obscures the primarily political power relation between America and Japan—transpacific complicity—which contains and in many ways dictates the new flows that emerged in the remake economy. In fact, these new flows, and what Wada-Marciano calls evidence of a "new geography" in film production and distribution (Wada-Marciano 2009, 32), fall neatly into what Sakai describes as an "old cartographic imaginary" of flows of knowledge between a centralized "West" and its peripheral areas (Sakai 2010 a, 28). He claims this old cartographic imaginary consists of two complementary flows:

> The first is a centripetal flow of "raw" and particularistic factual data from peripheral sites to various metropolitan centers "in the West." The second is a centrifugal flow of "advanced" information about how to classify domains of knowledge, how to evaluate given empirical data, how to negotiate with the variety and incommensurability inherent in the body of empirical data from the peripheries, and how to render intelligible to "a Western audience" the peculiarities and trivia coming from particular peripheral sites. (Sakai 2010 a, 27–28)

While Sakai is referring to academic knowledge in this case, his model is quite suitable for understanding the J-horror remake economy. Wada-Marciano and similar-minded academics are correct in pointing out the increase in centripetal flows and new possibilities that entails, but this greater emphasis on Japanese productivity and creativity conforms to a hegemonic structure that dictates what role periphery regions play (providing cultural "peculiarities") and what role the center region plays (translating or "rendering intelligible" those peculiarities into a "universal" Western format). Whether the critic sees Hollywood as exploiting Japanese cinema or sees a reversal of power and influence in which Hollywood reacts to Japanese productions, in both cases the critic fails to point out how the flows of particularized Japanese films and their American translations are part of a regionalizing network of power that is of political origin. Similarly, while critics have taken note of the ways in which remakes of J-horror films reveal differences in cultural expectations, most fail to point out how these remakes work within a framework of, and contribute to the global cultural image of, a peripheral-particular Japan interacting with a central-universal America.

PRODUCTIVE TEXTS: CREATIVE JAPAN AND COMFORTABLE AMERICA

One possible counterargument would be to highlight that the American studio involved with *The Grudge* (Takashi Shimizu 2004), the most commercially successful Hollywood remake alongside *The Ring*, was Columbia Pictures, a subsidiary of the Japanese conglomerate corporation Sony. The argument would be that Sony's position puts Japan at "the center" of the Hollywood filmmaking apparatus after all, or at least offers an instance of the remake economy working against the dominant structures of regional hegemony. However, in the context of filmmaking, Sony's relationship to the Hollywood *Grudge* series of remakes is more of an ironic coincidence than an example of Japanese corporate influence in the sphere of the American film industry. To understand why, we must understand Sony's history with Hollywood: in 1989, during the short-lived period of Japan's economic asset bubble, Sony bought Colombia Pictures, one of the major film studios of Hollywood. This move was indeed of great significance in the early days of corporate globalization, and it remains an example of the way in which globalization de-territorialized the traditional flows of power. Tezuka Yoshiharu writes that it not only "heralded the globalization of Japanese film finance" but also "marked the beginning of the conglomeration of media corporations and the era of a global culture industry" (Tezuka 2012, 3–4). However, the economic asset bubble collapsed in early 1992, coincidentally (or not, as some have argued [Wada-Marciano 2009, 16]) around the start of the J-horror movement in Japan. This marked the end of the time in which Japanese companies sought to buy up powerful American assets such as film studios, and so Sony's position of ownership is not reflective of the changes that took place during the remake economy of the 2000s.

Furthermore, Sony has no involvement in the production side of Columbia Pictures or its other American studio, Sony Pictures. The main players in the production of *The Grudge* were figures like Roy Lee, Ichise Takashige, and Sam Raimi of the newly formed independent American Studio Ghost House Pictures. Sam Raimi's brand image, heavily tied to the film's marketing, in a sense prefigured the status-shift of *The Grudge* and J-horror films in general: originally famous for directing *The Evil Dead* (1981), an icon of low-budget, creative independent horror cinema, Raimi had recently directed the Hollywood blockbuster *Spider-Man* (2002), helping to reignite popular interest in high-budget superhero spectacles and introducing his name to a younger audience. When *The Grudge* transitioned from Japanese film to American film it followed this trajectory, and so was able to appeal to both cult and mainstream audiences. Without going into the film's content, we can see how both the division of labor in the film's production and the final product sold to audiences therefore functioned under the same image: Japanese creative material in the service of Hollywood's global role as entertainer. The success of the film only further propagated the necessity of these roles amongst audiences and filmmakers, in which Japan provided originality and Japan-specificity, and Hollywood provided familiarity, spectacle, and a global platform.

The paradox of the remake economy is that it pressured Japanese filmmakers to produce original or "different" content, while at the same time pressuring Hollywood filmmakers to translate that original content into a familiar, homogenized framework. This can be understood as an effect of the framework of transpacific complicity that exists between Japan and America, and more generally as the "West and the rest" dichotomy that influences the globalization of regional cultures. While some commentators have framed the increasing use of the "Japan-specific" image within global popular culture as evidence of a pushback or Orientalist/nationalist reaction to the forces of globalization, Chika Kinoshita suggests that rather than evidence of friction within a global-local dichotomy, the Japan-specificity of the J-horror discourse shows that "globalization is constitutive of local culture" (Kinoshita 2009, 122). When we examine the financial logic of the remake economy, we can see material and ideological examples of how this constitution takes place. What must be taken into account is not only the constitutive power of globalization on both Japanese and international popular culture, but also the way in which it reinforces and re-creates an older regional distinction between the West as center and Japan as periphery. In this specific context, we can also say that globalization is not opposed to but constitutive of culturalist ideologies like Orientalism and Japanese nationalism.

The transpacific complicity of the remake economy has not only been a determining factor in the production and distribution of J-horror in Japan and abroad, but also in retrospectively manufacturing the status of Japanese horror auteurs. Tsuruta Norio's trajectory is revealing in this respect: he first directed the influential *Honto ni Atta Kowai Hanashi / Scary True Stories* (1991, 1992) on a tiny budget from Japan Home Video for a domestic audience, then struggled to find work; he was later considered as a potential director for *Ringu / Ring* but was passed over due to his lack of filmmaking experience (Zahlten and Kimata 2005); during the J-horror boom he was asked by *Ring* scriptwriter Takahashi Hiroshi to direct *Ringu Zero: Bāsudei / Ring 0: Birthday* (Tsuruta, 2000) (Zahlten and Kimata 2005); and then by producer Ichise Takashige to direct the "original story" of *Yogen / Premonition* (Tsuruta, 2004) which was then remade as a thriller in Hollywood (Zahlten and Kiamta 2005); and finally asked by American producer and director Mick Garris to direct a television film as part of his *Masters of Horror* series, which resulted in *Dream Cruise* (Tsuruta 2007) (Kehr 2006). His career and auteur status have thus bloomed in tandem with the global success of J-Horror, rather than due to the creative content of his films, which have consistently garnered mild critical approval at best.

Let us re-summarize this career trajectory in a broader context: when J-horror was in its formative stage in the 1990s Tsuruta was respected by the directors and filmmakers he had inspired, but failed to find work due to his "inexperience." When J-horror boomed at the turn of the millennium, he was invited onto projects and discursively reinstated as a horror auteur by the Japanese filmmakers and producers who recognized his role in their successes. Finally, during the remake economy of the 2000s, he was marketed as a "master of horror" internationally, both as part of Ichise's "J-Horror Theatre" labeled series of films (2004–2010) and as part of Garris's *Masters of Horror* television film series (2005–2007). In other words, the transformations in the cultural image of Tsuruta as Japanese auteur have been effected in the first place by changes in market and industry practices in Japan and America, which in turn are expressions of the power relation of transpacific complicity.

From this perspective, Garris's *Masters of Horror* series is also interesting in two other ways: how it presents Japanese auteurs alongside their American counterparts, and how those auteurs have followed Shimizu's *The Grudge* in adapting their styles to make J-horror films for an American audience. The second case will be examined closely in the next section. As for the first case, Japanese auteur Miike Takashi was invited to direct the final film of the first season of *Masters of Horror*, and Tsuruta was invited to direct the final film of the second and final season. With the exception of Hungarian Peter Medak and Italian Dario Argento, all of the other directors were American. In addition, unlike the Japanese films, the others were shot and set in America, obscuring Medak and Argento's signs of foreignness. However, by including one representative of Japan per season, the use of regional context as a structuring device becomes apparent. Either the "masters" are chosen based on the quality of their work regardless of region and the Japanese directors just happen to have been awarded parallel positions in the programming, or an unusual kind of regional imaginary is being used to determine the show's content. The former seems unlikely given the clear image of a "Westerners-plus-one-Japanese" line-up for each season, as well as the specific placement of each Japanese film as the final film of each season. What this format suggests then is indeed a new regional imaginary ostensibly based on horror auteurship, with the new auteurs of J-horror being invited into the ranks of American horror auteurs, much as the remake economy was figured as an integration of specific J-horror aesthetics and filmmakers into general American cinema—with the condition in both cases that Japanese-ness is marked and differentiated from the whole.

Positioning the Japanese films at the end of each season has the advantage of multiple connotations: the "grand finale" that provides an affective climax overshadowing the earlier films; but also the addendum or appendix, existing outside of the main content as "bonus material" or an afterthought. While the former connotation furthers a cultural narrative that exalts the superior qualities of J-horror and Japanese genius, the latter connotation keeps it at a wary distance by positioning it as an "outside" of the American television series—but both connotations construct a regional imaginary in which Japanese horror is fundamentally different from general American content, and in which the Japaneseness of the work is emphasized by its repeated placement in the programming schedule. The Americanness of the other works, however, remains unmarked and therefore universal, in contrast to the national specificity assigned to Miike's and Tsuruta's films. Dario Argento and Peter Medak's entries are haphazardly mixed in with the others, showing their equal status as "one of the boys." Alternative programming schedules could have placed the Japanese films haphazardly among the American ones, or invited auteurs from a larger variety of countries to participate, and so on, so why this particular configuration of Westerners-plus-one-Japanese? As a cultural text, the programming schedule of *Masters of Horror* clearly demonstrates the hegemonic status of the "old cartographic imaginary" in the way it organizes the representation of J-horror as a marked national-cultural region attached to an unmarked American universalizable region.

THE SHIMIZU FORMULA: TRANSPACIFIC COMPLICITY EMBODIED IN FILMIC CONTENT (*DREAM CRUISE, BLONDE KAIDAN,* **AND** *SHUTTER*)

In fact, the *Masters of Horror* programming schedule was never fully actualized as a televised viewing experience, as the Miike film ultimately was not aired due to its violent content (it was later made available as a DVD) (Kehr 2006). That film was notable for following the formula of Shimizu's Hollywood remake *The Grudge* in having a white American protagonist facing terrors in a Japanese context—specifically an American journalist searching for a Japanese prostitute during the 1800s (it departs from J-horror conventions, as Miike normally does, by eschewing contemporary urbanity and including scenes of violence). Tsuruta's film, *Dream Cruise* (2007) also followed the formula of a white American protagonist in Japan, presumably on the assumption that audiences will better relate to characters that look, act, and speak like them, and that its main audience would indeed be white Americans. However, this thematic formula also clearly derives from the image of universality associated with American protagonists established by Hollywood's global hegemony. We must therefore consider what functions it serves within filmic narratives and as an image being reproduced in global popular culture.

At the turn of the millennium, the success of J-horror had led to a new combination of Western audiences becoming fascinated with Eastern horror, and this fascination was aligned with Orientalist discourses in order to market DVDs and so on (Dew 2007). However, this new cultural image of Westerners coming into contact with a mysterious, terrifying East would soon be appropriated by J-horror filmmakers themselves. In a strange twist, the audience-spectacle, consumer-producer, Westerner-Asian binaries that had been conflated to sell J-horror became filmic content themselves. The most successful iteration of this image came in Shimizu Takashi's Hollywood remake of his own J-horror original, *The Grudge*. His positioning of Western protagonists coming into contact with a haunted Japan was a winning formula, and another example of how the aesthetics of J-horror embodied the material processes of their reproduction (much has already been made of the affinity between the J-horror ghost as technological virus and the spread of J-horror through new media and technology [Wada-Marciano 2009]). Indeed, the new aesthetic formula of developing the affect of alienation and isolation through the depiction of being a white American in an incomprehensible Japan went beyond the horror genre, as in this context *The Grudge* can be considered Hollywood's low-brow horror version of its high-brow drama *Lost in Translation* (Sofia Coppola, 2003), which had been released a year earlier to critical acclaim. Director Sophie Coppola has described her film as a portrait of two characters "going through a similar personal crisis, exacerbated by being in a foreign place" (Tezuka 2012, 127). While the use of an East Asian metropolis to exacerbate white American characters' alienation had arguably become a trope since the Techno-Orientalism of *Bladerunner* (Ridley Scott, 1982) (Morley and Robins 1995, 147–173), the focus on modern "Japaneseness" in particular as the source of disorienting Otherness for white Americans had probably never been so central and so aestheticized in a Hollywood film as it was in *Lost in Translation* and *The Grudge*, and to a lesser extent in later remakes that imitated Shimizu's specific appropriation of "culture shock" as a tool in the horror genre.

As much has been said about *The Grudge* already, I will focus instead on the less well-known *Dream Cruise* (Tsuruta 2007) to highlight the use and impact of the Shimizu formula. Like *The Grudge* and Shimizu's Hollywood follow-up *The Grudge 2* (2006), the transnational production and distribution of *Dream Cruise* also disrupted normative notions of national cinema as well as global flows. These kind of films were described in the Japanese press as "Hollywood production[s] made in Japan by Japanese filmmakers" (Tezuka 2012, 116) and were all released first in the USA and then some months later in Japan. In fact, most Hollywood remakes of J-horror films transposed their settings to an American context like *The Ring* (Verbinski 2002), and only a small but significant subset of films produced under the remake economy replicated the Shimizu formula of changing protagonists into Americans while retaining a Japanese setting. *Dream Cruise* is notable for being an entirely original film (though based on a Japanese short story) produced under these remake economy-induced narrative conditions, for example, a "new" J-horror film made in the first place for an American audience.

From its opening shot of the busy Shibuya pedestrian crossing that has come to visually signify to viewers, "we are in Japan," *Dream Cruise* has much in common with *The Grudge*, which indulges in Orientalist stereotypes through its positioning of American sympathetic subjects navigating an alien and hostile world of Japanese objects (McRoy 2008, 100–102). However, *Dream Cruise* varies in that it contains hints that Tsuruta was aiming to express, in some scenes, a space of "Japanese subjectivity," perhaps with the film's secondary Japanese audience in mind. The film, an adaptation of a story by *Ring* author Koji Suzuki, depicts the tensions of a love triangle between three passengers on a boat at sea: wealthy Japanese businessman Eiji; his unsatisfied wife Yuri; and the hero Jack, an employee of the company of which Eiji is a client and also Yuri's lover. As it begins to become clear that Eiji is aware of the affair, he makes several references to "Japan" and "America," telling Jack: "A Japanese lover would improve your Japanese"; "Just being an American in Tokyo means there are plenty of girls whose eyes will land on you"; and "In the old days in Japan, people who committed infidelity were sliced into four parts." Eiji rhetorically aligns himself with the image of an old and vengeful Japan in contrast with Jack and the image of an American foreigner both lustful for and desired by Japanese women. This depiction is notable in that this common stereotype and anxiety toward foreign white men in Japan is rarely depicted in films (Kelsky 2001, 198), but also in that, by allowing Eiji to express his jealousy and anger, a subjective, relatable space coded as "Japanese" is opened within the film's narrative. Unlike the un-subtitled anger of a Japanese taxi driver who complains about Jack the "*gaijin*" (foreigner), Eiji's anger against Jack can be read and understood by the primary American audience as well as the secondary Japanese one, indeed viewers may feel sympathy for the cuckolded husband, despite the more numerous narrative devices which position Eiji as a villain and Jack as a hero.

For example, the film opens by presenting Jack as a thoughtful young man getting by in a foreign country and struggling to overcome the trauma of having lost his brother in a boating accident at a young age (he has been scared of the ocean ever since). When it comes to adultery, we only ever see Jack looking regretful and troubled, or chastely pledging his love to Yuri and asking that she leave Eiji. Yuri herself is presented as having married Eiji for money and status, but claims that Jack has shown her the error of her ways and that she wants to be with him, if only she could get away from the possessive and dangerous Eiji. The typical love triangle plot of dramas interestingly recreates the "white savior" narrative of popular culture in which ethnicized women are saved from the patriarchal men of their culture by a white foreign male (Hughey 2014), as well as the gendered power dynamic Eve Kosofsky Sedgwick describes as a traditional facet of the love triangle plot in which a female object is competed over by two male subjects, a villain and hero (Sedgwick 1985, 21–27)—only in this case, the villain space of subjectivity is figured as "Japanese" and the hero space of subjectivity as "American."

The plot is too long and convoluted to fully detail here, but I will mention some key elements that show how the addition of "Japanese subjectivity" to this J-horror Hollywood film is quickly and overwhelmingly diminished as the film unfolds. The ghost of Eiji's ex-wife, Naomi, appears on the scene with the intention of killing Eiji and Yuri. Eiji dies and his ghost returns with the intention of killing Jack. The ghost of Jack's brother Sean joins the fray to protect his older brother. Despite the tangled web of who-wants-to-kill-who, it is quite easy for viewers to register that the malicious and vengeful ghosts are Japanese, whereas the good ghost (Sean) is American. At one point even Yuri seems to become possessed and attack her lover Jack, who nearly kills her in self-defense before his brother's ghost stops him, and he realizes Yuri is on his side. (This is similar to the way in which his brother's ghost seems threatening in Jack's dreams at the start of the film, but assumes his status as protector once the boat journey begins.) Therefore, all of the Japanese characters are portrayed as threatening ghosts at different points during the boat journey, whereas the American characters, Jack and Sean, are positioned as good throughout this journey. When the film ends, Jack and Yuri are seen happily together on a different boat, with Jack having overcome both his guilt over his brother's death and his fear of the ocean, while Yuri is pregnant. Jack says, "If it's a boy, we'll know what to call him," to which Yuri replies, "Yeah, his name works for me." This ending reframes the entire film as a dramatic adventure in Japan which allows an American man to overcome his personal trauma, a process which includes acquiring a Japanese wife who may provide him with a son to be named after his dead brother, Sean, as part of his healing. The very thought that Yuri might want to name her half-Japanese son something like Kosuke or Taro is laughable in this context. The film's narrative thus works to eventually convert all aspects of Japanese subjectivity into objects within the heroic subjectivity of the white American male hero.

Despite the figuring of Eiji's subjective space at the start of the film, the overall narrative of *Dream Cruise* demonstrates a power dynamic in which Japan is figured as the object of an American subjectivity, which maps neatly onto the image of Japan as culturally-coded particularistic elements interacting with a generalized America presumed to be a source of empathy for international audiences. Of course, films like *Dream Cruise* which follow the Shimizu formula reconstitute an Orientalist framework of Japan as the Other, simultaneously an object of desire and fear to be contrasted with a Western subjectivity. This Orientalism, however, also operates as a function of transpacific complicity, replicating the flow of specific cultural data towards a universal Western audience that can make sense of these foreign peripheral objects—just as Sakai describes the flow of academic information above.

This relation is even more obvious when we consider its inverse: the filmic construction of a Japanese subjectivity coming into contact with an objectified Western context, as seen in the parodic *Kinpatsu Kaidan / Blonde Kaidan* (Shimizu 2004), impressively (perhaps tellingly) also directed by Shimizu Takashi. In fact, Shimizu directed this short vignette for one of Ichise's domestic anthology productions, *Sekai saikyō J horā SP: Nihon no kowai yoru / Dark Tales From Japan* (2004), released in Japan one month before Shimizu's *The Grudge* was released in the United States. In *Blonde Kaidan*, a Japanese assistant director has been sent to Hollywood to assist with a Japanese production being made there. Despite being in awe of his surroundings, he complains to his taxi driver that Hollywood "has gone downhill. It's all Japanese horror movies now." This is a prime example (and one of the only examples) of the "reversal of global flows" understanding of J-horror, as espoused by Wada-Marciano and others, being manifested within the filmic content itself. The amusing situation is amplified by the fact that the character is speaking Japanese to an American taxi driver who presumably can't understand a word he is saying, the assertion of Japanese dominance within Hollywood literally falling on deaf ears. At the same time, an audience savvy to genre conventions will realize that our assistant director will soon fall victim to his hubris. His denigration of Hollywood is seamlessly followed by his exclamations of approval for the blonde women he sees in the street, saying they're "not like the girls in Tokyo" who dye their hair blonde, but rather "the real thing." In a reversal of regional power dynamics, the assistant director longingly cries out, "*Neitibu*! *Neitibu*!" ("Natives! Natives!"), as he watches the blonde women walk by.

While embodying a certain fetishistic attitude toward white Westerners that exists in Japan, this moment is a partial reversal of both the gendered and ethnicized power dynamics present in *Dream Cruise*, as well as a total reversal of the anthropologist's gaze that Shimizu turns on Japanese culture in *The Grudge*. That film begins with a scene of Sarah Michelle Gellar's character Karen and her boyfriend peering over a wall and into a cemetery while a small ceremony is being held at a grave, in which the camera stays firmly on her side of the wall and voyeuristically frames the mourning Japanese family as Karen explains, to her boyfriend and the audience, that "they do it so their dead can rest," exoticizing mundane rituals and setting an ominous tone at the same time. Just as Japanese ghosts soon haunt their objectifying observers that watch from the "outside" of Japanese culture in *The Grudge*, so too does the ghost of a blonde white woman terrorize the objectifying Japanese assistant director, who is in Hollywood but not of it, in *Blonde Kaidan*. In his short film for a domestic Japanese audience, Shimizu expertly mocks the same fetishistic conventions and industrial changes that he espouses in his feature length film for American/universal audiences.

Blonde Kaidan is less a horror film than a self-reflexive joke, amusing rather than scary, and an enlightening contrast to transpacific power dynamics under the remake economy. Subversions of these dynamics have also, to a much lesser degree, become manifested in "serious" horror films under the remake economy, perhaps most notably in *Shutter* (Ochiai 2008). A transnational production, *Shutter* is the Hollywood remake of Thailand's most successful horror film during the horror boom, but directed by J-horror auteur Ochiai Masayuki and filmed using the Shimizu formula, for example, white American protagonists in a Japanese setting. In *Shutter*, an American woman and her fiancé are haunted by a female Japanese ghost who is eventually revealed to be a clingy ex-girlfriend of the American man. She kills off his American male friends one by one, and haunts the protagonists in ways reminiscent of *The Grudge*, for example by scaring the American woman on a train so that she screams and then is stared at by uncomprehending Japanese bystanders, her status as "foreigner" used to amplify her isolation and fear. Eventually the ghost appears to be subdued after her spirit is "put to rest," and the American woman and her fiancé return to the safety of America, in keeping with the regionalization of Japan as a space of strangeness and danger and America as the audience's normalcy and "home." Rupturing this tranquility, the Japanese ghost appears again, disrupting the image of monstrous objects and suffering subjects as contained within their national boundaries of Japan and America respectively. In an even more radical departure from the aesthetics of transpacific complicity, the Japanese ghost reveals to the American woman that the American men she had killed had gang-raped her, and that the fiancé had photographed the event in order to blackmail her. Horrified by this revelation, and realizing that the ghost has been trying to warn her rather than harm her, the American woman decides she cannot marry her fiancé anymore, and deliberately leaves him to be further haunted by the vengeful ghost. Whether or not it is intentional, the ending of the original Thai film is quite significantly altered due to the use of the Shimizu formula in the remake. The remake's twist creates a sympathetic bond not just between ghost and hero, but between the Japanese female ghost and the American female protagonist, with the role of villain being suddenly cast onto an American man. By turning to the typical narrative of the rape-revenge subgenre, the anthropologist's gaze of *Shutter* is overcome by unexpected international female solidarity, and rather than "a clingy Japanese girlfriend," the film's monster is revealed to be white and patriarchal in nature.

IMAGES OF TRANSPACIFIC COMPLICITY AFTER J-HORROR

Shutter's ending reveals new possibilities for the remake economy, and creates the potential for further subversions of the Shimizu formula in which new international connections and subjectivities are explored without the necessity of Orientalism under the overarching structure of transpacific complicity. It is probably the only Hollywood film produced within the remake economy that has an element of active resistance to transpacific complicity. However, *Shutter* was made at the tail-end of the remake economy, and since then Hollywood has turned away from East Asia as a source of original scripts and horror auteurs. However, the passing of the remake economy does not entail the passing of embodiments of transpacific complicity in the sphere of genre films produced in both Japan and Hollywood.

For example, Japan's *Shin Gojira / Shin Godzilla* (Anno and Higuchi, 2016) is a perfect example of transpacific complicity becoming manifest in both production and filmic content. The film was very much designed and marketed as a nostalgic "return" to Japan's original *Gojira / Godzilla* (Honda 1954) and as a rebuttal to recent Hollywood portrayals of the monster (*Godzilla* [Emmerich 1998]; *Godzilla* [Edwards 2014]).[1] The "return" to the Japanese past was marked by a similar plot (rather than battling other *kaiju* [giant monsters], Godzilla simply emerges from the sea and walks into Tokyo, causing destruction by virtue of his size and power alone) and similar themes (contemporary political responses and the trauma of nuclear disaster—the images reminiscent of the atomic bombings of Japan replaced by images reminiscent of the Tōhoku and Fukushima disaster here). The film's narrative portrayed a Self-Defense Force restrained by hesitant and bureaucratic politicians, and the threatened bombing of the creature (and by extension Japan) by the United States unless the Japanese government can work out a solution by itself within a given time frame. Ultimately, the Japanese government prevails, defeating the monster created by nuclear waste dumped into the sea, while at the same time standing up to the United States and reaffirming its sovereignty through ingenuity and strong coordination between the government and an efficiently militaristic Self-Defense Force. The specific brand of nationalism espoused by the film is therefore illustrative of exactly that which is complicit with the hegemony of the United States in the East Asia region, a nationalism which demands sovereignty while at the same time paradoxically being "an ideology of colonial dependency" in that the conceptual positioning of Japan "outside" of the West makes it all the more dependent on the foreign policies of the United States (Sakai 2010 b, 261). Even without the driving force of the remake economy, the relevance of transpacific complicity to popular culture remains undiminished.

This structure also continues to be embodied in other forms of popular culture, such as in an episode of the popular Netflix science fiction anthology *Black Mirror*. In "Playtest" (Trachtenberg 2016), an American backpacker named Cooper becomes stranded in London, and volunteers to test a new type of video game technology for money. He is introduced to a man called Shou Saito, the owner of a video game company called "saitoGemu" renowned for its horror games. Throughout the episode, Saito frequently speaks Japanese with his British assistant, and the plot follows the typical "mad scientist" plot that has been popular since Mary Shelley's novel *Frankenstein* (1818), in which a creative genius takes on a morbid technological project (in this case, a horror game) which will ultimately fail in the manner of Greek tragedy-derived hubris. In "Playtest," it is of course the experimental horror game that eventually proves fatal for its American consumer, rather than its eccentric Japanese creator. In emphasizing the Japaneseness of Saito—not only through his appearance, speech, and so on, but also by his implausibly greeting Cooper with a deep bow and "konnichiwa"—writer Charlie Brooker clearly aligns Saito with video game horror auteurs such as Mikami Shinji, and more generally with the "horror genius" image of Japan that continues to be reproduced long after the J-horror movement has faded. More specifically, "Playtest" depicts a creative Japanese genius torturing an unsuspecting American with new technology and horror media, an image evocative not only of the standard discourse of the globalized J-horror boom but also of older strands of Orientalism in popular culture, such as the villain Fu Manchu who gained immense multimedia popularity in the West during the first half of the twentieth century as an embodiment of the "yellow peril" anxiety of the time.

Whether or not this more modern image will survive, transform, or disappear in the arena of global popular culture, and whether or not its intersection with Orientalist exoticism as a function of transpacific complicity will become more problematic, will have to be observed in the years to come. The fact that as "Playtest" approaches its climactic moment of horror, Saito's Japanese (deliberately un-subtitled for the viewer) prompts Cooper to frantically ask, "What's he saying? What's he saying?" suggests that the Shimizu formula of American-subject-encountering-scary-Japanese-object remains a viable resource for popular culture.

REFERENCES

"GFW Update: Godzilla vs Zilla." 2004. *Monster Zero*. Accessed 04/05/2018. http://archive.li/vSovU.

Balmain, Colette.2008. *Introduction to Japanese Horror Film*. Edinburgh: Edinburgh University Press.

Dew, Oliver. 2007. "'Asia Extreme': Japanese Cinema and British Hype." *New Cinemas: Journal of Contemporary Film*, 5:1 (April): 53–73.

Hughey, Matthew W. 2014. *The White Savior Film: Content, Critics, and Consumption*. Philadelphia: Temple University Press.

Iwabuchi, Koichi. 1994. "Complicit Exoticism: Japan and its Other." *Continuum: The Australian Journal of Media & Culture*, 8:2 (1994): 49–82.

Kalat, David. 2007. *J-horror: The Definitive Guide to The Ring, The Grudge and Beyond*. New York: Vertical.

Kehr, Dave. 2006. "Horror Film Made for Showtime Will Not Be Shown." *The New York Times*. Accessed 02/08/2018. http://www.nytimes.com/2006/01/19/arts/television/horror-film-made-for-showtime-will-not-be-shown.html.

Kelsky, Karen. 2001. *Women on the Verge: Japanese Women, Western Dreams*, Durham: Duke University Press.

Kinoshita, Chika. 2009. "The Mummy Complex: Kurosawa Kiyoshi's *Loft* and J-horror." in *Horror to the Extreme: Changing Boundaries in Asian Cinema*, edited

by Jinhee Choi and Mitsuyo Wada-Marciano, 103–122. Hong Kong: Hong Kong University Press.
La Porte, Nicole and Gabriel Snyder. 2006. "Fox holding 'Grudge' Guy to New Deal." *Variety*. Accessed 02/02/2018. http://variety.com/2006/film/features/fox-holding-grudge-guy-to-new-deal-1200505999/.
Lee, Vivian P. Y. 2011. "J-Horror and Kimchi Western: Mobile Genres in East Asian Cinemas." In *East Asian Cinemas: Regional Flows and Global Transformations*, edited by Vivian P. Y. Lee, 118-144. London: Palgrave Macmillan.
Lowenstein, Adam. 2009. "Ghosts in a Super Flat Global Village: Globalization, Surrealism, and Contemporary Japanese Horror Films." *The Free Library*. Accessed 04/28/2018. https://www.thefreelibrary.com/Ghosts+in+a+super+flat+global+village%3A+globalization%2C+surrealism%2C+and...-a0200723441
Mackie, Vera. 2009. "Transnational Bricolage: Gothic Lolita and the Political Economy of Fashion." *Intersections: Gender and Sexuality in Asia and the Pacific*, 20 Accessed 03/02/2018. http://intersections.anu.edu.au/issue20/mackie.htm.
McRoy, Jay. 2008. *Nightmare Japan: Contemporary Japanese Horror Cinema*, New York: Editions Rodopi B.V.
Miller, Toby, Nitin Govil, John McMurria, and Richard Maxwell. 2001. *Global Hollywood*, London: British Film Institute.
Morley, David and Robins, Kevin. 1995. *Spaces of Identity: Global Media, Electronic Landscapes, and Cultural Boundaries*. London: Routledge.
Rose, Steve. 2002. "Nightmare Scenario." *The Guardian*. Accessed 02/08/2018. https://www.theguardian.com/culture/2002/sep/20/artsfeatures.dvdreviews.
Sakai, Naoki. 2010 a. "Civilizational Difference and Area Studies: Pan-Asianism and the West." In *Whither Japanese Philosophy? II: Reflections through other Eyes*, edited by Takahiro Nakajima, 27–42. Tokyo: UTCP.
———. 2010 b. "Transpacific Complicity and Comparatist Strategy." In *Globalizing American Studies*, edited by Brian T. Edwards and Dilip Parameshwar Gaonkar, 240–65. Chicago: The University of Chicago Press.
Schilling, Mark. 2004. "Takashige Ichise Interview." *Mark Schilling's Tokyo Ramen*. Accessed 04/08/2018. http://japanesemovies.homestead.com/ichiseinterivew.html.
Sedgwick, Eve K. 1985. *Between Men: English Literature and Male Homosocial Desire*. New York: Colombia University Press.
Tanaka, Yuki. 2017. "A Critique of an Open Letter to Prime Minister Shinzo Abe." Accessed 02/02/2017. http://yjtanaka.blogspot.jp/2017/01/a-critique-of-open-letter-to-prime.html.
Tezuka, Yoshiharu. 2012. *Japanese Cinema Goes Global: Filmworkers' Journeys*. Hong Kong: Hong Kong University Press.
Wada-Marciano, Mitsuyo. 2009. "J-horror: New Media's Impact on Contemporary Japanese Horror Cinema." In *Horror to the Extreme: Changing Boundaries in Asian Cinema*, edited by Jinhee Choi and Mitsuyo Wada-Marciano, 15–38. Hong Kong: Hong Kong University Press.
Zahlten, Alex and Kimata, Kimihiko. 2005. "Norio Tsuruta." *Midnight Eye*. Accessed 02/04/2017. http://www.midnighteye.com/interviews/norio-tsuruta/.

NOTES

1. Various critics and filmmakers related to the Godzilla franchise have expressed their disdain for the 1998 Hollywood Godzilla, but sometimes by extension the concept of an "American Godzilla" in general. For example, director Kitamura Ryuhei said of his 2004 film Gojira: Fainaru Wōzu / Godzilla Final Wars, "I want to compete with America. I want to overwhelm the American Godzilla (which is a symbol of CG) with the Japanese technique of suitmation."

Chapter 12

Revisiting the Orphan Girl Narrative in *Rule of Rose*

Ingrid Butler

Punchline's *Rule of Rose* (2006), with its abundance of fairy-tale trappings—its deceptively simple storybook narration, allusions to well-known fairytales, and reliance on the tropes of princesses, princes, witches, mermaids, knights, and the like—may be one of the more overt examples of Japanese horror video games influenced by children's literature. *Rule of Rose* ostensibly follows a delicate, nineteen-year-old English woman named Jennifer who is kidnapped by a group of abusive children and subsequently imprisoned on an airship *en route* to India.[1] There she attempts to survive her indoctrination into their cult by following their rules of a monthly tribute on pain of death; as the story unfolds, however, it becomes clear that *Rule of Rose* is a trauma narrative where Jennifer's childhood memories of experiencing and witnessing abuse at a rural orphanage converge and weave in dense metaphors, symbolism, and moments of surreal violence, eventually concluding with the wistful epilogue "Once Upon a Time."

Rule of Rose belongs to what Bernard Perron identifies as "the antipodal clusters" of the survival horror video game genre (2006 to 2016) (Perron 2018, 218–219). While heavily influenced by horror films, the genre typically "modifies the experience" of horror films, "exploiting both fear and the urge to fight back" (Chien 2007, 64). The focus of such gameplay, whose protagonists are often "rather ordinary people" with makeshift or limited weapons, is generally "the hero's perseverance" over "relentless enemies and seemingly overwhelming odds" while navigating "dark, claustrophobic interiors" (Ibid). As the survival horror genre became deeply influenced by immensely successful *Resident Evil 4* (2005), subsequent games in the genre tended toward either "fight or flight" as a core feature of their gameplay (Perron 2018, 219). The gameplay of *Rule of Rose* in particular tends towards "retreat and avoidance" (Perron 2018, 218–219) with Jennifer herself part of the tradition of "[w]eak and frail-looking" young female protagonists in survival horror, along with Fiona of *Haunting Ground* (2005), Heather of *Silent Hill 3* (2003), and Miyo and Maya Amakura of *Fatal Frame II: Crimson Butterfly* (2003) (Perron 2018, 371). For all its horror trappings, *Rule of Rose* is, curiously, a partial ludic descendent of the perennially popular, turn-of-the-century orphan girl novels. The turn-of-the-century orphan novel (e.g., *A Little Princess* [1905] or *Anne of Green Gables* [1908]) features a relatively simple narrative structure, as Claudia Mills notes: beginning with an orphan girl who "is placed in a situation where she is initially unloved or unwanted," the narrative follows her as she wins over the people in her new home, ending with her love being "the dearest of all objects to its possessor" (Mills 1987, 228–229). As a literary manifestation of "the innocent, unspoiled, Romantic child" philosophical notion, the orphan girl does not experience any "moral growth" throughout the narrative, as she "already represent[s] a kind of moral perfection" (Mills 1987, 230). Key to the orphan girl novel is her "almost magical qualities" that transform the characters around her for the better (Nodelman 1979, 147). In his study of orphan girl novels from 1850 to 1923, Joe Sutliff Sanders identifies these miraculous qualities as affective discipline, locating the orphan girl narratives as the continuation of a cultural dialogue about affective discipline that begin in sentimental novels of the mid-1800s (2011, 8–9). Affective discipline, or moral suasion, was a feminine-coded form of discipline that encouraged the melding of identities; the outcome of successful affective discipline was that the one being disciplined unconsciously molded their own desires, thoughts, and behavior after that of the beloved discipliner (Sanders 2011, 15–16). Initially considered a more humane and successful form of discipline in contrast to physical discipline (e.g., hitting), affective discipline gradually became an uneasy means of behavioral control, and after the 1920s, it "becomes difficult to determine exactly in what arena that post-suffrage debate about affective discipline has been carried out" (Ibid). I argue that *Rule of Rose* resurrects the conversation about affective discipline and the fictional girls who wield this uneasy social power. *Rule of Rose* is a curious entry in the survival horror genre, torn between two worlds on multiple levels. It is a Japanese video game whose historical British setting and trappings is meant to appeal to Japanese audiences (Wales 2016), and a horror narrative about the simultaneous violence and helplessness of children meant for an older teen/adult audience, written at least in part by a Japanese man,[2] who borrowed the literary conventions of the orphan girl novel, a genre dominated by women writers (Sanders 2011, 179). The orphan girl novel might seem a strange topic for a Japanese horror video game to address, but consider the sheer and enduring popularity of *Anne of Green Gables* in Japan, which at one point warranted its own theme park attraction in Hokkaido (Baldwin 1993, 123–124). Similarly, many of the best-known orphan girl novels were adapted into relatively straightforward anime shows during the late 1970s to early 1990s.[3] By transposing the narrative expectations of the turn-of-the-century orphan girl story into the interactive format of the survival horror video game, *Rule of Rose* interrogates the failings of affective discipline as simultaneously an unambiguous site of horror that inspires acts of violence and cruelty in the name of love and admiration and also as an ultimately futile and gossamer means to power. Through its gameplay mechanics and narrative, *Rule of Rose* engages with the failings of the orphan girl story from both perspectives: Jennifer, the orphan girl unable to impose any modicum of affective discipline on the other characters, and the Princess of the Red Rose, the orphan-girl leader of the children's cult, who successfully wields affective discipline for the worse. In rejecting affective discipline, *Rule of Rose* then turns to remembrance as a potential source of power for the orphan girl, shifting the preoccupation from controlling others to an internal focus on memory.

"STRANGE, BUT FAMILIAR": REWORKING THE ORPHAN GIRL NARRATIVE

As a medium, video games allow for a greater degree of interactivity than other, more static media such as novels or television. Aubrey Anable writes that, as "affective systems," "[v]ideo games ask us to make choices, and they ask us to operate within the sets of constraints or rules that govern those choices" (Anable 2018, xii). It is through the player's character, also called the avatar, that the player interacts in the virtual world of the video game. In doing so, "[t]he gamer is significantly more than a mere audience member, but significantly less than a diegetic character. It is the act of doing, of manipulating the controller, that imbricates the gamer with the game" (Gallaway 2006, 83). As a result of this unique, interactive relationship between player and video game, *Rule of Rose* thus allows for the potential to experience affective discipline on a more immediate level,[4] whereas previously, a person might have only experienced affective discipline secondhand through the filter of reading (Sanders 2011, 181). Survival horror games require an additional layer of interactivity from the player in regards to its narrative. As Marc C. Santos and Sarah E. White argue in their psychoanalytic reading of the immensely influential *Silent Hill* and *Resident Evil* survival horror series, the player becomes the "champion of the symbolic order" as they "piece together narrative order" through the various in-game textual documents (Santos and White 2005, 72). Adding to this narrative complexity, the protagonist's "inward trauma" can also spill out into the game world, coloring it in horrifying and surreal ways, as in *Silent Hill* 2 (2001) and its tormented protagonist James Sunderland (Santos and White 2005, 75–76). Despite her in-game appearance as an adult, Jennifer can be read as an orphan girl throughout the game, especially given that the game's epilogue reveals that she was actually a small orphaned child all along. As such, she is probably the most overtly connected to the traditional orphan girl novel. The title of the beginning chapter of *Rule of Rose* and its associated storybook,[5] "The Little Princess," recalls *A Little Princess*,[6] while the game's opening features a nod to the traditional start to orphan-girl novels that typically begins with the girl *en route* to her new home (Nodelman. 1979, 146). Jennifer dozes as she rides the bus to a new life, her suitcase visible beside her. The narration, overlaying onto these visuals, tells of "a precious little girl" whose "mummy and daddy died suddenly," resulting in the girl being "sent away to a strange house." After Jennifer is freed in her new home, the airship (in actuality, the Rose Garden Orphanage, transformed by the children's collective imagination), she demonstrates all the attributes of the kindly orphan girl: she pays attention to the needs of the weak and (more) helpless, rescuing the dog Brown from his confinement and restoring the head of the Bucket Knight—a sort of omniscient protector made from a bucket, cloth, and sticks that is dubbed the "keeper of promises." Yet, for all her kindness, her dignified lack of retorts to the endless verbal abuse she endures from the other children and adults, and the grace she extends to another child who gleefully brushes a live rat against her face, she is unable to move the other children to model themselves after her—or even to stop abusing her.

While *Rule of Rose* is more or less an exercise in experiencing the agony of helplessness, being unable to end the abuses committed against Jennifer despite her kindness and goodwill, one moment stands out from the rest: the interlude of "The Gingerbread House" chapter. Set in June 1929, "The Gingerbread House" is notable in that it focuses on Jennifer's backstory before she came to the orphanage. In this chapter, *Rule of Rose* provides a microcosm of her life as a newly made orphan and her subsequent informal adoption by the alcoholic pea farmer, Gregory Wilson, who treats her as a replacement for his dead son, Joshua. "The Gingerbread House" chapter thus posits two questions to the genre: what happens when the child, reimagined in contemporary turn-of-the-century thought as "the center of domestic life" (Tribunella 2017, 140) is no longer there? And secondly, what if the orphan girl, meant to ultimately enable "emotional and spiritual uplift of adults" (Nelson 2003, 7) fails to do so?

Drawing on Henry Jenkins's concept of "embedded narrative," Ewan Kirkland writes that survival horror games frequently use their mise-en-scène as part of their narratives (Kirkland 2009, 70): these settings "function largely as static tableaux for players to move though," with the stories contained within them "firmly embedded in the past, closed off to player involvement" (Kirkland 2009, 71). The titular setting of the "The Gingerbread House" chapter, Gregory's house which Jennifer wakes up in front of at the beginning of the chapter, invites players to make sense of it as they move through it. The setting itself is a testament to loss: dilapidated, cluttered with mess and signs of grief—giant holes in the plaster, a messy kitchen, empty beer bottles scattered throughout. More than anything, it is a testament to the dead child and how cherished he was. The only photograph is a happy one of Gregory and Joshua, while Joshua's boarded-up bedroom is curiously well furnished with toys and trinkets, given the bleak poverty and sparse rooms of the rest of the house. Gregory's diary makes clear that he subscribed to the Victorian-era notion of "sacred childhood" with children being "sources of affection and delight" who were supposed to be spared physical work in favor of "leisure and education" (Tribunella 2017, 140). Joshua never worked in the fields, and he was the recipient of fantasy stories specially created for him by his father. "Nothing pleases me more than to see my son happy" goes the conclusion to one diary entry. Exploring the house, however, is fraught with tension: Gregory is a strange character who elicits both pity and terror. Before Jennifer enters the house, he can be seen in the basement, slowly reciting a gruesome rhyme about a cannibalistic man-monster named Stray Dog while holding a gun to his own head, and several shaky flashbacks within the house show Gregory in a drunken, despondent state. More so than merely grief, a loss of identity pervades the house: without the child, the center of the house simply does not hold. A tension thus emerges between the trappings of the orphan girl novel and the survival horror game. Given that Jennifer is a kind orphan girl, her arrival should signal a shift in Gregory's misery, even as the static environments of the survival horror game suggest otherwise. Here is a father waiting to be restored to his position within the house through the love of an orphan girl. However, upon approaching Gregory in the basement, he only locks her in, wishing "Joshua" a goodnight. Intrigue is met with horror. Ghostly artifacts of Joshua persist here: the dead child's clothes under the bedcovers, a sight that elicits "a sudden pain in [Jennifer's] chest"; a torn-up teddy bear named after the dead child perched high on a wardrobe; and most poignantly, a newspaper clipping of the airship crash that orphaned Jennifer, grimly ending the story about the airship's maiden voyage that begun with the clipping in Joshua's room. Survival horror games often feature "collaborative storytelling" which "invites[s] or conscript[s] the player into the narrative process," with the player progressing the story by obtaining certain documents or triggering certain events, for example (Kirkland 2009, 72). In *Rule of Rose*, the player is helpless to leave the basement and in fact must trigger the appearance of Wendy, the only friendly child from the orphanage, to have any hope of escaping the room. Even then, a considerable amount of in-game time is spent waiting for her to unlock the door once she disappears from view. If video games ask their players to make choices within the bounds and limitations of the software, as Anable writes, the only choice in "The Gingerbread House" chapter is to stay in the miserable house and continue to be (mis)identified as the dead child, or to flee it and progress the game but in doing so, also abandon Gregory to a misery that Jennifer cannot alleviate. The player's reward for leaving the house with Wendy is a final, gut-wrenching glimpse of Gregory wandering the perimeter, calling out for his dead son.[7] The Bucket Knight recognizes this internal dilemma, telling Jennifer that while she has "gained [her] freedom," she has also "betrayed" Gregory and "denied him even death" now that Wendy has possession of his gun. Even as the structure of the game allows for one narrative path, that of captivity and escape in this chapter, the game guilts its player for being unable to fulfill the impossible task of the orphan girl.

It is here that the meaning of the chapter becomes starkly clear. Not simply only an intertextual reference to the *Hansel and Gretel* fairytale,[8] the title recalls the site of attempted cannibalism in the fairytale, a motif reinforced by Gregory's rhymes in the basement about how Stray Dog partially eats and partially buries the children he finds. The narrative thus implies that there is something deeply cannibalistic about using children to replace other children as if they were merely interchangeable, that it is a form of violence and death even. In discussing affective discipline within the temperance novel, a literary genre that "The Gingerbread House" also borrows from, Karen Sánchez-Eppler argues that the child becomes "simultaneously victim of abuse and agent of discipline" within the genre (Sánchez-Eppler 2003, 86). While the child can affectively discipline her drunkard father into sobriety, "a power they too often and painfully lacked" (Ibid) in reality, the children ultimately fails to better their status within the patriarchal household, unable to "empower themselves" (Sánchez-Eppler 2003, 100). By dispensing with the transformative power of the child, *Rule of Rose* focuses on the abuse inherent in such a dynamic—the impossible bind of having to improve someone you are frighteningly dependent on. Even the relief of escape is, horrifically, tinged with guilt.

"GUIDE US! WE NEED YOU!": LONELY PRINCESSES AND ADORED MOTHERS

If Jennifer's storyline is about her inability to change the children and adults around her, despite being an ideal orphan girl, *Rule of Rose* also provides an example of the orphan girl who can wield affective discipline well—the mysterious Princess of the Red Rose, the largely unseen heart of the orphanage and leader of the children's secret cult. Like Sara Crewe of *A Little Princess* before her (Sanders 2011, 78), the Princess of the Red Rose affectively disciplines through storytelling, weaving a blend of cautionary tales about the monstrous Stray Dog who kidnaps misbehaving children and must be appeased through animal sacrifice, and the particularly potent notion that the children are all one family, with the Princess as their mother. A drawing of the Princess's royal lineage places her as the motherless mother of all the children, who are ranked in accordance with her favor. She alone is the focus of the children's unbridled adoration, with the majority of one child's notebook dedicated to her, complete with a crayon portrait and extensive notes on due deference towards her. In short, the Princess carries on the post sentimental literary lineage of orphan girls taking on "the responsibility of using the power inherent in affective discipline to rule over the people within that space" (Sanders 2011, 162). As Sanders chronicles, by the end of the genre, orphan girls had more or less assumed "the role of mothers as they took responsibility for the girls around them—and themselves," ultimately "confirm[ing] the disposability of mothers" (2011, 168).

If the aim of the affectively disciplining girl is to meld her identity with those she is disciplining, as Sanders has written, *Rule of Rose* posits the question of what happens when the orphan girl's wishes and thoughts are selfish, self-serving, or possessive, for example, anything else than the lofty, pure, and well-meaning thoughts of the turn-of-the-century orphan girl. While the children of the cult see themselves as a family, they are a wicked one, turning on each other in turn and devising hurtful plans, often including off-screen animal death. When the Princess's "companion," a stuffed bear, is stolen and later returned, the children translate her feelings of betrayal into expressions of outrage and violence meant to correct the behavior of the one they suspect to have stolen it—Jennifer. They escalate their harassment, giving her the silent treatment, kicking her down the stairs, and throwing notes with deeply disturbing, all-capitalized insults and death threats at her. They then make her the monthly tribute, implementing the ultimate form of behavioral correction—death. This sparks a horrific sequence in which Jennifer must evade waves of grotesque imps (hideous, eyeless creatures that shriek and grab at her) to escape to the orphanage's courtyard and the safety of Wendy's presence.

Throughout the game, Wendy has been a sympathetic figure, given the epithet of "the lonely princess" by the narrator. As an interactive, nonplayable character, Wendy seems to be designed to elicit sympathy: seemingly fragile in her light blue dress, she appears to be the perfect orphan girl: delicate but not needy, friendly but not clingy. Her gentle nature inspires a wish to listen to her, take her feelings into account, and most of all, to make her happy, even though the game's mechanics did not allow for that. Frequently bedridden, she is an object of pity but also interest and friendship: seemingly the only orphan girl not involved in the cult, she disciplines affectively with stories,[9] as well, spinning a fantasy where she is a princess and Jennifer is her prince, bound together by the titular rule of rose, the oath of "everlasting, true love." It is a fantasy she spins into reality when she rescues Jennifer (and by extension, the player) from captivity in Gregory's basement, and it is this promise of protection, love, and security that sends Jennifer into the courtyard to meet her. Survival horror narratives require players to analyze "game cues" and respond accordingly, thus helping to "produce the story in real time" (Kirkland 2009, 74). To progress in *Rule of Rose*, the players must have recognized Wendy as both a kind, harmless child and a gentle respite from the cruelty of the other children, and thus want to be around her, this time with devastating results. Going to her in the courtyard results in Brown being taken to the attic and killed by the children off-screen in Jennifer's place. Only in the attic is the truth finally revealed: Wendy is the Princess of the Red Rose.

The dichotomy between the sweet orphan girl and her sinister counterpart, the evil child, collapses with this revelation. Perhaps it is even a reprimand to the adult player that the notion of "the innocent, uncorrupted" Romantic ideal of the child underpinning the orphan girl narrative (Mills 1987, 228) is only a cultural construction of other adults, just as much as its inverse, the evil child, as James Kincaid has written; both represent the inability of adults to see children as fully human (Kincaid 2015, 7). Wendy, in fact, is actively harmful to the adult player: the discovery of Brown's corpse is a moment of visceral horror for the player, who has spent the game with Brown at their side, fending off the imps and guiding their avatar with his tracking abilities. The price for succumbing to the affective discipline of an orphan girl is the death of a beloved companion and protector. But in doing so, Wendy's actions also constitute the logical end to the other side of the orphan girl narrative that Jennifer's character arc has been tracking—that trying to make your abusers love you and thus change their ways does not translate to the real world. It is also here that the mythos of the orphan girl as mother narrative finally shatter. Jennifer, in a moment of horror and anger, symbolically drops the pretense of adulthood and reverts back to her true child self, as she slaps Wendy and knocks her to the ground. The guise of the benevolent mothering girl slips in front of the other children as they look on in silence: Wendy was only a child, capable of all the same selfish actions as they were, and her childlike tears as she runs away, sobbing from her humiliation, betray her true form.

While Wendy's loss of face as a mother figure directly leads to her ostracization by the other children, her effects on the other children persist in a more sinister way. "Stray Dog and the Lying Princess," the chapter after Wendy's humiliation, opens with Jennifer being whisked into a secret meeting with the other children, as they unnervingly smile and curtsey before her. Crowning her their new princess, the children ask for her forgiveness and beg her to devise a new game for them. Wendy's stories may be denounced as merely lies now, but the structure and purpose she gave to their lives through her stories and affective discipline fulfilled a deep emotional need in the lives of these otherwise neglected and abused children. One child in particular, Amanda, captures the voice of the room when she pleads with Jennifer to lead them: "Princess, go ahead! Guide us! We need you! We don't know what to do!" As Wendy's successor, Jennifer is swept into a role she never asked for, now idolized by the same children she was abused by, not only suggesting a deeply dehumanizing element to the notion of being a moral center for others, but also the return of being disposable. It is not Jennifer that they love, but what she represents to them—the promise of a new mother, a better one this time. Wendy's epithet, "the lonely princess," reflects this notion. She was only loved as long as she could perform motherhood for the other children; without that reverence, she becomes a pariah. Whereas fathers in the game may be terrifyingly unreachable (e.g., Gregory) or cruel and abusive disciplinarians (e.g., the headmaster Hoffman), *Rule of Rose*'s narrative suggests that mothers are a necessity for children; it is the one facet of domestic life that the cult reproduces in their fantasy world and after that fantasy has dissipated, they seek to recreate it.

More than just resonating with children as fulfillment of a deep emotional need, Wendy's stories find a second expression in the game's fairytale-esque narration. The narrator, as evidenced in the game's opening voice-over narration, is ultimately Wendy, whose voice takes on a different cadence when pretending to be the dead child Joshua. Her stories thus pervade not only the game world of *Rule of Rose*, where orphanage and airship graffiti relay fragmented stories about Stray Dog, but also the framing device that only the player interacts with, covertly shaping their point of view.

The covert influence of her stories manifests in the game's hidden choice of whether to kill Gregory in "Stray Dog and the Lying Princess." The chapter ends with Wendy's revenge on the other children, using Gregory, whom she has physically disciplined into becoming Stray Dog, to massacre them. Wendy's use of a father's body to enact violence backfires, however, and in the moments before her death, she begs Jennifer to kill him for her, returning his gun. If the player follows her guidance in the final boss fight and kills him, then they will be presented with the "bad" ending in which Wendy, cackling, berates Jennifer for being unable to "keep her promise, nor [. . .] save anyone." The only way to the "good" ending, the hidden epilogue, is to counterintuitively allow the events of the orphanage massacre to end with Gregory's murder-suicide. The player, as Jennifer, must shrug off the remnants of Wendy's affective discipline, her stories about Stray Dog, even as she has seemingly brought them to life, and refuse to continue the simplistic roles that Wendy has assigned them all through her stories: the loyal princess, the dutiful prince, and the murderous monster. Rather than killing him and thus symbolically rewriting the ending of her own trauma narrative, making herself into the heroine she was not, Jennifer must make a leap of faith, trusting Gregory to not hurt her once he sees her for who she is—his adopted daughter.

The good ending depends on the ability of the orphan girl to correctly tame her own father. Jennifer offers one shred of redemption to the fallen father as she returns his gun, his so-called "instrument of justice," trusting him to act well—in short, to revert from his feral state and act as a father should. Whereas Wendy's physical discipline transforms him into a murderous, dirty, and scarred creature that crawls on all fours, grabbing at Jennifer and knocking her to the ground, Jennifer's trust in his judgment briefly restores him to his position within the (fractured) household as father. The restoration of his humanity and position within the child-adult hierarchy is closely linked with Jennifer's own redemption, as she finally comes to the end of her trauma narrative by correctly remembering her past. All is not well, however. Gregory's newly returned humanity is marked with horror: the chapter ends with him apologizing to "Joshua" and then fatally shooting himself, abandoning his fatherly duties. Even as Jennifer restores his humanity with her own brave display of trust, she fails to attain a surrogate father to protect her, still unable to achieve the happy ending of the traditional orphan girl, in which the orphan girl's love becomes "the dearest of all objects to its possessor" (Mills 1987, 229).

CONCLUSION: THE TIES THAT BIND

As a game that takes the trappings of what has been described as simultaneously "power fantasies for an oppressed cultural minority *and* an endorsement of the status quo" (Sanders 2011, 185) and remakes it into a site of interactive horror, *Rule of Rose* aligns itself with what may be the current prevailing thought on the matter, namely that affective discipline does not empower girls and is a form of manipulation (Sanders 2011, 188). *Rule of Rose*, however, is still invested in interrogating the limitations and power of the orphan girl. Love in the game's epilogue becomes synonymous with remembrance and intertwined with nostalgia, shifting the preoccupation of control and power from trying to influence others via affective discipline, regardless of whether it is done consciously or not, to focusing on one's own locus of control, locating one power in the orphan girl—remembrance.

The recovery of a protagonist's memory is a common survival horror trope (Kirkland 2009, 75), but *Rule of Rose* imbues the act of remembering with power, whereas other examples in the genre often tend to link it with guilt (*Silent Hill 2* and *Amnesia the Dark Descent* [2010]), horror (*Silent Hill 3*) or danger (*Haunting Ground*). The crux of Jennifer's trauma narrative rests on her ability to remember things correctly, with multiple characters reminding her of her task, from the amnesiac Bucket Knight's gentle reassurances that they will "recall [their] memories together in order to remember [their] promise," to mockery from Wendy, disguised as Joshua, over Jennifer's failure to "remember now what a bad girl [she was]." In keeping with earlier survival horror games such as *Resident Evil 4* and *Silent Hill 2*, *Rule of Rose* follows the "day/night cycle" (Niedenthal 2009, 176) beginning at night and ending with the gentle sunrise in the epilogue, associating the symbolic end to the earlier horrors with her recovered memories.

Remembrance thus marks an end to a narrative about control. In Jennifer's final promise to remember the other children, whom she claims "don't deserve to be forgotten," the narrative subtly raises the possibility that she might have chosen otherwise, thus consigning them to the ultimate death in the game—to be forgotten. Even as Brown is preserved forever inside the shed of Jennifer's memories, unharmed, he is still bound by the chain that Jennifer affixes to his collar, illustrating the inherent contradictions of her promise: love, memory, and control tangle together in a chain that cannot be separated. While the control imbued in remembrance might more be subtle (and considerably less harmful) than in the forms of discipline (affective and physical) explored throughout the game, it is still existentially troubling. The lives and identities of the dead characters are not only defined by Jennifer's own memories of them, but also bound by the existential limits of her own life. Perhaps this is the new domain of the orphan girl, as she is continually re-written for a new audience.

REFERENCES

Anable, Aubery. 2018. *Playing with Feelings: Video Games and Affect*. Minneapolis: University of Minnesota Press.

Baldwin, Douglas. 1993. "L.M. Montgomery's Anne of Green Gables: The Japanese Connection." *Journal of Canadian Studies* 28, no. 3 (Fall): 123–133.

Bogost, Ian. n/d. "Videogame Adaptation and Translation." Accessed April 18, 2021. http://bogost.com/teaching/videogame_adaptation_and_trans/

Chien, Irene. 2007. "Playing Undead." *Film Quarterly* 61, no. 2 (December): 64–65. Accessed May 12, 2021. https://filmquarterly.org/2007/12/01/playing-undead/

Gallaway, Alexander R. 2006. *Gaming: Essays on Algorithmic Culture.* Minneapolis: University of Minnesota Press, 2006.

Gandolfi, Enrico. "Game on the Press, Between Prejudice and Technology." In *Assessing Communication: Integrated Approaches in Political, Social, and Business Context*, edited by Michele Sorice, 137–151. LUISS University Press, 2012.

Kincaid, James. Foreword to *Monstrous Children and Childish Monsters: Essays on Cinema's Holy Terrors*, 7–8. Edited by Markus P.J. Bohlman and Sean Moreland. Jefferson: McFarland, 2015.

Kirkland, Ewan. "Storytelling in Survival Horror Video Games." In *Horror Video Games: Essays on the Fusion of Fear and Play*, edited by Bernard Perron, 62–78. Jefferson: McFarland, 2009.

Mills, Claudia. 1987. "Children in Search of a Family: Orphan Novels Through the Century." *Children's Literature in Education* 18, no. 4 (December): 227–39.

Nelson, Claudia. 2003. *Little Strangers: Portrayals of Adoption and Foster Care in America, 1850—1929.* Bloomington: Indiana University Press.

Niedenthal, Simon. 2009. "Patterns of Obscurity: Gothic Setting and Light in *Resident Evil 4* and *Silent Hill 2*." In *Horror Video Games: Essays on the Fusion of Fear and Play*, edited by Bernard Perron, 168-180. Jefferson: McFarland, 2009.

"Program." *Back catalog*. Accessed April 15, 2021. http://www.nipponanimation.com/program/classic/.

Nodelman, Perry. 1979. "Progressive Utopia: Or, how to Grow Up Without Growing Up." *Children's Literature Association Quarterly* (1979): 146–154. https://doi.org/10.1353/chq.1979.0006.

Perron, Bernard. 2018. *The World of Scary Video Games: A Study in Videoludic Horror.* New York: Bloomsbury.

Sánchez-Eppler, Karen. 2003. *Dependent States: The Child's Part in Nineteenth-Century American Culture.* Chicago: University of Chicago Press.

Sanders, Joe Sutliff. 2011. *Disciplining Girls: Understanding the Origins of the Classic Orphan Girl Story.* Baltimore: John Hopkins University Press.

Santos, Marc C. and Sarah E. White. 2005. "Playing With Ourselves." In *Digital Gameplay: Essays on the Nexus of Game and Gamer*, edited by Nate Garrelts, 69–79. Jefferson: McFarland.

Staksrud, Elisabeth and Jürgen Kirksæther. 2013. "'He Who Buries the Little Girl Wins!' Moral Panics as Double Jeopardy: The Case of Rule of Rose." In *Moral Panics in the Contemporary World*, edited by Chas Critcher, Jason Hughes, Julian Petley, and Amanda Rohloff, 145–167. New York: Bloomsbury Academic.

Szczepaniak, John. 2014. *The Untold History of Japanese Game Developers.* SMG Szczepaniak.

Tribunella, Eric. 2017. "Pedophobia and the Orphan Girl in Pollyanna and A Series of Unfortunate Events: The Bad Beginning." In *Gender(ed) Identities: Critical Readings of Gender in Children's and Young Adult Literature*, edited by Tricia Clasen and Holly Hassel, 136–149. New York: Routledge.

"Unused Rule of Rose Cutscene with the Official Audio." 2017. *Rule of Rose Decrypted*. Accessed May 12, 2021. https://ruleofrosedecrypted.tumblr.com/post/156180807063/unused-rule-of-rose-cutscene-with-the-official.

Wales, Matt. 2006. "Rule of Rose Interview." *IGN*, September 13. Accessed May 12, 2021. https://www.ign.com/articles/2006/09/13/rule-of-rose-interview.

NOTES

1. *Rule of Rose* now is best known for the moral panic it caused in Europe, no doubt partially fueled by its provocative trailer almost made entirely of scenes that do not appear in the final work. It should be noted that European, American, and Japanese video game regulatory organizations found the game acceptable for older teenagers and adults to play. See Elisabeth Staksrud and Jorgen Kirksæther (2013) for an account of the moral panic, and Enrico Gandolfi's (2012) account of how the game was received in Italy, one of the European regions most alarmed by the game, or rather the rumors circulating about it.

2. Determining the authorship of *Rule of Rose* is a fraught endeavor, but Yoshiro Kimura takes credit for the early drafts of *Rule of Rose*, as well as shepherding the game through a reportedly troubled production (SMG Szczepaniak, 2014, 280–281). Furthermore, of the three officially credited on the screenplay (Tomo Ikeda, Hideki Okuma, and Shuji Ishikawa), two have traditionally masculine names, suggesting a potentially masculine slant to the storyline.

3. Nippon Animation alone lists several well-known orphan girl novels that it has adapted into anime in the 1970s, '80s, and '90s, possibly as the copyrights to the original novels expired: *Heidi*, *A Little Princess*, *Daddy Long Legs*, *Anne of Green Gables*, and *Pollyanna*. Nippon Animation, "Program," Back catalog. Accessed April 15, 2021. http://www.nipponanimation.com/program/classic/.

4. It would not be accurate to describe *Rule of Rose* as a straightforward procedural translation, as defined by Ian Bogost, of the orphan girl novel. While the game is deeply concerned with inner rules and workings of the genre, it transplants them into a traditional survival horror setting, complete with screeching monsters to fight or avoid—something entirely foreign to the orphan girl novel (Bogost 2021).

5. I use chapters to refer to the eleven named narrative segments of *Rule of Rose*, each corresponding to a linear moment in time (e.g., March 1930 for "The Little Princess"), as that is how the game itself refers to those, in a no doubt deliberately literary gesture. In each of the chapters, Jennifer is given a new (but sometimes incomplete) storybook that crudely illustrates the upcoming events and themes. The storybook that represents the overall narrative of the game, *The Little Princess*, gradually fills in as the player progresses through the game.

6. A considerable number of narrative elements in *Rule of Rose* overlap with *A Little Princess*, from the role of storytelling to the role of dolls, a preoccupation with India, attics, thinking of children as princesses, and more.

7. Unused cut scenes found in the Japanese edition of the game suggests a more violent end to Jennifer for leaving the house. In it, she wanders to the backyard to find Gregory digging a grave and burying something. Upon noticing her, he easily dispatches Brown (who is not present in the final version of the chapter) and then moves to kill her. Truly, a horrible end for the kind orphan girl. "Unused Rule of Rose Cutscene With the Official Audio," *Rule of Rose Decrypted*, https://ruleofrosedecrypted.tumblr.com/post/156180807063/unused-rule-of-rose-cutscene-with-the-official.

8. Several of the chapter titles are references to relatively well-known children's fairytales or literature: among them, "Mermaid Princess" is an allusion to *The Little Mermaid*, "Sir Peter" to *The Tale of Peter Rabbit*, "Stray Dog and the Lying Princess" to *The Boy Who Cried Wolf,* "The Rag Princess" to *Cinderella*.

9. Wendy's name aligns her with another character from children's literature, Wendy from *Peter Pan & Wendy* (1915), who is taken from her comfortable home to be a surrogate mother to the Lost Boys.

Chapter 13

Idol Culture and Gradations of Reality in Japanese Found Footage Horror Films

Dennin Ellis

Found footage horror films destabilize Derrida's (1987) concept of the frame—the material essence that draws off a boundary between an art object and the rest of the world. Films like *The Blair Witch Project* (1999) and the *Paranormal Activity* series (2007–present) serve as ontological playspaces by ostensibly crossing over into the real world in order to address issues of reality vs. fictionality, the symbolic vs. the material, etc. But the genre can also have greater relevance to specific culture. For instance, the films of Japanese director Koji Shiraishi—specifically, *Noroi: The Curse* (2005), *Cult* (2009), *Shirome* (2010), and *Occult* (2013)—are complicated by the presence of representatives from another ontological playspace. In both found footage horror films and Japan's idol culture,[1] the Derridean frame is elastic and permeable, allowing for the potential of ontological transgressions, which can be either repulsive (in the case of the former) or inviting (in the case of the latter). The presence of both within the same ontological playspace, manifested as a commodified object (film and/or idol) forces viewers to interrogate fear and desire, and therefore interrogate their own position as objects in an increasingly commodity-driven world.

Both found footage horror films and idol culture are impositions of a similar, albeit somewhat-different reality onto our own world, and therefore constitute the two main approaches to an ontological incursion (here made literal as a penetration of the Derridean frame from art object into the real world). In the case of idol culture, the imposition of a world that is brighter, more colorful, happier and more exciting poses the possibility of ontological incursions as being desirable—replacing an old ontology with one more amenable to the realization of one's hopes and dreams. Found footage horror, through its notion of being "presented not as mere artifact but as a fragment of the real world, and the implication that its material might well spill over into it" (Sayad 2016, 45), symbolizes the existential threat of ontological annihilation by an invading force. As such, found footage horror films metaphorically (if not literally) conform to "cosmic horror" a la H.P. Lovecraft, wherein a seepage of the unknown into the real world is interpreted as threatening and ominous.

BORDER-CROSSING: ONTOLOGY, REALITY AND FICTIONAL WORLDS

Shiraishi's films combine these two reactions, of desire and repulsion, through their combination of cosmic horror, played out by a number of Japanese idols whose characters are in fact "themselves." In doing so, Shiraishi's films are much more interesting than he likely intended them to be, as his modus operandi often slips into extreme gore (such as 2009's *Grotesque*, which was banned in the UK). This bizarre juxtaposition in Shiraishi's films suggests that the realization of one's dreams can become a nightmare, and conversely, that a nightmare can be fertile ground for the realization of one's dreams. These two functions are analogous to the basic functions of the documentary, "long[ing] for a sense of continuity with the external world . . . or instead highlighting discontinuities" (Sayad 2016, 52). If the documentary form is a filmic attempt to either "repair" or "highlight" a fracture in reality, the pseudo-documentary of found footage horror is a deliberate attempt to create such a fracture (or at least suggest the potential for such a fracture)—often by suggesting that one's ontology, whether in the form of belief, action, or their roots in some objective reality, can be overwritten.

The possibility that one will be "ontologically erased" is inherently frightening, while also undoubtedly proving alluring for anyone who has ever desired a fresh start, or simply to live in a reality that is a little different. The conceit of found footage deliberately plays with this possibility of ontological erasure, first by presenting fictitious events as real, and then through the implicit understanding of the audience that at least *some* of what they're seeing on screen *is* real[2] —the bodies, the spaces, the objects, all do exist. In fact, pseudo-documentary filmmaking techniques (such as those in Shiraishi's films, where there is never any doubt that a camera is pointed at the action) are often employed just for the purpose of further blurring the lines between fiction (the diegetic world) and reality (the extradiegetic world). Found footage films, then, are at least one degree closer to "real" than most films.

What compounds this elasticity, blurring, and breaking (or at least fracturing) of the frame that separates these two world are notions of what actually constitutes reality and how it is perceived and represented. The reason American found footage films represent reality as the realm of the everyman, and Japan understanding reality as the realm of the idol, comes down to cultural factors.

Whereas the overt presence of "reality" in American entertainment media such as television is arguably recent (with a good starting point being the premiere of *Survivor* in 2000) and niche (although certainly trends in broadcast television have been moving in that direction as scripted programs increasingly move onto streaming platforms), "reality television" is far more prevalent in Japan—at least in a form that would likely appear somewhat bewildering to American audiences.

Despite the numerous genres of Japanese television, there is nothing identified as "reality television." While one is unlikely to find reality TV featuring ordinary people in Japan, the same qualities that define reality TV are central to Japanese television programming and its celebrity system [. . .] Japanese variety shows, with their endless parade of idols and celebrity guests and regulars, incorporate all the elements associated with reality TV. Like reality TV, the genre of variety TV in Japan is a hybrid format that combines factual and entertainment programming [. . .]. These shows are often bifurcated into segments that involve a panel of celebrities who discuss and interpret the informational content in an entertaining way (Galbraith and Karlin 2012, 26).

This use of *tarento*, "celebrities who perform in various media genres simultaneously" (Lukács 2010, 13), is the largest difference between Japanese and American "reality" programming—*tarento* act not only as a mediator between audience and content, but as audience representative. "*Tarento* color the Japanese media landscape, obviating the need for ordinary people, whom they represent. They perform as a responsive audience for the media content that features them, talking to and about one another in shared or viewed media appearances" (Galbraith and Karlin 2012, 26).

It is this intermediary, representative role that reconstitutes the American "star system" upon which "idol industrial complex" is based—both are celebrity ontologies, but their systems of function and meaning have been re-calibrated according to their respective cultures, with the latter most certainly aided by Japan's postwar "hyper-Westernization." "In the postwar era, 'things Japanese' carried a negative connotation because of wartime memories, while 'things Western (American)' were sought after. From the mid-1950s, as Japan entered an era of high economic growth, Westernized (Americanized) consumerism and urban cultures were firmly established within Japanese cities" (Daliot-Bul 2014, 45). And following a severe backlash to "hyper-Westernization" in the 1960s and early 1970s, the apolitical nature of Japan's youth has largely remained the same. The substitution of idol culture for true political participation has undoubtedly helped to nurture this.

As such, Japanese culture at large has replaced the nation's "eight million gods" ("an ancient expression describing the many islands constituting Japan in which gods coexisted and competed against each other") (McVeigh 2006, 464) with just a handful, the veneration of whom was only available through proscribed rituals of capitalism—"a hegemonic, commonsensical concept of cultural identity. . . of imposing norms, styles, values or ends [. . . that] constrain[ed] actions of all individuals and groups by providing a limited set of resources from which they could construct strategies of action" (Daliot-Bul 2014, 54).

INHABITANTS OF THE BORDER-LANDS

This was, in other words, an ontological erasure—the "eight million gods" of Japan swiftly being replaced by a monolithic hegemony. A central plot point in *Noroi: The Curse* is centered on the discorporation of one such "local rural" culture, making this erasure quite literal. Kagutaba, the demon that is being investigated, originated in a small village named Shimokage. Documents dating from over two hundred years ago (roughly the beginning of the Industrial age, when the tools of capitalism become exponentially greater) show that the villagers had annually been performing a "demon ritual," a sort of performance that required a young woman from the village to act the part of Kagutaba in order to pacify it and prevent it from causing natural disasters. However, Shimokage Village was ultimately submerged in 1978 to make way for the Shikami Dam, and the "demon ritual" was discontinued.

Ultimately, it is only through the intervention of another young woman, an idol who appears to have some sensitivity to the "spirit world" (Marika Matsumoto, playing "herself") that the demon is once again pacified, albeit temporarily. The use of a pliable young woman with amorphous abilities to soothe the violent tendencies of a similarly amorphous "entity" points directly toward the function of idols as "depoliticizing agents." That Japan has not since had a prolonged period of general political unrest suggests that the combination of affective and commodity culture have had the desired effect of transferring the population's unrealized political energy into a safer avenue—capitalist consumption and production,[3] of which idols act as an intermediary to "ward off" bad energy, not unlike the young woman of Shimokage village whose participation in the "demon ritual" ensured peace throughout their ontological realm. As the villager performs a "ritual," so does the idol "curate" methods of capitalist consumption.

This curation is a central feature to Shiraishi's films, where they are meant to play out as they would on a Japanese variety program. *Shirome* and *Cult* are even presented as such. That the action happening on the screen is "curated" to some degree by the same idols who frequently appear on Japanese television, where their function is largely the same, only further obscures these films as fictional narrative—if anything, this "curation" by well-known faces reinforces the suggestion that the supernatural events are not illusory (Sayad 2016, 55). These four films, with their centering of the idol figure, can then be read as a metaphorical "ritual" to ward off certain "spirits," which then points to a larger role for the idol as a participant in an arcane ritual of modern capitalist Japan.

Taken together, these four films suggest a character arc, not for any single young woman, but for the "idol" as an archetype. This journey begins with *Shirome*, starring the members of Momoiro Clover, who were all between the ages of thirteen and fifteen at the time. In *Cult*, the action centers on three idols firmly in the middle of their careers—Yu Abiru, Mari Iriki and Mayuko Iwasa. Lastly, *Noroi:The Curse* stars Marika Matsumoto, at a phase in her career when she is slowly transitioning out of more traditional idol work and into primarily acting. Played in this sequence, and with the understanding that all of the idols in these films are actually the same "characters," a rather traditional narrative of the idol's career unfolds in a three-act structure, with a clear beginning, middle, and end. The presence of young actress Rio Kanno (playing Kana Yano, a girl who gains television notoriety due to her aptitude for psycho-spiritual abilities)[4] in *Noroi: The Curse* suggests this narrative's regeneration—here, the twelve-year-old Kanno is perhaps a "pre-idol" in one of her first roles of what has since been a long and fruitful career. *Cult* follows along a similar vein, with the initial subject of supernatural possession being a young girl named Miho Kaneda (played by Natsumi Okamoto, roughly fourteen at the time, who would also go on to a greater idol career). As such, the intertwined narratives of Kanno's character with Marika, and Okamoto's character with Yu, Mari and Mayuko, where a "circle of possession" is formed between idols at the start of their career and closer to the end, could easily be interpreted as a passing of the baton, as new idols appear to replace old. And this is to say nothing of the extradiegetic interpretation of this "baton-passing," with Kanno and Okamoto being initiated into the idol system partially under the supervision of Marika, Yu, Mari and Mayuko—that the former are playing characters, while the latter are playing "themselves" suggests this diegetic environment to be a training ground for the younger idols before they "grow into" playing "themselves" in later roles.

However, these films also contain a far more difficult narrative to uncover. If the idols of *Shirome, Cult and Noroi: The Curse* represent the female half of Japanese social makeup, several male figures[5] form an analogous male archetype—the "freeter," a term used to describe young people (almost always typically men) who are chronically underemployed and often described as "parasitic, ambitionless, irresponsible, plagued with little perseverance, and lacking a work ethic" (Cook 2013, 30). In *Noroi: The Curse*, there is Shin'ichi Osawa (Takashi Kaziawa), one of the cult members—a young man who spends his free time capturing pigeons and getting into fights with his neighbors. There is also Mitsuo Hori (Satoru Jitsunashi), a paranoid shut-in with mental health issues who has lined everything in his home (including himself) in aluminum foil in order to fend off the "worms." The most interesting "freeter," however, is *Occult*'s Shohei Eno, an unemployed young man who claims that "miracles" happen to him, and who gradually becomes the main character before morphing into a sort of villain.

The overall premise of these four films stays largely formulaic—a documentary film crew is investigating paranormal events. In *Cult* and *Shirome*, Shiraishi is more or less a background character, while in *Occult* he is arguably the second main character, as his personal interaction with Eno, his subject, drive the narrative. This premise of the "active director" also appears in *Noroi: The Curse* in the form of Masafumi Kobayashi (Jin Muraki). Both "Shiraishi" and Kobayashi churn out cheaply made videos in which they investigate paranormal phenomenon, thereby providing yet another barrier crossing between the diegetic and extradiegetic worlds—whereas the fictional Shiraishi exploits the supernatural (and his idols stars) in pursuit of a cheap buck, the real-world Shiraishi largely does the same thing, even as his films and the films of his fictional counterpart reach out to each other by portraying the events as real. There is nothing within the paratextual elements of *Cult*, *Shirome* and *Occult* that would suggest it is a fictional film, instead being presented as the end product of the the fictional Shiraishi's work (and similarly, *Noroi: The Curse* is presented as the work of the deceased Kobayashi). Only occasionally does the veil slip in the diegetic world, revealing the artifice—if not for these slips, it would take only a modicum of suspension of disbelief to read these films as non-fictional (especially if one is already predisposed toward a belief in the supernatural). In *Occult*, the fictional Shiraishi is sent to prison for twenty-one years for his role in abetting the terrorist attack carried out by Eno. The action picks up when he is released, decades after the film itself is released, creating an irreconcilable time paradox that undoubtedly signals the fictionality of the "documentary" (perhaps a wise choice on the real-world Shiraishi's part, as he thereby definitively absolves himself of his fictional counterpart's crimes).

THE BLURRING OF REALITY AND
FICTION IN THE BORDER-LAND

As with the idols, Shiraishi's status as a public figure complicates the blurriness between the diegetic and extradiegetic worlds in these films. Just in the last several minutes of *Shirome* (of which the central plot is Momoiro Clover investigating a wish-granting entity named "Shirome" at an abandoned school in order to ask for their wish to further their careers), which "world" the audience is looking into is reversed several times. In chronological order (as opposed to the order in which they appear in the film), the events are as followed:

1. Upon finishing their investigation into the haunted school, Momoiro Clover are leaving, but are stopped by Shiraishi, who holds up a sign informing them they've just been pranked, and all of what they had just experienced was staged (the members later informed the press that they had been fooled into believing the supernatural events were real).[6] The crew congratulate them for being good sports.
2. Upon concluding their second anniversary concert, Momoiro Clover are greeted by Shiraishi backstage. He asks if they'd still be willing to sell their souls for their careers. They answer affirmatively and Shiraishi falls to the floor, howling and spasming, startling the girls. Group member Akari then screams and falls to the floor.
3. Continuing immediately from (2), Akari continues to scream. Shiraishi yells "Cut!" but Akari continues screaming. Shiraishi runs forward, visibly frightened.

Which world is real? The best answer is that there are no answers—mutliple "worlds" suggested here have equally valid claims at being "real." In one world, only Shiraishi (along with his crew) is "in on the joke" during the post-concert scenes. In another world, both Shiraishi and Momoiro Clover are. In another, Shiriashi and Momoiro Clover are in on the initial joke—that Shiriaishi is being possessed—but only Akari is in on the second joke, that *she* is being possessed. Perhaps this is her own private revenge for being put through the wringer earlier at the school—pranking Shiraishi even past the point when he has called the scene to a close, perhaps attempting to make *him* believe in some supernatural force. Or yet another world, where *all* the girls were in on the second joke, and played along with Araki's "possession" to better fool Shiraishi.[7]

This plurality of coexisting dimensions, situated within the lore of monstrous, unknowable, otherworldly beings, points to the true horror of these films. Reality itself has been decentered, and anyone, even the famous and influential, may find themselves unmoored from the foundations of their own senses, and therefore call into question their own existence. Rather than having control over our own lives, that power has been ceded to forces outside of ourselves, larger than ourselves. Diegetically, those in control are malevolent demons such as Shirome, or Kagutaba from *Noroi: The Curse*, or the unnamed "leech god(s)" that appear in both *Cult* and *Occult*. As the girls of Momoiro Clover learn, the system they've found themselves in places a number of demands on them, not only by allowing outside forces to control them, but fragmenting their own identities into at least two distinct parts— their public selves and their private selves, while maintaining the illusion that these are one and the same, despite the limitations imposed on idols by their managers. Furthermore, there is the crushing weight of spatiotemporal limitations imposed upon them—idol culture is born of the unique qualities of Japan, making its transnational success limited, and the idols themselves are often compelled to "graduate" at the age of twenty-five, before their attractiveness fades and they become "leftover Christmas cake" that no one wants (ReCupido 2009). What this means (especially the aspect of "aging out") is that the idols are, by design, disposable. There are a few in the grand scheme of things that ultimately "survive" the "survival entertainment" of idol culture—for every Seiko Matsuda (Japan's "Eternal Idol") (Baseel 2016), there are thousands who fade away into obscurity. And for those thousands, their very existence only matters for a few fleeting moments, if at all.

It is this compounded series of existential crises that manifest in Shiraishi's diegetic worlds as demons and malevolent gods. In the extradiegetic world, though, it is figures like Shiraishi himself who pose an existential threat to the idols.

THE AFFECTIVE ALLIANCE OF IDOL AND OTAKU

Although he is a small fish in this big pond, Shiraishi (and his fictional counterpart in *Cult* and *Shirome*) are part of the *keiretsu* system wherein "independent firms cluster into informal business groups through establishing network ties, interlocking business relations and cross-shareholding," a system that is itself modeled after the greater Japanese industrial system (Shin 2017, 18). As a content producer, Shiraishi is beholden to the *jimusho*, "various promotion agencies and management companies [that] emerged to devise systematic idol production strategies" (Ibid).

Once the "commodity" of young girls looking to make it has been acquired, the business strategy of the *jimusho* is two parallel processes: 1) exhibit the girls as the embodiment of abstract hopes and dreams by making the public invested in their success, and 2) create a sense of "intertextuality" for the "character" by spreading them across multiple media that must be "collected" by their fans. The hidden process here is that everything is attached to a process of consumption, not just of material goods and media, but of the girls themselves—"idols not only promote the sale of goods and services, but actually *are produced* by the goods and services that they sell [. . .] T]he capitalist system too needs idols to advertise the products that it produces. The idol, then, is but a node in the network of the capitalist system" (Galbraith and Karlin 2012, 28. Their emphasis).

The question as to *why* idols are so appealing, specifically to middle-aged men, is far more complex than sex—as well as that being far too obvious an answer.[8] As previous scholars have noted,[9] commodities meant for sexual consumption are in abundance in Japan, and many *otaku*[10] do not consider the commodities of idols to be sexual in nature, even videos of the girls, some of which have them in swimsuits.[11] This is not to suggest there is no sexual component to idol culture, as there obviously is for many men. But this explanation can't account for *all* consumption, and it's likely impossible to say how much is sexual in nature vs. other. Instead, the idol presents an opportunity for "ontological play" that allows a form of personal escape to a reality that is more preferable—one that is bright, colorful, cheerful, exciting, and possibly (but not necessarily) sexual. "[T]he perception is that [idols] are not playing characters so much as they are playing themselves. As a result, the real world and the onscreen world cease to be different and instead a deeply intertextual form of televisual pleasure is created between the performer and audience" (Galbraith and Karlin 2012, 33).

There exist a number of deeply existential longings connected to five aspects of this consumption and the desires they are associated with—(1) youth, nostalgia and the potential for success and/or recovery, (2) intimacy, (3) ontological play, (4) meaning-making, and (5) catharsis of energies that would otherwise be expended on the political. The end result is an *otaku* who has become almost completely apolitical and deeply infantilized, obsessed with certain embodied objects (in this case, the living form of the idol), and has largely (and happily) fallen into the concurrent "grand narrative" of capitalist consumption, albeit one that is dressed up as a bright, colorful, exciting, cheerful playground. The *otaku* seemingly exists in a simulacrum of an alternate dimension.

Otaku who overindulge in idol culture do, in many ways, resemble a deviation from the real world, an imposition of another ontology onto the real world—one with its own norms, rituals, relationships and even politics. However, it is this fact—that they *do* exist in the "real world"—that forces us to acknowledge the unreality of their "alternate universe" and instead understand *otaku* culture as a form of "cult"—one built around commodity and "affective capitalism," wherein "lifestyle collectivities and brand communities" (Galbraith 2018, 206) become more integral parts of business, as commodities are fetishized and, with respect to idol culture specifically, "business interests stage the appearance of youth resistance, i.e., corporations utilize youth for their own profit-making purposes" (McVeigh 2006, 464). A particular idol's fans are then merged into an "affective alliance" where the purest form of "worship" involves acquisition of material goods, which are transmuted into a "worship" of the idol herself, who cannot be separated from such goods and has successfully transported fans to this "alternate universe"—"Idol pop stars are only considered a finished product when they are able to successfully suspend the outside realities of their fans" (Covington 2014).

Kano, the super-fan of "Rio" who is featured in *Storyville: Tokyo Girls* (at the beginning of which he tells an interviewer "This isn't a fad, it's a religion"), takes part in a number of rituals at Rio's shows, with the *shineitai* (cheering group) participating in synchronized movements and cheers before and during her performance, as Rio sings in call-and-response with her fans. "Faith, faith! Worship, worship! Pilgrimage, pilgrimage!" More choice lyrics—"Make a donation, say a prayer, don't listen to reason."

After the show, Kano addresses the other members through a megaphone, sharing the news that Rio has been signed to a label—"Everyone gathered her today, brothers from all over the world, greetings to you all! It's only the beginning! May Rio's magical smile and radiant power bless the whole world!" As another fan describes his "brothers" later on, "They looked happy and desperate at the same time. It was so moving. You don't often see such joy and release [. . .] If it wasn't for this, I'd be alone forever" (*Storyville: Tokyo Girls*).

Members of this "affective alliance" "are empowered by the idol's successes (within the group and industry), willingly subjugate themselves to the idol, and do not get bored with interactions with the with idol, interactions between members of the group, or interactions between groups" (Galbraith and Karlin 2012, 52). The "cult" of the idol replaces normal avenues through which the fan interacts with the world as the "responsibilities" of the group come to take up more and more of a "worshipper's" time—"Good fans, its implied, will attend every department store rooftop concert, get in line at every meet-and-greet, get an autograph whenever one is available" (Sevakis 2015).

"THIS WORLD IS JUST SHIT, ISN'T IT?"

Although never explicitly referred to as such, Shusei Eno from *Occult* fits the profile of the shiftless, underemployed young man approaching middle age whose prospects continually dwindle from bad to worse. His status as a believer in a superior alternate universe positions him as the stand-in for "freeters," "salarymen" and "otaku" who worship a foreign ontology that opposes the "real world." He enters the orbit of Koji Shiraishi (playing a version of himself in the film, not unlike an idol) as the latter's production team are investigating the 2005 stabbing spree of a man named Ken Matsuki. Eno is the only victim who survives. This is not accidental—Matsuki deliberately left Eno alive, carving a strange petroglyph into his back (the same one that Matsuki himself had as a birthmark) and telling him "It's your turn now, OK?" before jumping off a cliff.

When Shiraishi meets Eno, the latter is a typical "freeter." His situation is explained not by himself, but by the film's captions—"When you reach thirty, temporary jobs rapidly become scare. This is also influenced by downsizing tendencies of corporations [. . . Eno] buys groceries based on whether they will fill his stomach or not. He doesn't have his own apartment. He spends his nights at a manga cafe. He is a so-called internet cafe refugee," where nightly rent is ultra-cheap. "The good thing about manga cafes," Eno explains, "is that you can take a shower, you can use the air conditioner, and you don't have to spend money on things like fuel and electricity. They also have beverages that you can drink as much as you like."

Eno claims that, since the stabbing, he has been witnessing unexplainable phenomena about once a day—disembodied voices, poltergeist activity, and unidentified objects flying in the sky. He confides in Shiraishi that he understands what the voices mean, believing them to be a supernatural entity ("God," as he describes it) and that they have given him a mission—he is to set off a bomb in Tokyo famously busy Shibuya Crossing, which he believes will not kill anyone, but rather transport them to another dimension akin to heaven—"That world is so much better than this one. This world is just shit, isn't it?" he remarks.

Eno's clear desire to escape a world he finds to be "shit" is analogous to the position of the *otaku*—albeit in much simpler, more nihilistic language. As *otaku* find meaning in their higher purpose of "crossing over" to a different "dimension," so too does Eno. What also links *Occult* to the greater "mythology" of idol culture that is on display in *Noroi: The Curse*, *Cult* and *Shirome* is the actual manifestation of this supernatural "dimension." The psychically attuned idol is key in those three films, but the material makeup of the various demons, gods and entities are highly similar, with "Kagutaba" (*Noroi: The Curse*) and "Hiruko" (*Occult*) appearing in the form of massive leeches—sometimes singular, sometimes as a cluster that writhes around each other. The nameless creatures in *Shirome* and *Cult* can be described similarly, with other manifestations resembling tentacled underwater creatures that look not unlike the mass of wriggling leeches that appear elsewhere in the films (and despite the description of "Shirome" as a butterfly, the final scene where it appears to be possessing Akari makes it seem more like a squid).

Extradiegeticaly, the explanation seems obvious, if a bit cynical—Shiraishi's films were pumped out on a shoestring budget, and a generic "worm" shape is very easily created through rudimentary computer-generated special effects. Diegeticaly, though, the symbol of the "worm/leech" has multiple signifiers. The entity Eno is interacting with in *Occult* is referred to as "Hiruko."[12] In the Japanese creation myth, Hiruko (literally translated to "leech child") is the first son of the gods Izanami and Izanagi, born deformed and therefore cast aside by his parents. Secondly, the leech itself as a creature that subsists off the blood of other animals—with multiple points of analogy here, such as the idol sapping the financial reserves of her fans, the fans sapping the idol's emotional, mental, spiritual and physical energies, and the capitalist system surviving on the "blood" of a dehumanized labor force that includes both idol and *otaku*. Thirdly, the leech, as it appears in the films, is a rather nondescript phallic symbol, and indeed, the 'leeches" spend much of their time pursuing, attacking, inserting themselves into and protruding from female bodies. The leech, then, is weaponized masculinity.

COMMODIFICATION AND HUMAN SACRIFICE

Idol culture also, as a rule (hegemonically created by "producers" and largely carried out by fans and idols themselves), is centered on masculine control of the female form.[13] Ostensibly under the auspices of keeping them "pure," idols are forbidden from certain behaviors such as smoking, drinking alcohol and taking drugs. In addition, "the girls are forbidden to have boyfriends, lovers or any kind of sexual relations" no matter their age (Yamamoto and Adelstein 2019). In *Cult*, this extreme control manifests as existential danger—when Mayuko is caught having eaten a hamburger, she is told it has opened her up to possible demonic possession.

The amount of control exerted over idols has led to a number of high-profile scandals. Minami Minegishi of AKB48 issued a public apology when it was discovered she had a boyfriend, and publicly shaved her head as penance.[14] When Maho Yamaguchi of NGT48 was assaulted by two fans near her home (who had supposedly been given her address by one of Yamaguchi's co-workers), Yamaguchi came forward to highlight the danger she had been put in (after which her own managers "contacted reporters at tabloid newspapers and suggested that Yamaguchi was mentally ill, hoping to discredit her"), but was soon forced to issue a public apology for "causing a commotion" (Yamamoto and Adelstein 2019). After being overworked, harassed and threatened, sixteen-year-old Honoka Omoto of Enoha Girls committed suicide. And then there are the routine aggressions of management against their *tarento*—being given assignments with no room for negotiation, regardless of their comfort level. Yumeno Nito, who works with "Colabo. Charity" in order to fight against the exploitation of young women, reported "one girl was taken to a venue without receiving a job description and then suddenly forced to wear a swimsuit. According to Nito, the girl was crying because she didn't want to participate in the event [. . .] Nito explains that the teens are convinced into believing that this is what working as an idol involves. But she confirms that it is abuse" (*The Mainichi*, 2018).

Both *Shirome* and *Cult* contain such scenes. In the former, the girls cry, whine, scream, and plead to not be made to take their assignment. Ultimately, they acquiesce, only under the premise that doing so will gain them a chance to advance their burgeoning careers. This is made all the more disturbing knowing that, at the time, the girls had not been informed they were only being "punk'd."

In the latter, Yu, Mayuko and Mari are told of their latest assignment, "something to do with the spiritual." They learn they are to investigate a demonic possession, and immediately voice their displeasure. However, they are handed documents explaining what they are supposed to do. Bound by contracts, the girls have no choice, despite the danger they face. They read the documents—"This reads 'shouldn't be any harm.' That's not a reassuring statement!" Still, they accept the assignment, because they are legally obligated to do so. Later, when Mari meets with her manager, trying to quit the assignment, he lays into her—"How can you quit a job so easily?" he shouts at her. "It's not just me you put in trouble, there's a lot of staff on this project. Do you get it?" Here, Mari functions as an object of sacrifice—the toll the work is taking on her must be endured for the good of others, who are likely not under the strain she is.

The idol, then, is simultaneously an object of worship and an object of sacrifice—created by managers and producers, who throw them to rabid fans for consumption, whose act of consumption is a futile attempt to stave off their existential crises. The *otaku* salaryman is likewise an object of sacrifice, whose labor potential is used up for the good of others—the *keiretsu* who, in Shiraishi's films, take the form of mostly invisible, monstrous super-gods who leech off others for survival. The motif of "possession" in these films is mostly one of "positioning"—placing the "victim" in circumstances that are most amenable to the process of "leeching." As this is true for the idols, so it is for the salarymen, for whom idol culture functions as an "expensive mirror" (*Storyville: Tokyo Girls*).

If the lives of idols are dramatized by the Japanese media [. . .] in what might be called "life theater," those who lead less glamorous, more mundane lives must stage their own selves in order to satisfy corporate culture (appropriate dress, correct speech, company loyalty, etc.). If "personal image" is the most important commodity of performers, then there is a good chance that the same holds true for everyone else. In other words, the "simulation" and "packaging of self" are not limited to the entertainment world; they impact everyone. Indeed, the great concern with the self is a postmodern leitmotif: establishing the self, disciplining the self, developing the self, discovering the self, renewing the self, evaluating the self, recovering the self." (McVeigh 2006, 466–467)

Essentially, "the idol's lack of an autonomous existence makes her an interchangeable and disposable image commodity" (Galbraith 2018, 268). However, this is true for the salarymen, as well. This, of course, begs the question—if the self of the everyday person is "packaged," what world are they really living in? Were they born into the capitalist dimension, or were they, little by little, compelled to cross over? And in that case, does the escape to the "idol dimension" constitute a return, or a second crossing-over, to yet another dimension? In other words, does an escape to the "idol dimension" suggest a recovery of human nature (however temporary), or another manufactured reality, not unlike the "capitalist dimension"?

Ultimately, it is impossible to tell, as these three ontological landscapes are inextricably intertwined. However, modern social, political and economic forces suggest that we are all doomed to return to one of them. As Eno learns, the world he believed to be "so much better than this one," is in fact a hell (and raises another question—has he returned to the "capitalist dimension" or crossed over into one reserved for that dimension's refuse?). As Kano, the superfan from *Storyville: Tokyo Girls* remarks, he has no real prospects and will likely succumb to old age and disease before long. The question is, who will take care of him? It seems unlikely that Rio, the object of his worship and affection, will become his caretaker, or will even send a bit of money for his care. If she is lucky enough, she will have moved from the idol world into more "sophisticated" entertainment, becoming a singer, actor, and so forth. But it's far more likely that, like thousands of idols before her, she will "graduate" to life as a housewife shortly after her twenty-fifth birthday. Kano and Rio will continue to inhabit the same ontological space, albeit now a different one from the "idol universe"—instead, they'll both be relegated to the hellish limbo of capitalism's discarded detritus.

CAPITALISM AS COSMIC ENTITY

The final scene of *Occult* returns to Eno's suicide bombing. He has been carrying a camera with him, recording the consummation of his "mission" to help others cross over to the world of the gods. The camera is still filming as he crosses over, now finding himself in a floating hellscape, surrounded by shrieking, dismembered human heads. On all sides of him, massive jellyfish-like creatures float past him and monstrous black worms wriggle. "It's hell!" he shouts. "Shiraishi-kun! Help me!" His head is severed and joins the others around him before they are all subsumed by the demonic creatures, which seem to not even notice him.

If there are indeed "gods" of capitalism, and they've replaced the old gods, not only of religion but of pre-Enlightenment reasoning, we can make a series of insights into their nature, all of which further the comparison between a personification of "capitalism" and the "cosmic horrors" that populate Shiraishi's films.

First, these are gods of not only creation but destruction, their processes a closed loop of production and consumption, "creating performers from zero, full coordination of artistic content by company employees, long-term market planning, and demands to control all media content pertaining to the idol [. . .] then forcefully pushing their talent out into the wider popular culture" (Marx 2012, 64) and squeezing as much out of the resource as possible before it spoils, and is then "destroyed." For idols, this spoilage has a mostly clear date, sometime around their twenty-fifth birthday. Young workers have roughly until the age of thirty to settle into a salaryman job, where they will likely remain until the age of sixty-five (although recent changes in law have upped that to seventy, thereby allowing more labor to be wrung out of "human resources") (Hughes 2020).

Second, these gods are unknowable. In Japan, the loose *keiretsu* system of business alliances is negotiated well outside of public view. The exact relationship between any two firms is rarely explicit, and to what degree any and all *keiretsu* have created a de facto monopoly over an industry (or *all* industry) is largely impossible to know (Shin 2017, 18–19). Furthermore, the "source" of all the malaise created by these gods is often shifted onto the individual—"In Japan's neoliberal media system, criticism of producers is almost always taboo. If fans are pathologized in the media, it is often because criticism of the media industry is strictly proscribed" (Galbraith and Karlin 2012, 49).

Third, the gods are the only true power. The order has been established, the hierarchy is firmly in place, and attempts at overthrowing it have become increasingly difficult due to the co-opting of youth culture, and therefore of the most potent source of revolutionary power. Moreover, the removal of the political as a publicly-tread realm assures that those who already hold the power retain it. Idols can be "poor actors, bad singers, and unskilled dancers, but they can certainly not be controversial, unattractive, or otherwise disruptive" (Marx 2012, 84). Their ubiquity and their apolitical status combine to influence an apolitical public—idols "tend to avoid deep meanings and lasting associations, which are divisive (and bad for business). Maybe idols can only express moral truisms (e.g., killing is evil, life is beautiful) and sufficiently general principles (e.g., we should help others). Maybe in order to secure mass appeal idols can only ever be conservative" (Galbraith and Karlin 2012, 54), thereby helping to maintain the status quo.

Fourth, the gods are eternal. Stardust Promotion, the company that managers Momoiro Clover, among many, many others, was founded in 1979. Johnny & Associates, who manage many of Japan's biggest idol groups, were founded in 1962 (and up until his death in 2019, was run by Johnny Kitagawa for over forty years). Many of the largest talent agencies in Japan have held their positions for decades. "The general industrial structure of the *jimusho* world, especially the fact that new firms have a hard time entering it, essentially means that the same people have been responsible for crafting new stars decade after decade" (Marx 2012, 82).

Fifth, the gods' appetite is never sated. As there will always be profit to be extracted, and labor to be squeezed out, the gods will continue to consume. The religion of consumption demands insatiability, and this aspect of the system trickles down to everyone within it, thereby propagating it - "as the object [of desire] can never be fully possessed, the climax is indefinitely deferred and the continuation or serialization of interaction can be sold as harmless fantasy to both children and adults [. . .] The idol is a symptom not just of man, but also of consumer-capitalist society" (Galbraith 2018, 273–274).

Sixth, the gods are inescapable. Even a seeming escape into the "idol dimension" is only a temporary journey into a "pocket dimension" created for further extraction of wealth and influence

> [T]he technologies of governmentality produce a citizenry to serve the policies of neoliberalism through the linking of the capitalist state and the ideology of consumerism. The state does not police these policies through the threat of force, but relies on corporations and the techniques of marketing and the subjugation of bodies. The biopolitics of this regime cultivates the mimetic desires of the masses by channeling their energies into ritualized forms of consumption. Celebrities are the enforcers of the regime of capitalism through their signification of the ideology of consumption. The mimetic desire to appropriate the image of the celebrity operates in the sphere of economic processes for the controlled insertion of bodies into the routinized repetition of the consumption of goods.(Galbraith and Karlin 2012, 44)

Capitalism is an abstract, and yet horrifically material, manifestation of the Cthulhus of the world, as well as the Kagutabas—not for nothing do the characters of the latter's name translate to "demon, tool, spirit [. . .] A tool that's capable of causing disasters" (as the historian of *Norio: The Curse* tells Kobayashi) an apt description of commerce and capital if there ever was one. Ironically, what leads us to a number of these conclusions is itself a commodity—Shiraishi's cheaply made found footage horror films. The conceit of found footage, the overlapping of ontologies it centers, and the gradations of reality it highlights, all point toward a horrific truth—we are living in this world populated by such gods, and this world may very well be of their creation. However, the conceit of found footage also contains within it a possible means of counteracting their influence. If indeed the "real world" is a confluence of ontologies, film (and found footage in particular) presents an opportunity to craft a utopian image populated by the true representation of ontologies people wish to exist in, rather than the "pocket dimensions" manufactured for us.

REFERENCES

"AKB48 pop star shaves head after breaking band rules." 2013. *BBC*. Filmed February 1. Accessed May 12, 2021. https://www.bbc.com/news/world-asia-21299324.

Baseel, Casey. 2016. "Pop Singer Seiko Matsuda, 54, still turning heads as a lingerie model." *Japan Today*. Accessed May 1, 2021. https://japantoday.com/category/entertainment/pop-singer-seiko-matsuda-at-54-still-turning-heads-as-a-lingerie-model.

Cook, Emma E. 2013. "Expectations of Failure: Maturity and Masculinity for Freeters in Contemporary Japan." *Social Science Japan Journal*. Vol. 16, no. 1 (Winter): 29–43.

Covington, Abigail. 2014. "Unraveling a fantasy: A beginner's guide to Japanese idol pop." *The AV Club*. Accessed May 12, 2021. https://music.avclub.com/unraveling-a-fantasy-a-beginner-s-guide-to-japanese-id-1798270934.

Daliot-Bul, Michal. 2014. "The Formation of 'Youth' as a Social Category in Pre-1970s Japan: A Forgotten Chapter of Japanese Postwar Youth Countercultures." *Social Science Japan Journal*. Vol. 17, No. 1 (November): 41–58.

Derrida, Jacques. *The Truth in Painting*. Translated by Geoff Berrington and Ian McLeod. Chicago: University of Chicago Press, 1987.

Galbraith, Patrick W. 2012. "Idols: The Image of Desire in Japanese Consumer Culture." In *Idols and Celebrity in Japanese Media Culture*, edited by Patrick W. Galbraith and Jason G. Karlin, 255–275. New York: Palgrave McMillan.

_____. 2018. "'Idols' in Japan, Asia and the World." In *Routledge Handbook of Celebrity Studies*, edited by Anthony Elliott, 202–214. Routledge.

Galbraith, Patrick W. and Karlin, Jason G. 2012. "Introduction: The Mirror of Idols and Celebrity." *Idols and Celebrity in Japanese Media Culture*, edited by Patrick W. Galbraith and Jason G. Karlin, 19–60. New York: Palgrave McMillan.

Hughes, Clyde. 2020. "Japan approves laws to raise retirement age to 70." *UPI*. Accessed March 20, 2021. https://www.upi.com/Top_News/World-News/2020/02/04/Japan-approves-laws-to-raise-retirement-age-to-70/2741580840804/.

Jozuka, Emiko. 2019. "Why a pop idol's stand against her assault sparked outrage in Japan." *CNN*. Accessed May 16, 2021. https://www.cnn.com/2019/01/16/asia/japanese-pop-idol-sexual-assault-apology-bullying-intl/index.html.

Lukács, Gabriella. 2010. *Scripted Affects, Branded Selves: Television, Subjectivity, and Capitalism in 1990s Japan*. London: Duke University Press.

Martin, Ian. 2013. "AKB48 member's 'penance shows flaws in idol culture." *The Japan Times*. Accessed April 29, 2021. https://www.japantimes.co.jp/culture/2013/02/01/music/akb48-members-penance-shows-flaws-in-idol-culture/.

Marx, W. David. 2012. "The *Jimusho* System: Understanding the Production Logic of the Japanese Entertainment Industry." In *Idols and Celebrity in Japanese Media Culture*, edited by Patrick W. Galbraith and Jason G. Karlin, 62–90. New York: Palgrave McMillan, 2012.

McVeigh, Brian J. 2006. "Island of Eight Million Smile: Idol Performance and Symbolic Production in Contemporary Japan." Review of *Island of Eight Million Smile: Idol Performance and Symbolic Production in Contemporary Japan*, by Hiroshi Aoyagi. *Journal of Japanese Studies*, Vol. 32, no. 2 (2017): 462–467.

"Momoiro Clover, the first stunning movie that includes a stunning recording is decided." 2010. *Oricon*. Accessed April 26, 2021. https://career.oricon.co.jp/news/77570/.

Nagaike, Kazumi. 2012. "Johnny's Idols as Icons: Female Desires to Fantasize and Consume Male Idol Images." *Idols and Celebrity in Japanese Media Culture*, edited by Patrick W. Galbraith and Jason G. Karlin, 142–163. New York: Palgrave McMillan.

ReCupido, Amanda. 2009. "'Leftover Christmas Cake' and Other Anti-Feminist Expressions." *Huffington Post*. September 8, 2009. https://www.huffpost.com/entry/leftover-christmas-cake-a_b_248364.

Sayad, Cecilia. 2016. "Found-Footage Horror and the Frame's Undoing." *Cinema Journal*. Vol. 55, no. 2 (Winter): 43–66.

Sevakis, Justin. "Why Can't Idol Singers Have Lives of Their Own?" *Anime News Network*. July 24, 2015. https://www.animenewsnetwork.com/answerman/2015-07-24/.90830.

Shin, Solee. 2017. "Niche, Ethnic and Global Operations: Models of Production and Circulation of East Asian Popular Music." *European Journal of East Asian Studies*. Vol. 16, no. 1 (2017): 5–35.

"Suicide of teen draws attention to poor working conditions, harassment of idols." 2018. *The Mainichi*. November 18, 2018. https://mainichi.jp/english/articles/20181118/p2a/00m/0na/005000c.

Yamamoto, Mari and Adelstein, Jake. 2019. "Inside the Weird, Dangerous World of Japan's Girl 'Idols.'" *The Daily Beast*. January 21, 2019. https://www.thedailybeast.com/look-but-dont-touch-inside-the-weird-dangerous-world-of-japans-girl-idols.

NOTES

1. "The role of an idol is much closer to that of a beauty pageant winner: they're in the business of selling dreams. The product is the illusion of a cute, slightly idealized person who is there for you, the fan. Idols are prohibited from dating anyone because if word got out, that would ruin the illusion that they're there JUST FOR YOU. Likewise, any sex life, alcohol use, or anything else that would be seen as "impure" to fans that want this perfect, innocent little china doll (male or female) would ruin the illusion, and therefore render the idol useless" (Sevakis 2015). "Idols make themselves accessible to fans through live performances, small venues and special events where contact and communication are possible" (Galbraith 2018, 202).

2. Barring animated films and computer-generated imagery, among other things.

3. "Youth's means of self-definition have been commodified since the 1970s, leaving very little room, if any, for expressive tools beyond the scope of consumer culture. . . [I]n late capitalist societies, those who wish to distinguish themselves from the homogenizing effects of mass society (such as rebellious youths) do so almost exclusively by consuming products and practices that seem to them to be nonconformist, although they are marketed by the same production and distribution channels that produce mass society" (Daliot-Bul 2014, 56).

4. The connection between idols (past, present and future) and psychic abilities provides a rich metaphor for the central work of idols to connect fans with their own dreams. In *Noroi: The Curse*, psychic affinities are displayed by both Rio Kanno's character and "Marika Matsumoto." The same is true for three characters in *Cult* (Natsumi Okamoto's character, "Mari Iriki" and, to a lesser degree, "Mayuko Iwasa") and one in *Shirome* ("Akari Hayami").

5. Despite their similar titles of *Cult* and *Occult*, one is not the sequel/prequel of another. If anything, they function as spiritual companions, as *Cult* centers on female experience while *Occult* does the same for male experience.

6. "Momoiro Clover, the first stunning movie that includes a stunning recording is decided" (*Oricon* 2010).

7. In yet another world (albeit one that's rather far-fetched), the spirit "Shirome" truly exists in the extradiegetic world and has come to claim Akari.

8. Focusing solely on idol culture as one of "perversion" and sexual exploitation risks approaching a "neo-Orientalist discourse . . . If Japan is branded as the nation of idols, then this can quickly transform into Japan being branded as a nation of normalized sexual exploitation of women. And because idols are understood to be young, Japan is further branded as a nation of normalized sexual exploitation of children" (Galbraith 2018, 209).

9. See (Aoyagi 2003) in addition to the Galbraith works (2018; 2012) noted elsewhere.

10. Otaku is a term that can be applied quite broadly ("hard-core fans" [Daliot-Bul 2014, 42]) and specifically ("a derogatory term for antisocial maniacs, who are obsessed with one particular thing, especially areas of pop-culture such as manga and anime" [Nagaike 2012, 161]). "Unlike normal guys with a mainstream hobby who have a real girlfriend and a proper job" (*Storyville: Tokyo Girls*. Directed by Kyoko

Miyaki. BBC, 2017). What is especially relevant here is the idea of otaku as "those with an affinity for 'fictional contexts'" (Galbraith 2018, 257).

[11.] Reasons given for watching such videos include "(1) it heals me to be taken out of my stressful day . . . (2) it energizes me to see the young and happy idol . . . (3) it allows me to see the idol's growth, keeping me connected and close to her" (Galbraith 2018, 270).

[12.] The amateur historian who identifies Hiruko is Kyoshi Kurosawa, director of *Pulse* (2001) and *Tokyo Sonata* (2008) among other films, playing himself here much like several others.

[13.] While there are plenty of male idols, in terms of sheer numbers, female idols are far more prevalent and arguably exponentially more influential and profitable.

14. See "AKB48 pop star shaves head after breaking band rules." *BBC*. February 1, 2013. https://www.bbc.com/news/world-asia-21299324.

Chapter 14

Obscure, Reveal, Repeat

Hidden Worlds and Uncertain Truths in Kōji Shiraishi's The Curse *and* Occult

Lindsay Nelson

In the first book of Eugene Thacker's *Horror of Philosophy* trilogy, *In the Dust of This Planet*, the author defines "occult" as "something hidden, concealed, and surrounded by shadows" (Thacker 2011, 52). He goes on to say, though, that "that which is hidden implies that which is revealed . . . just as that which is already apparent may, by some twist, suddenly become obscure and occult" (Ibid). Drawing on the work of H.P. Lovecraft and others, Thacker imagines "fissures, lapses, or lacunae" between what he calls the "world-in-itself" and the "world-for-us" (Thacker 2011, 8). These gaps are the Planet, the "world-without-us . . . the 'dark intelligible abyss' that is paradoxically manifest as the World and the Earth" (Ibid). In this context, horror "is not simply about fear, but instead about the enigmatic thought of the unknown" (Ibid). Horror, Thacker argues, is a means to help us understand the limits of our own humanity, and to break down and confront our fear of the unknown, which is often manifested in these "fissures, lapses, or lacunae" that reveal a world beyond our comprehension.[1]

J-horror as a genre has always been deeply concerned with the occult, with confronting the unknown and the limits of our own understanding, and with revealing things once obscured, often with deadly results. In Hideo Nakata's *Ringu* (*The Ring*, 1998) the sight of the ghostly Sadako and her single, staring eye is enough to kill her victims, and also to render photographic images of them warped and distorted. In more recent films like Yoshihiro Nakamura's

Zan-e: Sunde wa ikenai heya (*The Inerasable*, 2015) we wait for the horrifying thing to be revealed, but for much of the film we see very little: terror comes instead from ghosts and presences that lurk but are almost never seen, revealing themselves through faint, repeated sounds, and leaving the rest up to our imaginations. In Kiyoshi Kurosawa's *Kairō* (*Pulse*, 2001), one character attempts to stave off his fear of ghostly apparitions by saying repeatedly that they are only "phantoms" (*maboroshi*)—only to find that he is able to touch one of them. The ghostly presence then tells him, "I am not a phantom" (*maboroshi de wa nai*). It is arguably this knowledge, that the world is full of things beyond his comprehension, that drives this character mad, condemning him to the madness that defeats so many of Lovecraft's characters when they are confronted with the "paradoxical thought of the unthinkable" (Thacker 2011, 9). The worlds presented to us in J-horror are worlds that, like the specter, are "both visible and invisible. . .a trace that marks the present with its absence in advance" (Derrida and Stiegler 2013, 38). They are entities and events that circle and repeat, that in their spectral fashion, "begin by coming back" (Derrida 1994, 11), and that exist in a world in which ghosts and the occult cannot ultimately be understood or defeated. Rather, they must be "lived with," in a manner similar to the way that spectrality "as a conceptual metaphor. . . (signals) the ultimate disjointedness of ontology, history, inheritance, materiality, and ideology" (del Pilar Blanco and Pereen 2013, 6).

Many of the found footage horror films and straight-to-video series of director Kōji Shiraishi are also deeply concerned with "revealing" hidden truths, both in their narratives (which often focus on the supernatural) and in the ways that Shiraishi often seems keen to let the audience in on the secrets of his filmmaking. The supernatural creatures and myths described in these films are a mix of invented Japanese folklore and Lovecraftian monsters, familiar images that are presented as taboo or too horrifying to be viewed. Shiraishi's camera acts as an instrument that reveals hidden truths but in the same moment undermines that "truthfulness" by mixing documentary-style footage with cheap visual effects, and by confusing the relationship between director and subject. Hidden entities and images are revealed visually, but, as in so many Japanese horror films, endings are often ambiguous, and the meanings of the monsters and supernatural happenings are never quite fully explained or understood. Visibility does not equal knowability.

In two of Shiraishi's films released in the 2000s, *Noroi* (*The Curse*, 2005) and *Okaruto* (*Occult*, 2009) we can see a contrast between a fairly standard found footage horror film (a "record" or document of strange events compiled by an investigative journalist) and a more complicated examination of visible / invisible and the nature of "truth" in found footage horror. This contrast is evident in the use and role of the camera and who wields it, the way that repetition and freeze frame serve to both clarify and obscure "truth," a gradual weakening of the divide between director and subject, and a rising tension between presenting a "realistic" documentation of events and repeatedly undermining that realism through the use of cheap visual effects. In *The Curse*, the camera exists purely to provide a record, and the cameraperson is mostly invisible. In *Occult*, though, multiple cameras are in play, multiple people are holding them, and the question of who has the final say when it comes to the "truth" being presented via the edited footage is unclear. *Occult* also makes its connection to a Lovecraftian mythos—and by extension the idea of "other worlds" and hidden things being revealed through narrative— more explicit.

This chapter will offer an examination of the ways that *The Curse* and *Occult* reveal and conceal hidden worlds and ideas both within their narratives and through their structure, use of repetition, references to a Lovecraftian mythos, and use of visual effects. In examining these two films, I hope to place them in the larger context of J-horror and found footage horror, as well as to reveal the ways that the films' narratives, camera work, and editing choices both reveal and obscure occultish "hidden" worlds and entities, forcing the viewer to constantly question the version of "truth" that is presented on screen.

Mockumentary and found footage are likely not the first genres that come to mind when one imagines the J-horror genre. But films like *The Ring* and Takashi Shimizu's *Ju-on (The Grudge*, 2002) still have a strong connection to the "true ghost story" tradition. As Steven T. Brown and Alex Zahlten have argued, the cheap, bare bones aesthetic of Norio Tsuruta's straight-to-video *Hontō ni atta kowai hanashi (True Scary Stories*, 1992) series, which depicted supposedly "true" supernatural events in everyday settings, had a strong influence on the aesthetic of J-horror (Brown 2018, 2; Zahlten 2017, 163). More specifically, *The Ring* screenwriter Hiroshi Takahashi argues that the *Hontō ni atta kowai hanashi* aesthetic was the inspiration behind Takahashi's and director Hideo Nakata's creation of *The Ring*, which would have a strong influence on J-horror as a whole (Brown 2018, 2–3). Japanese cinema and TV also have a long history of mixing documentary and fiction, as well as with "true ghost story" videos presented either as a film or TV episode / segment.[2] Shiraishi's found footage and mockumentary horror films, then, are drawing on a long "true ghost story" tradition that precedes the J-horror "boom" period of the late 1990s and early 2000s, even if at first glance Shiraishi's films might not seem to fit the J-horror model.

The films and video series that Shiraishi has created since his university days, with varying degrees of creative control, mix elements of comedy, horror, and drama, ranging from extremely violent and graphic films like 2009's *Gurotesuku (Grotesque)*, to retellings of urban legends like 2009's

Teke Teke (the story of a vengeful ghost who is missing the lower half of her body), to the much more conventional 2016 film *Sadako vs. Kayako*, a merging of the J-horror *Ring* and *Grudge* franchises. As outlined in his own *Feiku dokyuentarī no kyōkasho* (*Fake Documentary Textbook*, 2016), though, Shiraishi's passion seems to lie with the found footage / mockumentary genre, which he has explored with *The Curse, Occult, Bachiatari bōryoku ningen* (*Cursed Violent People*, 2010), *Chō akunin* (*Hyper-Villain*, 2011) *Aru yasashiki satsujinsha no kiroku* (*A Record of Sweet Murder*, 2014) *Karuto* (*Cult*, 2013) *Shirome* (2010), and his long-running original video series *Senritsu kaiki fairu: kowasugi!* (*Dreadful Mystery Files: Too Scary!*, 2012–present), a series of mockumentary-style paranormal investigation videos that focus on demonic possession and urban legends (Shiraishi 2016). Most of Shiraishi's found footage films involve the investigation of some form of paranormal activity, often with a connection to Japanese folklore and Buddhist or Shinto rituals, as well as images that recall Cthulhu and other Lovecraftian monsters.[3] Shiraishi often plays a version of himself in these films, and actors often play versions of themselves, using their actual names or slightly altered names (frequent Shiraishi collaborator Shōhei Uno, for example, is known as Shōhei Eno in *Occult* and *Hyper-Villain*, actress Marika Matsumoto plays a version of herself in *The Curse*, and film director Kiyoshi Kurosawa plays a version of himself in *Occult*). While *The Curse* and some entries in the *Dreadful Mystery Files* series seem to be trying for genuine scares, more often Shiraishi seems to be more focused on playing with the tension between reality and fiction that is inherent in the found footage genre. In a DVD that accompanies his *Fake Documentary Textbook*, Shiraishi and his team offer a mini-lesson in how to script, shoot, and edit a short found footage horror film in a single day, with the DVD divided between the finished product and a behind-the-scenes look at its production. In *Cursed Violent People*, much of the action centers around Shiraishi revealing to his subjects that everything he does is "a lie" (*uso*) and "fake" (*yarase*) and then working together with them to produce increasingly outrageous "fake" ghost story videos.

At first glance, Shiraishi's films seem to be borrowing a great deal from the found footage horror films that dominated the English-language film world for much of the late 1990s and 2000s. The found footage / mockumentary genre can be seen as far back as the 1960s in "mondo" films (a genre of "shocking" and exploitative pseudo-documentary that often focused on sex and violence) and in the early 1980s in films like Ruggerio Deodato's *Cannibal Holocaust* (1980), which was banned in multiple countries due to images of animal cruelty and rumors that people had actually been killed during the making of the film. The found footage genre truly gained international mainstream popularity, though, with *The Blair Witch Project* (Daniel Myrick and Eduardo Sánchez, 1999), which made use of the first internet-based viral marketing campaign, and continued with films like *Paranormal Activity* (Oren Peli, 2007) and *Cloverfield* (2008). Like those films, Shiraishi's films include shaky camera work, poor sound quality, little in the way of professional lighting or sound editing, an ad libbed style of storytelling, and intertitles that give us context for what is happening on screen. As Alexandra Heller-Nicholas notes, these particular aesthetic details have solidified over time as markers of the found footage / mockumentary genre, telling the audience that they are watching a particular type of horror film and thus allowing them to experience the enjoyment of viewing something that *seems* real (and reacting accordingly), even if modern audiences no longer suspect that what they are watching is "real" (Heller-Nicholas 2014, 8; Nelson 2016, 147). In found footage horror films, we are frequently told that what we are watching is an unedited "record" of some sort of frightening event, usually a supernatural happening or an act of violence. But, as films like *Occult* in particular are all too eager to reveal, what we are really watching is a piece of media that has been carefully edited to *resemble* an unpolished "record" of truth, one in which the seeming "cheapness" and amateur-looking aesthetics convince us that we can trust what we're seeing.[4] The knowledge that what we are watching is "fake" does not lessen our enjoyment of our investment in it—the intense feelings come from the "heightened perception of realism and subjectivity" that these films create, which "effectively allows the audience to experience horror on a deeper and more personal level" (Ancuta 2015, 153). Shiraishi himself has argued that he and other fans of found footage horror are drawn to the "humanity" (*ninjōkan*) that these films, which feel unpolished and not like something carefully created for entertainment, allow them to feel (Utamaru shinema hasurā 2016).

With their use of cheap-looking camera work and editing that draws attention to the construction of the films themselves, *The Curse* and *Occult* recall J-horror's longstanding connection to the notion of technology, particularly technologies connected to communication and visual media, as ghostly or haunted. In *The Ring*, the video cassette is not only haunted and cursed, it is an object that obscures and excludes certain things from the frame, given that VHS images are modified to fit a television screen (Benson-Allot 2010, 133). Unmarked video cassettes were also key to *The Ring*'s international marketing campaign, "(encapsulating) the regime of iterative reproduction around which the work itself revolves" (Rojas 2014, 435). In *Pulse*, a deeply lonely character reaches out to embrace what she thinks is a ghost, but at one point it appears as if she is embracing the film's camera, or perhaps her own reflection (Gerow 2002, 23). Cameras, computers, video cassettes, and phones in many Japanese horror films drive home a theme of endless copying, repetition, and virality that makes the distinction between self / other, original /

copy, and reality/fiction more difficult to parse. Films like *Occult* and *The Curse* continue this tradition, but now the technology is built into the construction of the films themselves—the "techno-horror" comes from the way that a cheap, hand-held camera seems to record everything, both illuminating and manipulating the "truth" that we have become accustomed to consuming via amateur video footage and "reality" television. Shiraishi's "digital horror" reminds us that even if "a fear of technology and the machine has lurked in horror for a long time—even inflecting its presentation—then digital horror makes this terror explicit and turns it into both an aesthetic and a narrative preoccupation" (Blake and Aldana-Reyes 2016, 3). Beyond being narratives *about* digital media and found footage, these are films that *use* cheap-looking visual effects, lighting, sound, and editing to construct stories that *appear* to be unpolished "documentaries" but are in fact fictional stories dressed down to look "authentic."

In *The Curse* and *Occult*, occult elements—ghosts, haunting, demonic possession, psychic energy—exist as both narrative devices and as a means for the films to comment, both within the narrative and through the process of their own creation, on the nature of spectrality and "truth" as presented through visual media. As del Pilar Blanco and Pereen note in their introduction to *The Spectralities Reader*, the use of words like "spectral" and "spectrality" to refer to all manner of haunting-and ghost-related phenomena arguably began with Derrida's *Specters of Marx*, which "uses the figure of the ghost to pursue (without ever fully apprehending) that which haunts *like a ghost* and, by way of this haunting, demands justice" (2013, 9). Derrida suggested that "rather than being expelled, the ghost should remain. . .as a conceptual metaphor signaling the ultimate disjointedness of ontology, history, inheritance, materiality, and ideology" (del Pilar Blanco and Pereen 2013, 6). The use of words like "specter" and "spectrality" "specifically evoke an etymological link to visibility and vision, to that which is both *looked at* (as a fascinating spectacle) and *looking* (in the sense of examining)" (2013, 2). Akira Lippit draws on Derrida's ideas concerning visuality in his analysis of a number of Japanese films, arguing that "Derrida's excess visualities might point to a category of complex visuality, a system of visuality that shows nothing, shows in the very place of the visible, something else: avisuality" (2005, 32). Noting that the cinema and the x-ray both came into existence in the same year (1895), he argues that both "offered extreme, even excessive modes of visuality that came to be seen, paradoxically, as modes of invisibility, or unseeability, challenging the notion of interiority. . .but also the conditions of visuality as such" (2005, 30). Films like Kiyoshi Kurosawa's *Cure* exist "between increasing clarity and deeper obscurity" (2005, 143), with the "x" mark of the hypnotist serial killer Mamiya serving as "a mark of erasure... but also an opening: the slices through which interiority escapes to the outside" (2005, 147). In the same way that classic J-horror has played with notions of visibility, invisibility, and avisuality, *The Curse* and *Occult* also force us to think deeply about "that which is both *looked at* (as a fascinating spectacle) and *looking* (in the sense of examining)" (2013, 2), and to think of ghosts, haunting, and the supernatural as both narrative subjects and "disjointed" metaphors that blur the lines between past, present, and future.

Circularity and repetition are also an important component of J-horror, especially films like *The Ring*, which tells the story of a cursed videotape that must be endlessly copied, and the *Tomie* series (1999~2011, Ataru Oikawa and others), the story of a demonic girl who is repeatedly reincarnated. In his early analysis of "circularity" in films like the *Ring* series, *Uzumaki* (Spiral, 2000, Higuchinsky) and *Pulse*, which echoes Derrida's notion of the specter as a ghost that "begins by coming back," Aaron Gerow invokes Deleuzian notions of difference and repetition to argue that repetition has structured much of the *kaidan* (ghost story) experience: "Audiences enjoyed the return of these repressed monsters not only by viewing them time and again, but by supporting a cyclical exhibition schedule which, for a long time, played *kaidan* films in the hot summer months... Contemporary urban legends with a horror twist... are fueled by the endless repetition of story telling that constitutes such social forms of transmission" (2002, 20). In her own Deleuzian analysis of the *Ring* and *Tomie* narratives, Raechel Dumas notes that the copy / simulacrum need not be "mere repetition of the same," but could instead be "a site of endless possibilities," imagining the vengeful Sadako and Tomie as "simulacratic girls" who endlessly self-replicate, with Sadako in particular "resisting through repetition the interpellation of her identity into an overdetermined narrative of victimization, vengeance, and resolution" (2018, 50). Similarly, Shiraishi's films frequently focus on repetition—often in the form of slowing down video footage and showing it again, or replaying video footage as characters watch and react to it. This alternate view of what we have already seen opens up the possibility of other perspectives, other realities, and other worlds, confirming what we have already seen but also offering a different version of it, showing us the possibility that the enigmatic "world-without-us" is within reach.

In their use of repetition, the way they play with the visible/invisible/avisual, and their emphasis on the tension between truth and fiction, *Occult* and *The Curse*, like so many found footage horror films, offer up "disjointed" narratives that force us to question the nature of what is being shown (and not being shown) to us, that blur the lines between director, subject, and audience, and that promise to "reveal" previously "hidden" things while simultaneously keeping much shrouded in secrecy. They remind us that "horror is not simply about fear, but instead about "the enigmatic thought of the unknown . . . the paradoxical thought of the unthinkable" (Thacker 2011, 9). Like the Lovecraftian worlds that inspired many of their supernatural elements, these films allow us to "enter the human world of hide-and-seek, of giving and withholding" (2011, 52). Violence is often obscured in Shiraishi's films, as in the stabbing incident at a cliffside resort that opens *Occult*, supposedly recorded on a handheld phone camera but with most of the specifics unclear. But monstrosity is also thrust into the audience's face, sometimes with graphic realism, as in a shocking rape scene at the end of *Cursed Violent People*, in the endless series of graphic images on display in *Grotesque*, or in the final shot of the main character floating in a hell-like "other world" surrounded by monsters in *Occult*. Like Thacker's conception of the occult and the "world-without-us," monsters and otherworldly things in Shiraishi's films are obscured, revealed, but also made "hypervisible," invoking a "dialectics of visibility and invisibility" which involves "a constant negotiation between what can be seen and what is in the shadows" (Gordon 2008, 17–18). In *Occult* and *The Curse*, we see not only an illustration of this tension between revealing / obscuring, visible / invisible, and truth / fiction, but also a steady progression from a more "standard" found footage horror story that "follows the rules" to one that gradually dispenses with certain conventions, leaving us questioning both the nature of the narrative and the filmmaking process itself.

The Curse begins in the manner of so many found footage horror films: with a story about a video cassette that apparently contains "the truth" about an investigation of paranormal phenomena by a well-known journalist. We learn that the journalist's house burned down and that he is still missing, with a video cassette labeled *noroi* (the curse), a record of one of his last investigations, being the only clue about what happened to him. After a brief voiceover introduction, the first bit of on-screen text is a quote from the journalist: "I want to know the truth. Even if it's horrifying," which could well be the central premise of many of Shiraishi's films, and much of found footage horror itself. The focus then shifts to the footage on the tape, which is a mix of interviews conducted by the journalist and television footage: a chronicle of the journalist's quest to uncover the truth about a series of supernatural events that may be connected to demonic possession and an ancient ritual performed in a small mountain community. At the very end of the film, we see footage from an extra video cassette that the producers supposedly received later, which appears to show the journalist's wife possessed by the demon and burning down their home. The final on-screen text tells us that the journalist is still missing.

Though Shiraishi had much less creative control over *The Curse* than he would have in many of his later films and straight-to-video series (Murata 2018), this film establishes many of the aesthetic details, structural conventions, and plot points that would be common in his later films. The opening voiceover tells us that what we are about to see was deemed "too disturbing for public viewing," establishing that we are watching something hidden that has been made visible. There is a focus on invented folklore mixed with Buddhist and Shinto rituals (we see characters in what appear to be temples and shrines taking part in rituals involving chanting and costumes resembling those worn by Buddhist and Shinto priests). Characters are haunted by an invented demon known as "Kagutaba," while some characters are more prone to possession or being able to see and hear spirits. There are references to "worms," images of spirals and hieroglyph-like drawings, and images of ropes tied in intricate loops and knots that recall images from Lovecraft's Cthulhu mythos. The camera work is shaky and awkward, with little in the way of professional lighting or sound editing. Actors perform in a decidedly "natural" style, reading scripted lines but sounding as if they are ad libbing. On-screen text tells us who everyone is and what happened to them. Much time is devoted to "verification" with the journalist consulting audio specialists, historians, psychics, and local villagers to get a clearer picture of "the truth."

The repeated scenes of "verification" are particularly significant and appear in many of Shiraishi's other films and video series.[5] These scenes further support the idea that these films are made in service of "the truth" and that they are engaged in scientific research and fact-finding (not simply speculation). In this way, they recall a long history in Japan of using "science" to both understand and de-fang superstitions surrounding concepts like monsters and the supernatural. This practice was most evident in the world of *yōkaigaku*, or "monsterology," which was promoted as a way to "bring apparently inexplicable objects into the purview of rational explanation" and turn monsters and other supernatural phenomena into "real and natural objects that can fall into fields of rational meaning" (Figal 1999, 46). Similarly, journalist Kobayashi seeks to provide viewers with clear, unemotional explanations for what they are seeing (and to provide "proof" that the supernatural events are legitimate). In one scene, for example, the journalist brings a mysterious recording of the sound of a baby crying to an audio specialist, who conducts a "spectrographic analysis" of the sound. As the camera zooms in on a computer image of the sound file, the specialist plays both the original file and a version of it with the background noise reduced, and we hear a clear sound of a crying baby. Though he initially describes it as an "animal" sound, further analysis of the pattern and rhythm of the noise leads the specialist to confirm that it is not the sound of an animal but a human baby—specifically, more than five babies. All of this happens in a room full of professional-looking audio equipment, with the audio specialist wearing a white lab coat and speaking in highly technical language. The message of the film is clear: what is unclear will be clarified, what is hidden will be revealed, and it will happen via science and reason. This is a film that is in service to "the truth," even if all the trappings of "truthfulness"—the rough editing, the poor visual and sound quality, and the seemingly unscripted acting style—are in fact careful choices to shroud a fictional narrative in a veneer of authenticity.

Repetition and "loops" are also a frequent sight in *The Curse*. In addition to hearing sound files multiple times (rendered clearer each time), we also watch other people watch themselves in video footage, as when Marika Matsumoto watches a tape made of herself in her room while she was sleepwalking and tying a cord into knots. When Kobayashi is walking outside after visiting a woman's home, the camera passes by a boy peeking through a window. Moments later, we see the footage again, this time slowed down and freeze framed—the boy's face is now clearer. Symbols drawn on surfaces, hanging talismans, and shapes made with yarn and cord by some of the film's subjects all take the form of circles and loops, a repeated motif that also calls to mind Cthulhu-like monsters. All of this points to a world in which ghosts and demons appear again and again, monsters that "should be past" but that "will only continue in the future" (Gerow 2002, 19). Though the repeated film footage is meant to clarify and rationalize, in the end it offers little comfort. We see what happened, but the *why* of it remains elusive, as does any hope of stopping the demon from "coming back" in the future. And the fact that all of this is presented to us via "found footage" (found by whom? presented for what purpose?) further muddies the timeline, presenting an electronic spectrality that forces us "to doubt this reassuring order or presents and, especially, the border between the present, the actual or present reality of the present, and everything that can be opposed to it" (Derrida 1994, 40).

The role of the camera and the director in *The Curse* is fairly straightforward. Though we know Kobayashi's name and also briefly see his cameraperson, Miyajima, the camera does not really focus on them as "characters"—we get no sense of their interior lives, and they simply exist to document and provide a record. The camera here looks almost entirely in one direction: toward Kobayashi and his documentary subjects, providing a record of everything that happened. The focus here is on this supposedly authentic "record" of supernatural happenings, with nothing to sow confusion about who is looking or being looked at. There is no real examination of what Shiraishi calls the *daisansha* (third party) in found footage horror: the person or entity who is responsible for editing or presenting the found footage (in *Cloverfield*, for example, the third party is the U.S. government, which has catalogued the tape a part of its collection of records related to an alien invasion) (Utamaru shinema hasurā 2016). The camera here exists only in service of "the truth," even if all of the "evidence" that it records is, of course, staged in the service of a fictional narrative.

Ultimately, *The Curse* does what so much found footage horror claims to want to do: it provides a record presented from a single perspective, with its cheap-looking visual style serving as a guarantee of its (fictional) authenticity. In its focus on occult practices like psychic predictions and demonic possession, it also makes the invisible visible, and in some cases hypervisible (allowing the camera to linger for a long period of time on a woman who is supposedly possessed by a demon, for example). But it also, in the manner of J-horror, found footage horror, and occult practices, obscures just as much as it claims to reveal. By the end of the film, we do not know what has happened to Kobayashi (who is listed as "missing") or what the "demon" wants. Endless scenes of investigation and verification ultimately end with many people dead and the feeling that the demon has not in any way been vanquished. This, too, is central to many J-horror narratives, which often end with the sense that we must "live with the ghosts," and that haunting is messy and complicated.

The complicated nature of haunting and the supernatural, as well as the relationships between director/subject and truth/fiction, get even messier in *Occult*, the 2009 film that Shiraishi counts as the first film in which he truly had creative control (Murata 2018). *Occult* begins in a manner similar to *The Curse*, with a story of one man's effort to find the truth (this time the man is Shiraishi himself, along with his assistant director and producer). The mystery this time is a stabbing incident at a fictional cliffside resort called Myōgasaki that appears connected to strange folk tales, symbols carved into people's skin and on the surfaces of mountain rocks, and the appearance of Cthulhu-like monsters hovering in the sky. The film begins, like *The Curse*, with a fact-finding mission: Shiraishi and his team interview various people about the stabbing incident, which was caught on camera. Their interviews lead them to stories about strange dreams and premonitions, as well as stories about the ancient Japanese legend of the *hiruko* (leech child), the first offspring of the gods Izanagi and Izanami, who was born without bones. Initially, the camera, the cameraperson (Shiraishi), and his team are not characters in their own right and serve only to document this fact-finding mission.

But then the role of the camera, the relationship between director and subject, and the focus of the film shift, effectively abandoning all of the fact-finding to zero in on one man, Shōhei Eno, who survived the stabbing incident but has become convinced that he is witnessing "miracles" (*kiseki*) and feels that committing a spectacular act of violence similar to the stabbing incident will allow him and others to escape to a "separate world." As Shiraishi's relationship with Eno deepens, he gives Eno a camera and tells him to try to document the "miracles" (supernatural events) that Eno claims he has been witnessing since the stabbing. The film then switches back and forth between Eno's footage of "miracles" (and of himself talking to the camera) and footage *of* Eno filmed by Shiraishi and his team. Finally, Eno straps a bomb to himself, hangs a camera around his neck, and walks into the middle of Shibuya Crossing to blow himself up. Some of the last footage we see is from this camera, staring up at Eno as he pushes the button to detonate the bomb. In the film's final moments, which take place twenty-one years after the bombing, the camera literally falls out of thin air and into Shiraishi's lap. The cassette tape inside reveals images of Eno floating in the "other world," a hellish void filled with Cthulhu-like monsters rendered with cheap visual effects.

Occult is even more concerned with repetition as a form of verification than *The Curse*. We see certain video footage again and again, with a slightly different focus and perspective each time. The opening footage of the stabbing at Myogasaki is first presented as a lighthearted video made by co-workers before cutting away at the sound of screams. Later, we see pieces of it slowed down and zoomed in on, allowing us to meet some of the people involved in the event (the murderer, Shōhei Eno, the women and men who witnessed the stabbing). We also get our first glimpse of a "miracle"—a black dot that flies across the sky—which will be slowed down, frozen, and shown again to us and to Eno. Later, when a paper hamburger wrapper flies off of a table, we will see it again, slowed down and with ominous music in the background. We see the footage of Eno preparing to blow himself up first from director Shiraishi's perspective, and then from Eno's. We see Eno documenting the appearance of strange, tentacled creatures in the sky, and then see the director and his team watching this footage and reacting to it. As in *The Curse*, all of this repetition is meant to verify, refine, and clarify, but in many cases it only serves to emphasize how "unreal" all of these occult happenings are (through zooming in on the very fake-looking visual effects used to create the Cthulhu-like monsters, for example). In the final scene, when the tentacled creatures that we have been seeing brief glimpses of are finally revealed in colorful (but very obviously animated) glory, the "truth" that we have been waiting for so long to be revealed turns out to be another lie. The "world-without-us" that Eno was so desperate to escape to turns out to be unknowable and hostile to human life, forcing us to "rethink the world as unthinkable" (Thacker 2011, 48) and deal with the Lovecraftian notion that becoming aware of all the horrors in the world (and our complete irrelevance in relation to them) will surely lead to madness.

Unlike *The Curse*, which keeps its director-subject relationship fairly distinct and focuses primarily on one POV (Kobayashi's camera) to present us with "the truth," *Occult* sees the subject (Eno) become a kind of co-director. The film shows us a mix of 1) footage presumably filmed by Eno (which includes his commentary) and 2) footage filmed by Shiraishi's director-character and his team. Eno also ultimately makes Shiraishi complicit in the act of violence that he commits, at one point telling him "Your job is to document everything." All these notions of truth and authenticity, though, are undermined by the film's use of cheap visual effects to represent the "miracles" that Eno documents—essentially stick figure animations and drawings of tentacled creatures superimposed over the sky, with truly ridiculous images of technicolor jellyfish and disembodied heads in the final scenes of "hell." In the midst of a film that places so much emphasis on revealing hidden truths and capturing previously unseen things on camera, Shiraishi also seems keen to remind the audience that everything they are seeing is a lie, something that also occurs in *Cursed Violent People* (when he breaks down and tells two of his subjects that everything is "fake" and "a lie") and in *Shirome* (when, at the end of the film, all of the "hauntings" are revealed to have been a hoax).[6]

This commitment to reminding the audience that what they are watching is false is also clear in a truly remarkable scene in which the well-known film director Kiyoshi Kurosawa appears briefly as a version of himself. During the production team's fact-finding mission, they are told that a film director has been researching Mt. Hiruyama (the location of some drawings that might be connected to the stabbing and Eno's "miracles"). That film director turns out to be Kurosawa, who is identified in on-screen text as a film director who researches ruins. He shares his "research" on Mt. Hiruyama's strange hieroglyphs with Shiraishi's team, playing the scene completely straight and claiming that he has been studying the mountain and its carvings for twenty years. Like "Myōgasaki" (the resort where the stabbing incident occurred), Mt. Hiruyama is not a real place, and of course its "hieroglyphs" are also completely invented. By inserting a well-known horror film director into the narrative and having him play a version of himself, but with certain fictional details added, *Occult* almost seems to be forcing the audience to remember that they are, in fact, watching a fictional horror film and should not trust anything they see.

Looking at *The Curse* and *Occult*, we can see a transition from a fairly standard work of found footage / mockumentary horror to a type of filmmaking that focuses on more fundamental questions about the nature of realism and filmmaking itself, as well as the tension between that which is hidden and revealed within "occult" practices. *The Curse* "follows the rules" in the sense that it presents us with a record (in the form of a videocassette) of strange happenings and allows us to follow an investigator's attempt to solve a supernatural mystery. Hints and threads ultimately add up to a story of demonic possession and the dangers of getting too close to secrets and hidden worlds. The cameraperson and the journalist provide our only perspective: the camera and the audience are looking in only one direction, toward the subjects.

Occult begins in a similar manner, but the focus shifts and becomes unstable. Instead of presenting us with an objective record of events, the camera turns backward to focus on the cameraperson and his team, who gradually become an important part of the narrative. The fact-finding is ultimately abandoned in favor of a much more intimate portrait of a single, disturbed person and the strange relationship he develops with "the truth," with the idea of other worlds and occult forces, and with the team who seeks to document him. And the "truth" of the film is repeatedly undermined by the presence of cheap visual effects and the presence of real people like Kiyoshi Kurosawa, who is presented as an "expert" in something that does not exist.

The "world-without-us" as defined by Eugene Thacker represents the "fissures, lapses, or lacunae" between the knowable aspects of the world, a space that reveals the horror of the unknowable and our own insignificance in the face of it. *Occult* and *The Curse* offer us glimpses of that world-without-us within their narratives, but also in the means through which those films were created: the use of amateur-looking aesthetics to create a narrative that simultaneously presents itself as truth and lie, and the continuous tension between "revealing" things deemed "too disturbing for public viewing" while at the same time undermining the authenticity of the reveal. Visible, invisible, and avisual, awash in repetition and motifs of loops and circularity, these films remind us that haunting dislocates not only our sense of real and unreal, supernatural and natural, but our sense that more images—more footage—add up to a more accurate and truthful picture of what happened. In the case of these films, what is illuminated serves to obscure just as much as it serves to reveal.

REFERENCES

Ancuta, Katarzyna. 2015. "Lost and Found: The Found Footage Phenomenon and Southeast Asian Supernatural Horror Film." *Plaridel* 12.2 (August): 149–177.

Benson-Allot, Caetlin. 2010. "'Before You Die, You See the Ring': Notes on the Imminent Obsolescence of VHS." In *The Scary Screen: Media Anxiety in The Ring*, edited by Kristen Lacefield, 115–140. Famham, UK: Ashgate.

Blake, Linnie, and Xavier Aldana Reyes. 2016. "Introduction." In Digital Horror: Haunted Technologies, Network Panic and the Found Footage Phenomenon, edited by Linnie Blake and Xavier Aldana Reyes, 13–31. London: I.B. Tauris."

Brown, Steven T. 2018. *Japanese Horror and the Transnational Cinema of Sensations*. New York, NY: Palgrave Macmillan.

del Pilar Blanco, María, and Esther Pereen. 2013. "Introduction: Conceptualizing Spectralities." In *The Spectralities Reader*, edited by María del Pilar Blanco and Esther Peeren, 1–29. New York, NY: Bloomsbury.

Derrida, Jacques. 1994. *Specters of Marx*. Translated by Peggy Kamuf. New York, NY: Routledge.

Derrida, Jacques and Bernard Stiegler. 2013. "Spectrographies." In *The Spectralities Reader*, edited by María del Pilar Blanco and Esther Peeren, 37–52. New York, NY: Bloomsbury.

Dumas, Raechel. 2018. *The Monstrous-Feminine in Contemporary Japanese Popular Culture*. New York, NY: Palgrave Macmillan.

Figal, Gerald. 1999. *Civilization and Monsters: Spirits of Modernity in Meiji Japan*. Durham, NC: Duke UP.

Foster, Michael Dylan. 2009. *Pandemonium and Parade: Japanese Monsters and the Culture of Yōkai*. Berkeley, CA: University of California Press.

Gerow, Aaron. 2002. "The Empty Return: Circularity and Repetition in Recent Japanese Horror Films." *Minikomi: Informationen des Akademischen Arbeitskreis Japan*. Vol. 64 (February): 19–24.

Gordon, Avery. 2008. *Ghostly Matters: Haunting and the Sociological Imagination*. Minneapolis, MN: University of Minnesota Press.

Heller-Nicholas, Alexandra. 2014. *Found Footage Horror Films: Fear and the Appearance of Reality*. Jefferson, NC: McFarland.

Lippit, Akira. 2005. *Atomic Light (Shadow Optics)*. Minneapolis, MN: University of Minnesota Press.

Murata, Ramu. 2018. "44-sai `horā eiga' o kiwameru otoko no namihazureta shūnen `senritsu kaiki fairu kowasugi!' o unda hassō [A forty-four-year-old horror master on what inspired his obsession with "Dreadful Mystery Files: Too Scary!"]." *Toyokeizai Online*. January 11.

Nelson, Lindsay. 2016. "Choosing Illusion: Mediated Reality and the Spectacle of the Idol in Kōji Shiraishi's *Shirome*." *Journal of Japanese and Korean Cinema* 8.2 (October): 140–155.

Rojas, Carlos. 2014. "Viral Contagion in the *Ringu* Intertext." In *The Oxford Handbook of Japanese Cinema*, edited by Daisuke Miyao, 416–437. Oxford, UK: Oxford UP.

Shiraishi, Kōji. 2016. *Feiku dokyumentarī no kyōkasho* [*Fake Documentary Textbook*]. Tokyo: Seibundō shinkōsha.

Thacker, Eugene. 2011. *In the Dust of This Planet: Horror of Philosophy Vol. 1*. Winchester, UK: Zero Books.

Utamaru shinema hasurā. 2016. "'Tokushū' Utamaru `feiku dokyumentarī' ni tsuite manabou tokushū by eiga kantoku shiraishi kōji [Utamaru Special Feature: Learning about "Fake Documentaries" from Film Director Kōji Shiraishi]." *YouTube*. YouTube, 5 Mar. 2016.

Zahlten, Alex. 2017. *The End of Japanese Cinema: Industrial Genres, National Times, and Media Ecologies*. Durham, NC: Duke UP.

NOTES

1. My thanks to Christophe Thouny, whose 2015 workshop at the University of Tokyo, *Planetary Love 1: Weird Realism*, led me to Thacker's work and my initial examination of the film *Occult*'s connections to it.

2. Particularly in summer, Japanese "wide shows" (lengthy television programs featuring many different segments) and variety programs often feature "scary story" segments with a mix of documentary footage and reenactments. Sometimes the focus is on urban legends or folklore, sometimes the focus is on "scary things that actually happened to everyday people." The long-running *Gakkō no kaidan* (*School Ghost Stories*) series of books, comics, and films also depicts familiar ghost stories set in schools. Some urban legends, like the story of *kuchi-sake onna* (the slit-mouthed woman), have been reported in mass media in ways that made her seem real, especially to children (Foster 2009, 184–194).

3. In a lengthy interview for *Toyokeizai Online*, Shiraishi himself noted the influence of Cthulhu on his films. Interviewer Ramu Murata also noted that Cthulhu-esque and Lovecraftian images are common in Japanese video games and manga (Murata 2018).

4. This disconnect is particularly evident in films like *Cloverfield*, which was made with a budget of $25 million, significantly larger than the budget of a typical found footage horror film. Though *Cloverfield* clearly had the funds to make its film look more professional, the use of a handheld camera and a seeming lack of professional lighting or sound editing helps to give the film the same "raw" feel of its much lower-budget predecessors *The Blair Witch Project* and *Paranormal Activity*.

5. In Shiraishi's *Dreadful Mystery Files: Too Scary!* series, for example, the videos often begin with the filmmakers conducting interviews, with the caption *kenshō* (verification) appearing on screen before these scenes.

6. For a more thorough examination of *Shirome* and the connections between found footage horror and Japanese idol culture, see (Nelson 2016).

Index

1950s, 193
1960s, 40, 151, 194, 214
1970s, 41–42, 45, 114, 125, 128, 150, 179, 189n3, 194, 209n3
1980s, 86, 88, 104, 114, 128n9, 150, 214
1990s, 76, 97, 114, 116, 120, 125–127n2, 128n14, 132, 157–158, 165, 179, 213–214
2000s, 53, 157–158, 164–165, 212–214
3.11 disaster, 22, 24–26, 28–30, 32, 34–36

abject, 47, 97–99, 101
animism, 85–88, 91, 94, 234
anti-American, 161
Anthropocene, 148
apocalypse, 65, 150–151
Argento, Dario, 14–15, 166
Asato, Mari, 97–101, 103–105, 107–110
atomic bomb, 25, 173

Bazin, André, 113–114
Bilocation, 98–101, 103–104, 110

The Blair Witch Project, 159, 191, 214, 226n4

Blonde Kaidan, 167, 170–171

The Boy from Hell, 100, 103

Buddha, 134, 147
Buddhism, 16, 42, 66, 78, 131, 133–134, 136, 145, 147, 151–152

cannibalism, 142, 181–182, 214
capitalism, 89, 95n1, 194, 200, 204–206
childhood, 43, 106, 177, 181
China, 9–11, 17, 19n3, 24, 69, 79, 81n7
Christianity, 131, 134, 142, 151
cinephilia, 117, 125
Cold War, 21, 161
commodification, 212
Cult, 191, 195–196, 198, 201, 203, 209n4–5
Confucianism, 133
countercultural, 98, 151
Creed, Barbara, 97–99, 107
Cthulhu, 206, 214, 219–222, 226n3
Cure, 76, 120, 124, 128n13, 216

dark ecology, 149–152
Dark Water, 77
deep ecology, 150–152
demons, 139–145, 147–149, 151–152, 198, 201, 220
Derrida, Jacques, 212, 216–217, 220
Devilman, 139–152

doppelgänger, 43, 101
Dream Cruise, 165, 167–168, 170–171

ecocide, 150
Edo period, 40, 66
EM: Embalming, 113, 115
environment, 54, 67, 122, 148–151, 181
Ero-Guro, 66, 74
Evil dead trap, 14–15, 20n6
exorcism, 108

fairy tale, 177, 182, 185, 190n8
fascism, 17, 139, 144, 150
Fatal Frame, 99–100, 105–108–110, 178
Fatal Frame II: Crimson Butterfly, 178
female body, 98–99, 107, 109
Flower of flesh and blood, 13
folklore, 52, 55, 65, 82n12, 212, 214, 219, 226n2
found-footage, 26, 28, 191–193, 207, 212–218, 220–221, 223, 226n4, 226n6
Fukushima, 22–25, 31, 35, 173

Gate of Flesh, 117
gender, 82n13, 93, 97, 99, 101, 104, 110, 134, 144, 169, 171
global economy, 85, 94
globalization, 25, 41, 157–158, 160, 162–165, 174
Godzilla, 21–22, 24–36, 172–173, 176n1
gore, 129n14, 192
Gothic, 85, 89, 91–92, 160
grotesque, 65–66, 74, 113, 141, 183
Grotesque (film), 192, 213, 218

The Grudge, 163–165, 167–168, 170–171, 213
The Grudge 2, 168

Gunning, Tom, 123

Halloween, 58

Hansel and Gretel, 182
hauntings, 67, 223
Haunting Ground, 178, 187
hell, 132, 134, 136, 141–142, 204, 205, 218, 222–223
hermaphrodite, 144

The Hidden Fortress, 158

Hiroshima, 15, 39
Hollywood, 16, 39–41, 44–48, 58, 128n10, 157–165, 167–173, 176n1
Hollywood remake, 46, 48, 158, 162–163, 167–168, 171
Holocaust, 10
homoerotic, 106

idol culture, 191, 194, 198–203, 209n8, 226n6
imperialism, 17, 43–44
industrialization, 86–88
isolation, 88–90, 167, 172
Itō, Junji, 65, 71, 79, 86, 131–132, 135–136
Iwabuchi, 161

Ju-On, 51–54, 61, 63n2, 98, 213
Ju-On: Black Ghost, 100, 108, 110
Ju-On: Origins, 51–52, 54–62
Ju-On: The Beginning of the End, 51
Ju-On: White Ghost, 51
Judeo-Christian, 131, 141–142
jump-scares, 60–61

kaidan, 40–42, 45, 65–67, 76, 79, 107, 217
kaiju, 28, 173
Keiretsu, 198, 203, 205
Kristeva, Julia, 97–99
Kuroneko, 40

The Kurosagi Corpse Delivery Service, 65–68, 81n2–3

Kurosawa, Kiyoshi, 53, 76, 114–115, 118–122, 124, 128n7, 128n9, 128n13, 128n14, 162, 210, 212, 214, 216, 223–224

lesbianism, 106–107
Lost Decade, 42–43
Lovecraft, H. P., 135, 192, 211–214, 219, 221, 226n3

manga, 65–67, 69, 73, 78–79, 81n12, 86–87, 133–134, 139–141, 143–145, 147–149, 152, 162, 201, 209n10, 226n3
masculinity, 202
Masters of Horror, 165–167
Meiji Restoration, 43, 86, 95n2

Men behind the sun, 12, 14, 20n4
Miike, Takashi, 66, 77, 129n14, 165–167
miko, 108
mise-en-scène, 51, 181
monstrous feminine, 98–99, 110

Nagai, Go, 139, 144–148, 151–152
Nagasaki, 39
Nakata, Hideo, 10–11, 14, 16, 39, 41–42, 53, 77, 114–115, 118, 129n14, 158, 162, 211, 213
Nanking massacre, 9–12, 15–17, 19n2, 20n8
National Resilience Policy, 22, 28–30, 33–35
nationhood, 39–40, 99
nazisploitation, 12–14
neoliberalism, 85, 88, 91, 94, 95n1, 205–206
Night of the living dead, 16, 18
Noroi: The Curse, 191, 194–196, 198, 201, 209n4, 212, 218
North Korea, 24

Occult, 191, 196, 198, 200–202, 204, 209n5, 212–218, 222–224, 226n1

oni, 141–143, 148, 150, 152
onryō, 40, 67, 76–78, 107–108
orientalism, 161, 165, 168, 170, 172, 174
otaku, 116, 199, 201–203, 209n10
Ōtsuka, Eiji, 65–66, 68, 70–79, 81n12

Our blood will not forgive, 117

Paglia, Camille, 98
posthumanism, 140, 142, 144, 149–150, 152
Pulse, 53, 115, 120–122, 124, 210n12, 212, 215, 217
Punchline (Company), 177

queer, 231

racism, 12
Rampo, Edogawa, 85–94, 95n3

The Rape of Nanking, 9, 19n4

reality TV, 193
Resident Evil (game), 177, 179, 187
Ring of Curse, 109
Ringu, 10, 39–41–42, 44–46, 48, 77, 115, 121–122, 124, 128n14, 158, 165, 211
Rule of Rose, 177–180, 182–187, 189n1, 189n2, 189n4–5, 190n6–7

sacred, 108, 181
Sadako, 10–11, 13–15, 41–42, 44–45, 77, 124, 211, 217
Sakai, Naoki, 160–161, 170
samsara, 131–136
Satan, 139, 144, 150–151
Scary True Stories, 127n2, 165
science-fiction, 173
Shigehiko, Hasumi, 114–119, 121–123, 125, 127n1, 127n5, 128n6–128n11
Shin-Godzilla, 21–22, 24–25, 29–30, 32, 35, 172

Shinto, religion. 16, 66, 86, 108, 133, 136, 214, 219
Shirome, 191, 195–198, 201–203, 209n4, 214, 223, 226n6
Shutter, 171–172
Silent Hill (game), 178–180, 187
Star Wars, 158, 161–162
Suicide Forest, 79–80, 81n11
survival horror games, 179, 181, 187
Suzuki, Koji, 10, 168

Taoism, 151
Thacker, Eugene, 211, 218, 224, 226n1
thriller, 45, 165
Toei Animation, 139
Toho, 21
Tokyo, 14, 25–28, 30–32, 35, 54, 71, 75–76, 81n7, 86–89, 168, 171, 173, 201
Tokyo Drifter, 117
Tomie (manga), 65

Tomie (film), 217
transnational, 15–16, 48, 158, 160, 168, 171, 198
tsunami, 21–24, 26, 29, 31, 79, 142

urban legend, 68–69, 73, 81n5, 81n12, 128n14, 213–214, 217, 226n2
Uzumaki, 65, 79, 131–132, 135–136, 161–162, 217

Verbinski, Gore, 40, 158, 168
Victorian, 181

western influence, 87
World War II, 9, 44, 81n6, 105

Youth of the Beast, 117
yūrei, 65–67, 71, 74, 78–79, 107

Zen, 78, 151
zombie, 65, 67

About the Editors

Fernando Gabriel Pagnoni Berns is an Assistant Professor at the Universidad de Buenos Aires (UBA)—Facultad de Filosofía y Letras (Argentina)-. He teaches courses on international horror film and is director of the research group on horror cinema "Grite." He has published chapters in the books *To See the Saw Movies: Essays on Torture Porn and Post 9/11 Horror*, edited by John Wallis, *Critical Insights: Alfred Hitchcock*, edited by Douglas Cunningham, *A Critical Companion to James Cameron*, edited by Antonio Sanna, and *Gender and Environment in Science Fiction*, edited by Bridgitte Barclay, among others. He has authored a book about Spanish horror TV series *Historias para no Dormir*.

Subashish Bhattacharjee is an Assistant Professor of English at the University of North Bengal, India. He edits the interdisciplinary online journal *The Apollonian*, and is the Editor of Literary Articles and Academic Book Reviews of Muse India. His doctoral research, on the cultures of built space, is from the Centre for English Studies, Jawaharlal Nehru University, where he has also been a UGC-Senior Fellow. His recent publications include *Queering Visual Cultures* (Universitas, 2018), and *New Women's Writing* (Cambridge Scholars, co-edited with GN Ray, 2018).

Ananya Saha is a PhD scholar in the Centre for English Studies, JNU, New Delhi. Her research is on the idea of the "outsider" in Japanese and non-Japanese manga vis-à-vis globalization. Other research interests include Fandom and Queer studies, Translation theory and practice, New Literatures and so on. She has published in international journals, including *Orientaliska Studier*, from the Nordic Association of Japanese and Korean Studies. She is the co-editor of the volume titled *Trajectories of the Popular: Forms, Histories, Contexts* (2019), published by AAKAR, New Delhi. She has been the University Grants Fellow, SAP-DSA-(I) in the Centre for English Studies, JNU (2016–17), and has been awarded a DAAD research visit grant to Tuebingen University, Germany under the project "Literary Cultures of Global South."

About the Contributors

Calum Waddell is a lecturer in film at the University of Lincoln and the author of *The Style of Sleaze: The American Exploitation Film 1959–1977* (Edinburgh University Press, 2018), *Images of Apartheid: Filmmaking on the Fringe in the Old South Africa* (Edinburgh University Press, 2021) and the forthcoming *South Africa in Horror Cinema* (Bloomsbury). He lived in China for three years, and has enjoyed many a trip to Japan, but his true East Asian passion is an undying love for K-pop.

Barbara Greene is an Assistant Professor at Tokyo International University, where she teaches courses on Japanese popular culture and literature. She received her Ph.D from the University of Arizona in 2017. Past publications have focused on postmodernity in contemporary Japanese literature and collective memory in popular manga series.

Bipasha Mandal received a Master's degree in English literature from Jadavpur University and a Bachelor's degree from Calcutta University. She is an avid reader, a football fanatic, and always keen on learning new languages. She is interested in pursuing a Ph.D. degree. She has published numerous papers mostly on her academic interests (postcolonialism, cultural studies, marginality studies, eco-criticism) in numerous journals, and books of academic repute.

Daniel Krátký is a PhD student in Film and Audio-visual Culture Studies at Masaryk University, Czech Republic. His main research interests are the Poetics and Cultural Transfer of Japanese Kaiju Eiga, Narrative and Stylistic Tendencies of Hollywood, Czech and Hong Kong Cinema, Film Criticism, and Film Festival Programming.

Megan Negrych obtained her BA in Japanese Language (2012) and MA in History (2014) from the University of Regina. Her thesis, "In the Shadow of Anxiety: The Detective Fiction of Akimitsu Takagi and Seichō Matsumoto and the Japanese Post-War Experience" evaluated the ability of Japanese detective fiction to function as an historical account. Her research interests include memory, trauma, and the legacy of World War II in Japan; folklore and horror; and the sociocultural history of horror in pop culture.

Leonie Rowland has an MA from the Manchester Centre for Gothic Studies at Manchester Metropolitan University, where she will begin her PhD in October 2021. She is currently researching commodity animism in the Japanese Gothic. Leonie is Assistant Reviews Editor at The British Society for Literature and Science and Editor-in-Chief of *The Hungry Ghost Project*. Her academic work has been published by *The Dark Arts Journal* and is forthcoming from *Fantastika Journal*. Her debut collection of prose is available from Dreich.

Canela Ailen Rodriguez Fontao is MA at the Facultad de Filosofía y Letras, Universidad de Buenos Aires (UBA), Argentina. She has published chapters in books such as *Bullying in Popular Culture: Essays on Film, Television and Novels*, edited by Abigail Scheg, and *Deconstructing Dads*, edited by Laura Tropp. Currently she coordinates, with Mariana Soledad Zárate, a free writing space called "La Monstrua cinefága" that specializes in making visible the role of women, on and off camera, in horror films.

Mariana Zárate is MA graduated from the Universidad de Buenos Aires (UBA)-Facultad de Filosofía y Letras (Argentina). She has contributed to *Racism and Gothic: Critical Essays*, *Projecting the World: Classical Hollywood, the 'Foreign' and Transnational Representations*, *Uncovering Stranger Things*, and *The Handmaid's Tale and Philosophy: A Womb of One's Own*. She works in cultural management programming film series in the city of Buenos Aires (Mondo Trasho) and is currently part of the organization of "La Monstrua Cinefaga," a space for writing about cinema with a gender perspective.

William Carroll is a Postdoctoral Associate at Duke University in the Department of Asian & Middle Eastern Studies. His current research focuses on the interactions between film production, film criticism, and film schools in contemporary Japan. His work has been published in *The Journal of Japanese & Korean Cinema*, *Cinéma&Cie*, and *Concentric: Literary & Cultural Studies*. His monograph on Suzuki Seijun is forthcoming from Columbia University Press in Spring 2022.

Dr. Wayne Stein, a professor at a university in the heartland, enjoys teaches courses on cinema, literature, and horror. In addition, he often publishes on Asian horror and films. Born and raised in Asia, he continues to study its cultures, discovering new insights all the time. Finally, for over twenty years, he enjoys practicing Kendo and Katori Shinto Ryu, Japanese sword arts.

Fernando Gabriel Pagnoni Berns (PhD in Arts, PhD Candidate in History) works as Professor at the Universidad de Buenos Aires (UBA)—Facultad de Filosofía y Letras (Argentina). He teaches courses on international horror film. He is director of the research group on horror cinema "Grite" and has edited a book on Frankenstein's bicentennial (Universidad de Buenos Aires) and one on director James Wan (McFarland, 2021). His last book is on horror Spanish TV series *Historias para no Dormir* (Universidad de Cádiz, España). Currently editing a book on the Italian giallo film (University of Mississippi Press).

Seán Hudson wrote his doctoral thesis on internationally popular Japanese cinema while studying at Kyushu University. He is especially interested in the production of popular films and visual media insofar as they pertain to geopolitical and ideological discourses such as Orientalism and nationalism.

Ingrid Butler is a Master of Library and Information Science student at the University of Missouri. She has previously earned an MPhil in Education, specializing in Children's Literature, from the University of Cambridge, and a Bachelor of Art in English from the University of California, Davis. Her contribution is partially drawn from her MPhil thesis, "'Always at Her Side': Affective Discipline in *Rule of Rose*.

Dennin Ellis is a PhD Student at The Ohio State University. He received his Master's at the State University at New York, Albany. His research interests include popular culture, narrative theory and postcolonial studies, with an emphasis on film, music and graphic narrative. His recent publications include papers on Aboriginal characters in Marvel Comics and the specter of communism in Andrei Tarkovsky's *Stalker*.

Lindsay Nelson is an assistant professor in the department of political science and economics at Meiji University in Tokyo. Her research focuses on Japanese horror films and Japanese popular culture. Her work has been published in *Journal of Japanese and Korean Cinema*, *East Asian Journal of Popular Culture*, and *Japanese Studies*. Her first book, *Circulating Fear: Japanese Horror, Fractured Realities, and New Media*, is forthcoming from Lexington Books in 2021.

www.ingramcontent.com/pod-product-compliance
Lightning Source LLC
Chambersburg PA
CBHW020116010526
44115CB00008B/855